Praise for Don Watson

DEATH SENTENCE

'The Book of the Year . . . witty, erudite and funny. Awfully funny' – *The Australian Financial Review*

'A funny and profound polemic' – *Times on Sunday*

'A marvelous polemic' – *Forbes* magazine

'Watson makes an eloquent, elegant, and sometimes scathing case for taking back language from those who would strip it of all colour and emotion and, therefore, of all meaning' – Booklist

'Don Watson has written a fine and necessary book. Any citizen who neglects to read it does so at his or her peril' – *Harper's Magazine*

'Captures the powerlessness and frustration we feel when confronted by meaningless words delivered with authority' – *Los Angeles Times Book Review*

AMERICAN JOURNEYS

'This is not travelogue, it is dazzlingly eloquent and perceptive; it is the Tocqueville of damaged but persistent and enduring dreams. Like Tocqueville, and unlike much writing by foreigners about the United States, it is affectionate and comes across the many Americas and their oddities with an uncondemning eye' – Tom Keneally

'The best book by an outsider about America since – forever' – David Sedaris

'Don Watson has written a profound and deeply personal work that makes for itself a place in the great tradition of American journeys' – *Australian Book Review*

RECOLLECTIONS OF A BLEEDING HEART

'A masterpiece . . . simply the best inside account of life, politics and combat inside the highest office of the land ever written' – *The Age*

'A classic: an insider's account of the working of the political process, with its paranoia, its envies, its fevered inconsequentiality, its joys, crammed with wisdom and a lovely detachment' – *The Sydney Morning Herald*

BENDABLE LEARNINGS

'The book is worthwhile just for Watson's hilarious introduction' – Adelaide *Advertiser*

'Watson offers witty, acerbic insights into an embarrassing use of language that bears no relation to real life' – *The Courier-Mail*

'He should have his own show' – Alan Jones, 2GB

WORST WORDS

Don Watson

with Helen Smith

VINTAGE BOOKS
Australia

A Vintage book
Published by Random House Australia Pty Ltd
Level 3, 100 Pacific Highway, North Sydney NSW 2060
www.randomhouse.com.au

First published by Vintage in 2015

Random House Books is part of the Penguin Random House group of companies whose addresses can be found at global.penguinrandomhouse.com.

National Library of Australia
Cataloguing-in-Publication entry

Watson, Don, 1949–, author
Worst Words: a compendium of contemporary cant, gibberish and jargon

ISBN 978 0 85798 344 2 (paperback)

English language – Terms and phrases
English language – Errors of usage
English language – Jargon

427.994

Cover design by Sandy Cull, gogoGingko
Cover image: Tyra von Zweigbergk/woo.se
Typeset in 10.5/14 pt Sabon by Midland Typesetters, Australia
Printed in Australia by Griffin Press, an accredited ISO AS/NZS 14001:2004 Environmental Management System printer

Random House Australia uses papers that are natural, renewable and recyclable products and made from wood grown in sustainable forests. The logging and manufacturing processes are expected to conform to the environmental regulations of the country of origin.

Don Watson's books, articles and essays have been widely acclaimed. His bestselling titles include *Recollections of a Bleeding Heart: A Portrait of Paul Keating PM*, which won *The Age* Book of the Year, the National Biography Award and several other awards, *Death Sentence*, which won the Australian Booksellers Association Book of the Year, *Watson's Dictionary of Weasel Words*, and *American Journeys*, which won *The Age* Book of the Year and Non-Fiction Book of the Year, the inaugural Indie Award for Non-Fiction and the Walkley Non-Fiction Award. Since 2003 his website weaselwords.com.au has been documenting the viral spread of management-speak and the decline of public language. His critically acclaimed 2014 book *The Bush* recently won the Indie Book of the Year and the NSW Premier's Literary Award.

KEATS
WORDS
IN
verb
CHURN
BLUE SKY THINKING
DISBENEFIT
PUSH THE ENVELOPE
INCENTIVISE
OPTIMALITY
TIME POOR
BOTTOM LINE
PR
$
LIFE
COMMUNICATE
Petty

Introduction

Graham Greene liked Fidel Castro. He even liked his four-hour-long speeches. They are 'not made up of evasions and oratorical tricks and big abstract words', he wrote in 1966, 'they are full of information, down to earth, filled with detail . . . he is the revolutionary brain in action, like one of those glass-sided clocks in which you can see the wheels in motion.' As Greene reported it, the (Spanish) language of the long-winded socialist revolutionary brain was everything the post-capitalist managerial brain is not.

We who are living the lifestyle need not fear socialist revolution or four-hour speeches: our modern leaders do not have enough concrete words at their command for either of them. Not even with PowerPoint. Remember *1984*: 'the whole aim of Newspeak is to narrow the range of thought. In the end we shall make thoughtcrime literally impossible, because there will be no words in which to express it.' In many organisations much of Orwell's fantasy has all but come to pass. As for the clock: try to think of its wheels in motion while reading this random sample from the base material of managerial language: 'In particular, the degree of formality evidenced across universities, regarding the documentation of risk strategy and risk appetite, processes to identify and manage risk, and reporting on new and emerging risks suggests that rigour in risk management is a key enabler in improving organisational performance.' Read it again, and try to think of *anything* in motion.

All public language inclines to pomposity and deceit, but modern public language inclines these ways acutely and nails it to the inclination. Unlike Greene's Castro, it is also evasive and dishonest in its essence; abstract, devoid of useful information and concrete example, remote from human reality, filled not with detail but with hogwash.

Being spontaneous, and burbling with quotidian life, Greene declared Castro's speeches were nearer to William Cobbett's than Winston Churchill's, 'and the greater for that'. He might have been right in general, but the most famous passage in Churchill's greatest – or historically most telling – speech could not have been plainer or more grounded in the lives of ordinary Britons. 'We shall go on to the end. We shall fight in France, we shall fight on the seas and oceans, we shall fight with growing confidence and growing strength in the air, we shall defend our island, whatever the cost may be. We shall fight on the beaches, we shall fight on the landing grounds, we shall fight in the fields and in the streets, we shall fight in the hills; we shall never surrender.' We shall fight in the places that we know, right up to our doorsteps.

No mention of a strategy. No action plan and nothing to be actioned. No enablers. No risk management. No accountability. No outcomes to be 'passionate' about. No 'Leadership is about making the right decisions for our country's future.' No 'That's what the government is working to deliver for you.' Compare the verbs with which Churchill tried to save civilisation, with those Tony Abbott chose when trying to save his skin in February 2015.

There is nothing very bad about that risk strategy passage. It is written in the language of the people we now call 'knowledge workers'. By knowledge is meant information or data (including metrics), and ideas about what to do with it. The workers are those whose job it is to make connections, understand processes, implement strategies, find synergies and iterate, iterate, iterate. In developed countries with 'knowledge economies' there are four or five times more knowledge workers than any other category of employee. To extract the last drop of value from them, knowledge and knowledge workers both need management. Business management, of which knowledge management (KM) and human resources (HR) are two burgeoning subsets, is a colossal knowledge industry in itself. Knowledge workers are the adepts of our time, the toiling masses of the modern century, even if they're just marking time before the robots.

It hardly matters that they do not speak a language that would be familiar to the great majority of English speakers fifty years or a century ago: this is a new world, and this is the English it speaks. Every day around the globe knowledge workers assemble a million paragraphs of the kind I quoted; and their firms exchange immense sums for them. Such paragraphs are the grist of modern commerce; they keep millions employed and able to buy houses and cars and holidays: they make *sovereign consumers* of them, make lifestyles possible. Even when the words are pure muck, we might conclude that the injury to language is a price worth paying for a sprightly economy and a great customer experience.

'The actions of men proceed from their thoughts,' wrote that same William Cobbett. 'In order to obtain the cooperation, the concurrence, the consent of others, we must communicate our thoughts to them. The means of this communication are words . . .' Management has decided that words such as align, output, input, outcome and buy-in are the best means of communicating thoughts and gaining consent to them. Yet professional translators have told me that the absence of meaning in business documents can make translation impossible: whatever the writers' thoughts are, they cannot be communicated in the words available to them. There are knowledge workers who say that they and the firms they work for are paid to mystify people. Some of their colleagues will argue with that idea. And some will argue that 'mystify' is too generous: that 'render insensible' is nearer to the truth.

The principal point to be made about management language is that the rot has set in. It is to the knowledge economy what 'miner's lung' was to mining, and just as much to be expected.

You cannot suddenly make out of the same person an empowered employee and a sovereign and delighted consumer without consequences for her language. New technology is transforming human communication. As much as we are citizens, we are consumers; as much as we live in a society, we now live in an economy which treats 'productivity' much as we used to treat religious observance. Private worlds have been upended; work and careers reconfigured; connections to history, literature, place and belief have been severed. Language must pay a price. The language of management is now inseparable from the lives we all lead and, unless in future human twaddle proves an impediment to artificial intelligence, there will be no stopping its advance.

So where's the harm? If universities want to pay half a million dollars for risk management, or a rebranding that leaves them with meaningless symbols and mottos – unless it can be said they symbolise the shell of their former meaningful existence – whose business is it but their own? The academics might be embarrassed for a while, but like other living things, they'll adapt. If every bank, government department, hospital and fire brigade feels that without 'a mission-driven streamlined process for revising its strategic plan' it can give up on going forwards, is anyone worse off? Apart from the employees, of course: as far as I know, no one has studied the effects on human beings of long-term daily exposure to jargon and clichés: but we may assume that a world whose language defies visualisation, and is stripped of all lyric, comic and descriptive possibility, is far from an ideal human environment and some kind of trauma may result.

The managerial echo in the empty cadences of politics might be counted as collateral damage. But management speak can scarcely be blamed for the crimes against language committed by politicians who have postured and evaded, and played all sorts of shameless oratorical tricks since the game of politics began. They have borrowed from wherever their needs took them: from literature and social theory and religion at times long ago, but more recently from marketing and advertising. That's where they learned messaging. They like the military too. How could a politician resist 'operational matters'? It's so lordly and owl-like, when, for all anyone knows, you haven't a clue.

Management's verbless pomposity has not conquered politics, merely found a grateful host: grateful for 'issues', and 'deliver', and 'challenges', and 'step up to the plate', and the 'bottom line', and 'starting a conversation', 'at the end of the day', and, of course, 'going or moving forwards'. More grateful than ever they are these days, because with media of all kinds now pestering them every minute they need new ways to say nothing gravely, or something that conceals something else.

Yet the crime is less in the evasion than in the platitudes that hollow out debate even as they talk about starting a 'conversation' with us. The first true crime of managerial politics is that we must push through so much flatulence and dross to reach the nub of it. Take Governor Nikki Haley of South Carolina the day a young white man killed seven black people worshipping in a church. She began by saying a 'conversation' was needed, that this was the South Carolinian way. She said 'conversation' three times in her first two sentences. The press then asked her if she would now do something about the Confederate flag flying at the state capitol. She replied: 'I think that . . . at a time like this, you have to look back at what we've done. Fifteen years ago the General Assembly at the time they had a *conversation*.' And she said conversation again and again until someone asked her to say what her position was. And she replied: 'You know, right now, to start having policy *conversations* with the people of South Carolina . . .' The 'conversation' has been going on since the Civil War. It takes in slavery, Jim Crow and the civil rights movement. But 'conversation' puts all that history to sleep: it puts the world to sleep and gives Governor Haley time to test the political waters.[1]

These suffocating words and phrases might serve communication within a business, but they thwart it in debate. That is the second crime of modern political language: it stifles thinking. For all the talk of diversity and flexibility, brainstorming and blue-skying, management language is designed to get everyone thinking the same way: or, more accurately, not thinking beyond the part each plays in the process. One *cannot* think in clichés, or in pure abstraction, or in messages: and to speak or write in these forms is to prevent others from thinking too. One can't think or convey thoughts without images. One can't think in the fog that management jargon deliberately creates. One can't *know* in it. Whatever else might be better for being process-driven, politics is not. Politics needs thought and language equally. Civil society does.

But where will we find the politicians who know anything else? Leave aside the contaminated areas of their working life if they have had one, the universities they attended have rolled over to the managerial cult. The education departments are infected, and schools write reports that leave parents wondering if the outcomes in outcomes-based education are outcomes for their children or for the educators. Even kindergartens send home folios headed 'Early Years Learning and Development Framework Outcomes.'

We cannot fail to notice the new technology, the new economy, the new ways of working. It's hard to miss the fact of the revolution we're living through. But we can easily miss the way the new language has crept into daily life. We scarcely recognise the change, and even less do we notice what we're

1 A few days later Governor Haley was brave enough to have the flag and the flagpole removed.

losing. We adapt to the new all-purpose words and forget the many old ones they've replaced. With their passing, meaning fades; poetry and other keys to human possibility, including irony and critical self-reflection, are lost. 'The limits of my language are the limits of my world,' Wittgenstein said. In this sense at least, so-called globalisation and the global revolution in technology and communications have not made for an expanded world, but a diminished one. The knowledge economy is a realm of *lost* knowledge, of assured ignorance.

We come to ignore what has no meaning. We bend our brains around the void, and stop wondering if such as this is an unwitting idiocy or something sinister: 'In the recent evaluation by the Australian Council for Educational Research, school and community members reported that Direct Instruction was having a positive impact on student outcomes, but the researchers were not yet able to say whether or not the initiative has had an impact on student learning.'

Read it five times and you will not find a sensible meaning. Not even if you *drill down*, *deep dive* or *unpack* it. The problem is less one of logic than of language. In your mind's eye try to attach that sentence to some familiar thing, the inside of a ticking clock, for instance. There is no movement: or flesh, or bone or blood. Like many of the entries in this book it is a little absurd: like all but a very few it is also lifeless, and that, as Graham Greene would have said, is the bigger failing and the chief cause of the absurdity.

A

absolute crap

1. Not the case. Without basis in science. Untrue. Irrefutably false. Lies, poppycock, flapdoodle, hokum, pap, puerility, etc. As, 'Astrology is *absolute crap*.'
2. Demonstrably the case. With overwhelming scientific evidence. *Irrefutable. Absolute fact.* As, 'The argument [for climate change] is *absolute crap*' (Tony Abbott, *Australian*, 12 December 2009).
C.f. Nietzsche, 'The falseness of a judgement is to us not necessarily an objection to a judgement . . . The question is to what extent it is life-advancing, life-preserving . . .'

See *gospel truth*, *very seriously*.

absolute fact

1. Not fiction; even more factual than a fact; incontrovertible, and there are pictures to prove it. As, 'Gravity is an *absolute fact*.' 'It is an *absolute* statement of *fact* that Australians would experience a much lower standard of living if there was no foreign investment, or even reduced levels of foreign investment' (Joe Hockey, 2013).
2. *Absolute* humbug, hogwash, eyewash, won't wash, dupery, flimflam, japery, lie, etc. *Absolute crap*. As, 'It is an *absolute fact* children were thrown in the water . . . if you don't accept that, you don't accept anything' (Peter Reith, September 2001).

absolute principle

1. A principle which cannot be qualified or compromised; from which there can be no deviation or departure. As, 'Universal adult suffrage is an *absolute principle* of Australian democracy.'

2. A passing or convenient principle; *non-core* principle; not the *gospel truth* principle; *absolute crap*. As, 'It is an *absolute principle* of democracy that governments should not and must not say one thing before an election and do the opposite afterwards' (Tony Abbott, August 2011).

absolutely calm, considered, etc.

Favourable to truth-telling. As, 'I know politicians are going to be judged on everything they say, but sometimes in the heat of discussion you go a little bit further than you would if it was an *absolutely calm*, considered, prepared, scripted remark' (Tony Abbott, ABC, May 2010).
C.f. 'So I responded in what I thought was the most truthful, or least untruthful, manner by saying "no" ' (US Director of National Intelligence James Clapper clarifying his claim that the National Security Agency does not collect information on millions of Americans, *Huffington Post*, 6 June 2013).

access

1. (n) Admittance, admission. Entry. As, 'gain *access*'. 'Easy *access* to the beach.' A noun for nearly all its life, but since mid-20th century also a verb. (v) To open, get into. As, '*access* the data', '*access* your account', your garage, lavatory, mind, etc. 'Windows cannot *access* the specified device.'
2. A right or entitlement to services. As '*Access* and Equity.' 'Drought-stricken SA farmers reveal unequal *access* to low-interest loans . . .'
3. Meet or meeting with another, or parts of oneself hitherto unknown. As, 'In Tibet, I managed to *access* the Dalai Lama for half an hour.' '*Access* Consciousness provides you with ways to become totally aware and to begin to function as the conscious being you truly are.'

4. A buzzword, as: Access Hollywood, Access Canada, Access Economics, etc.

> 'Language is a *key issue* of *access* for people from any non-English speaking culture. It affects the individual's ability to *access* and use services and knowledge of services.'
>
> Human Rights Commission

> 'Four score and seven years ago our fathers brought forth upon this continent a new nation, conceived in liberty, and dedicated to the proposition that all men are created equal and should have equal *access* . . .'

accountable / accountabilities

1. Liable to be asked to render an account; answerable (to God, for instance).
2. What every organisation must be, along with every employee. Hence *accountability* (*ies*), a *core value* to be spelled out in every public statement.
As, 'In keeping with our *commitment* to high standards of behaviour, *transparency* and *accountability*, we have undertaken to inform the public when an officer faces serious allegations of misconduct' (*MyPolice QPS News*, 30 April 2015).
3. The Great Financial Crisis was caused by a lack of *accountability* (and *transparency*) in certain great companies (including accounting companies *accountable* for their clients' *accountability*), even though in their mission statements they swore *accountability* was a *core value*. Since the Great Financial Bailout these companies have sworn to it again, and more avidly. As, 'a *re-commitment* to strong, *accountable* processes that reemphasize the importance of *appropriate*

behavior and doing the right thing' (Goldman Sachs). We may consider the problem remedied.

4. A requirement of service owners. As, 'The decision taken will *facilitate* this by giving service owners greater ability to influence required business *outcomes*, noting that service owners are ultimately *accountable* for ensuring *delivery* of service changes to their respective client groups' (Email from university Chief Information Officer).

5. A kind of football. As, 'Magpies set to play *accountable* football' (*Wangaratta Chronicle*, 11 April 2014).

accounting irregularity

1. Creative accounting. An indiscretion involving money.

2. An innocent mistake, error, anomaly, or accidental misapplication of accounting principles inadvertently leading to *great* wealth among certain *clients* of the auditor – and the auditor.

3. Equally inadvertent consequence of bonus hunting.

4. What, in a *decontextualised scenario* might be interpreted as approximating or simulating fraud. White-collar crime. Theft motivated by excessive zeal, *commitment*, *passion*, *core values*, etc., but unarmed and rarely requiring actual break-in. *Accountable* theft.

5. An 'egregious refusal to see the obvious, or investigate the doubtful', especially among well-respected if not downright *iconic* firms – Deloittes, Bear Stearns, etc.

(Note: The shredding of files by accounting companies is not called an *accounting irregularity*.)

> '*Accounting irregularity* may be death knell for World Com: World Com, the second largest US phone company, admitted on 25 June that it had improperly booked its operating

expenses in such a way as to hide $3.8 billion in costs over the last five fiscal quarters. The expenses were reported as capital expenditures to be depreciated over time, allowing the carrier to post $1.38 billion in net income for 2001 instead of more than a billion dollar loss.'

Spectrum online, 27 June 2002

'Thou shalt not *account irregularly* . . .'

8th *Core Value*

'Thou shalt not covet thy neighbour's accountant.'

10th *Core Value*

across the board

Everyone and everything; without exception. Sweeping, all-encompassing, etc. As, 'But what is happening now is we are gradually increasing – *across the board*. The challenge for Australian-made vehicles *across the board* has been that we were behind the curve in moving to more fuel-efficient cars' (Tony Burke MP, *Sunrise*, 16 November 2012).

'Of great importance is the reaction of the business community, with the government in need of a rise in confidence *across the board*.'

9news.com.au, 12 May 2015

'Thou shalt not covet thy neighbour's house, thou shalt not covet thy neighbour's wife, nor his manservant, nor his maidservant, nor his ox, nor his ass, *across the board*.'

'You took the part that once was my heart,
So why not take me *across the board*.'

action

(n) 1. An act of doing; a thing done, a deed, etc.
2. A deed not necessarily done.
3. An (*action*) item of an *Action Plan* or *Action* Statement.

> 'DSE has also developed the *Actions* for Biodiversity Conservation (ABC) system in which the *actions* in *Action* Statements are stored. Responsibility for undertaking *actions* are recorded and priorities for *action* set.'

(v) do (something about something). As in, 'Please urgently *action* the following *issue* with your online order' (Telstra). 'We don't have enough resource to *action* that initiative right now.'

> The *Action* Wheel illustrates the interrelationship between the *outcomes* and the *action* areas: achievement in any one action area will impact on more than one desired *outcome*, conversely, achieving sustainable *outcomes* requires activity in more than one *action* area.
>
> The *Action* Wheel also guides *implementation* of the strategy beyond the systemic priorities identified in the plan.'
>
> Indigenous Education Strategic Plan 2006–2009, NT

> 'Demonstrate and articulate *innovative* methodologies that will *enhance* your ability to have your ideas heard (influence), and *actioned* (*project managed*) [sic].'
>
> Melbourne University Leadership & Professional *Development* Program

> 'Thy kingdom come. Thy will be *actioned*.'
>
> Jesus

> 'If it were *actioned* when 'tis *actioned*, then 'twere well. It was *actioned* quickly.'
>
> Macbeth

actionable

1. Affording ground for a legal *action*, or subject to such.
2. Able to be *actioned* (or done, used, etc., if you're old fashioned).
3. A kind of intelligence or knowledge. As, 'helping to explain options and quantify *impacts* in order to identify and capture *actionable* insights' (KPMG). '*Actionable* Intelligence is a necessity in a *dynamic* world of massive information *growth* because it empowers organizations with crucial insights and enables decision makers to anticipate, respond, and take *action*' (www.verint.com).

> '*Actionable* knowledge products distil and package knowledge into forms which can be easily *implemented* in day-to-day frontline practice. They provide "*calls to action*" at point of clinical need.
>
> To see how *actionable* knowledge is being taken forward in NHS Scotland, as part of knowledge into *action*, go to: http://www.knowledge.scot.nhs.uk . . .'
>
> NHS Scotland

action item

1. Task, job, thing to do.
2. Items of *action*.
3. Disaggregated objective.
4. 'transaction-based tasks that are assigned for completion within an activity guide' (docs.oracle.com).

> 'The 2013 OECD BEPS *Action Plan* was released after the G20 Ministers called for a coordinated and comprehensive approach to address BEPS issues. The *Action Plan* has 15 *Action Items* . . .'
>
> www.ato.gov.au

> 'Don't send a boy on a man's *action item*.'

NOTE: Ten *Action Items* are listed in the Lifecycle Management *Action Plan* recorded in Exodus 20 and Deuteronomy 5.

action plan

1. Plan of *action*, plan to do something, plan, etc.
2. Plan of, or for, very little *action*. An In*action Plan.* Tosh.

As, 'The Aboriginal and Torres Strait Islander Education *Action Plan* is a national plan that *commits* all governments in Australia to a unified approach to closing the gap in education *outcomes* between Aboriginal and Torres Strait Islander students and non-Aboriginal and Torres Strait Islander students' (scseec.edu.au).

> 'Minister's foreword. I am pleased to present an updated ICT Renewal *Action Plan* that will guide the ongoing *transformation* of government ICT.'
>
> Ian Walker, Minister for Science etc., Queensland, 2014

> 'The Aboriginal and Torres Strait Islander Health Performance *Framework* monitors progress in closing the gap in Indigenous Australians' health *outcomes*, while for education *outcomes* annual reporting is carried out on the Aboriginal and Torres Strait Islander Education *Action Plan* 2010–14. Six-monthly reports are also made on *deliverables* and *outcomes*

under the Northern Territory's Stronger Futures *package*, including formal reporting by the Northern Territory Government on measures for which it is responsible.'

'Closing the Gap', February 2013

'The best laid *action plans* o' mice an' men,
Gang aft agley.'

'Lights! Camera! *Action Plan*!'

address

To speak to, confront, look at, look into, examine, consider, *engage*, solve, etc.

The only thing to do with a *problem*; or an *issue* or a *need* (the means of actualising it); or a *challenge*, or a *potential outcome* or an *agenda*. What one does with an *ongoing issue*. What one is determined to do when one intends to do nothing. As, 'Strategies for *Addressing* Common Challenges'. 'Tailored interventions to *address* identified determinants of practice.' 'The Evidence Base for Improving School Outcomes by *Addressin*g the Whole Child . . .'

'After a week of probing we determined that he had bigger problems: his *leadership team* was not *aligned* on the operating model, *vision*, *growth strategy* or *business strategy*. It was evident that they didn't have a *process* to *address* these *issues*.'

European Business Review

'I'll *address* that bridge when I come to it.'

addressable spend

1. (v) Lay out money, time, etc. As, 'Hey, big spender / Spend a little time with me.'

2. (n) What has been, can or will be spent; and 'addressable' – able to be addressed. 'The proportion of expenditure that is eligible for spend savings.' As, 'We aggregate further *addressable spend* to maximise the gain-share against the procurement spend baselines . . .'

> 'The problem with our current definition is that there's too much room for interpretation of what constitutes *addressable spending* . . .'
>
> Marco Sa

> 'I'll *address* that *spend* when I come to it.'

adverse patient outcomes

Sore leg, hives, runny nose, death, end of the journey, etc.

> 'Reviews and analyses *data* on all components of the patient *journey* and experience and recommends *strategies* to address patient concerns . . .
>
> *Implement* and *evaluate* the *framework* for the recognition and response to the deteriorating patient and clinical emergencies . . .
>
> Maintain standards of professional practice and system improvement through reviews of *adverse patient outcomes* . . .'
>
> Job ad for Sydney West Area Health Service

> '. . . our little lives are ended with an *adverse patient outcome*.'

See also *negative patient outcomes*.

advices

More than one *advice*. As, 'No further *advices* will be issued unless thunderstorms redevelop' (Bureau of Meteorology).

> 'Son, let me give you some *advices*. Be good *in terms of* your *behaviours*.'

agenda

1. Program, schedule, plan, list of items, esp. for a meeting, ambition or *strategy*. (Hence, *agenda* for *change* or *change agenda*, *agenda* for *reform*, etc.)
2. Secret, hidden, unconscious, self-interested, wicked, *plan*. As, 'But the real *agenda* is a takeover.'
3. An ideology, doctrine or obsession frequently opposed to one's own, or to common sense, or the broader interest (e.g. feminist, gay, environmentalist, *bleeding heart*, national, right-wing, left-wing, neo-liberal *elitist*, socialist (now rare), murderous – anything). As, 'The Gay *Agenda* is an elusive concept.'
4. Government *agenda*, as in: 'Consult with *stakeholders* to *advance* government *initiatives* to support the "smart state" *agenda*.' (Consultant to Queensland Studies Authority)

> 'Radical feminism, male lesbians, transsexuals, musical condoms with suspenders, and lots a drummers drumming are all manifestations of a political *agenda* with roots in the 1960s.'
>
> Rush Limbaugh, *See, I Told You So*

'What does it mean for Grade 6's *moving forward*? . . . Board view of *strategic challenges*, "Talent" debate, career management debate, People *Strategy*, *Flexibility* and *robustness agenda* . . .'

Office of Fair Trading, UK

'We are such stuff as *agendas* are made on . . .'

The Tempest

aggressive timeline

1. Who knows?
2. *Going forwards aggressively*; with intent, speedily. *Robust* timeline.
3. *Fast track*. Do it before you go home tonight. Get a wriggle on. Mush! Get your arse into gear, etc.

'It's very *key* so we want an *aggressive timeline* on the *implementation architecture*.'

Victorian Education Department

'Thus the heavens and the earth were finished to an *aggressive timeline* . . . and he rested on the seventh day.'

aggressively pursue

To seek cost reductions, performance *enhancement*, *value-adds*, *change agility*, *commitments*, *business opportunities*, *employment*, *performance targets*, *etc*. *Robustly* pursue. Go after issues, commitments, goals, etc., like John Wayne leading a posse, As, 'in the pursuit of relentless excellence [sic]'.

'Our mission is to *aggressively pursue* our *commitment* to source a percentage of our federal, state and local government contracts for goods and services from Disadvantaged,

> Women-owned, HUBZone and Service Disabled Veterans businesses.'
>
> CPS HR Consulting

> 'Mr McGowan said he and Mr Wyatt would meet with the GST Review Panel to *aggressively pursue* the issue and present the committee with a comprehensive submission.'
>
> *WA Labor*, 16 April 2012

> '*Aggressively pursue* and ye shall find.'

agile / agility

1. Nimble, spry, lithe, athletic. C.f. Nureyev, mountain goat, etc.
2. A Treasury official. As, 'Change. Definition: change reflects the ability to be *agile*, initiate or adapt to work effectively in a variety of situations and with different people' (Victorian Department of Treasury and Finance).

> 'The Australia of the future has to be a nation that is *agile*, that is *innovative*, that is creative. We can't be defensive, we can't future-proof ourselves. We have to recognise that the disruption that we see *driven* by technology, the volatility in change, is our friend if we are *agile* and smart enough to take advantage of it.'
>
> Malcolm Turnbull, Prime Minister, 14 September 2015

> 'Ms Larson has an MBA plus a second Masters in Organisational Development. She co-presents this simple, yet highly applicable *change* model with the intention that Black Belts add *change agility* to their *skill set*. Thus building nimble *change embracing cultures* that are based on discipline, facts and data.'
>
> *Developing* Black Belt *Change Agents*

'*Agile* and Scrum Workshop:

The course uses the principles of Scrum and *Agile*, where the *learning outcome* is driven by the needs of the participants through a combination of expert instruction and self-directed learning.

You recognize the need to employ people who display *agile* traits and characteristics. You need facilities that encourage *agility* and connectedness.'

humanresources.about.com

agreed outcomes

Whatever is desired in common. Outcomes there is 'agreeance' about (from 16th-century French). The *team* responsible for *achieving* the *outcomes* is in *agreeance in terms of* how *core* they are.

'. . . document *agreed outcomes* and *indicators* in a Commissioning for *Outcomes* Statement.'

www.atdc.org.au

'The COMET (Core *Outcome* Measures in Effectiveness Trials) Initiative brings together people interested in the development and application of agreed standardised sets of *outcomes*, known as "*core outcome* sets" . . . The existence or use of a core *outcome* set does not imply that *outcomes* in a particular trial should be restricted to those in the relevant core *outcome* set.'

Comet Initiative

'For the coach (especially early on in his/her coaching), it can be tempting to focus so hard on *agreeing an outcome* (because that is *best practice*) that *achieving* agreement becomes an end in itself. Under this model of thinking, the first ten or so minutes of a session become completely focused on *agreeing a desired outcome* for the client . . . now the real job of coaching can finally begin, and the coach can use all of their finely honed skills to help the *client* get to the *outcome just agreed.*'

The Empty Table

'Wilt thou, Nigel, take . . .'

Solemnisation of *Agreed Outcomes*

align

1. To arrange in a line as sometimes our stars are.
2. What you must do with your *core values* and a*ctions* if you're to be a useful member of the *team. Goals* also need to be *aligned* with *values*. So do *behaviours*, with both *values and goals*; and *goals* with *actions*. And skills with *behaviour*s, and *change*. And *strategy* with *outcomes*. And all of them with key business objectives, which is to say, the *bottom line*. As, '. . . we have *ensured* our *CSR* (*corporate social responsibility*) activities are fully *aligned* with our efforts to *deliver* our *key* business objectives' (BAE Systems).
3. A close relation of maximising *synergies* (distant relation of astrology and Maoism).

'Objective: To help *team* leaders review their *values* with their *teams* and ask for *input* on how well their *actions* are aligned with these *values*.'

www.leadershipchallenge.com

'So if one of my (the leaders) *values* is *relationships*, and you believe that I allow time for *team* discussion and fun to build our *relationships*, my *actions* would be *aligned* with that value.

> If, on the other hand, one of my *values* is honesty/integrity and you have noticed that I don't share information with you, that might mean my *actions* are not *aligned* with my *values*.'
>
> (How To Discover And *Align* Your Company's *Core Values*)
>
> www.7geese.com

alignment (mis)

Disagreement; at variance with others. As, 'Unfortunately Mick's obvious public *misalignment* with the football club has resulted in a loss of trust between the club and coach' (Carlton FC President, *Age*, 26 May 2015).

> 'I am *misaligned* with what you say, but I will defend to the death your right to say it.'
>
> Voltaire

all-hands meeting

An enthusiastic expression of *buy-in*. C.f. May Day in Tiananmen Square. As, 'Ah! The *All Hands Meeting*. What will you say when you get up to speak about the state of the organization? How will you stand and deliver a talk that perfectly frames the current *issues*, *challenging* people to *move forward* and redouble their efforts?' (The Bates Blog)

> 'A senior executive reportedly told "an *all-hands meeting* Amazon used to burn a lot of people into the ground."'
>
> *New York Times*, 17 August 2015

> 'The 2015 Gulf of Mexico Alliance annual *All Hands* meeting will be held June 16–18, 2015 in Biloxi, Mississippi. Much of the meeting will be devoted to *Action Plan* III development through the reorganized *Priority Issue Teams*.'

'Northwestern University welcomes you to the Open Science Grid *All-Hands Meeting* 2015 . . . The Open Science Grid (OSG) provides a common service and support for resource providers and scientific institutions using a distributed fabric of high throughput computational services.'

Amazonian

An employee of Amazon. As, 'The article doesn't describe the Amazon I know or the caring *Amazonians* I work with every day' (Jeff Bezos, Amazon CEO, *New York Times*, 17 August 2015).

'"If you're a good *Amazonian*, you become an Ambot," said one employee, using a term that means you have become at one with the system' (*New York Times*, 17 August 2015). 'Amhole' is also popular.

See *anytime feedback tool*; *manage out*

anytime feedback tool

Widget used by Amazon that allows employees to send praise or criticism about colleagues to management anytime. '. . . many workers called it a river of intrigue and scheming.'

'They described making quiet pacts with colleagues to bury the same person at once, or to praise one another lavishly. Many others . . . described feeling sabotaged by negative comments from unidentified colleagues with whom they could not argue. In some cases, the criticism was copied directly into their performance reviews – a move that Amy Michaels, the former Kindle manager, said that colleagues called "the full paste"' (*New York Times*, 17 August 2015).

'Workday, a *human resources* software company, makes a similar product called *Collaborative Anytime Feedback* that promises to turn the annual performance review into a daily *event*.' The very thought that his fellow 'caring *Amazonians*' should think their workplace a 'soulless' dystopia governed by 'purposeful Darwinism' caused Amazon CEO, Jeff Bezos, to publicly express dismay and to write to employees, '*Hopefully*, you're having fun working with a bunch of brilliant teammates, helping invent the future, and laughing along the way.' Bezos was an early investor in the Workday *tool*.

See *manage out*

appropriate

Not *inappropriate*. Not raping, molesting, harassing, assaulting, for instance.

> '"The department expects service provider staff to act *appropriately* and with integrity in all their dealings."'
>
> Immigration Department spokesperson 'in the wake of allegations three Australian guards who worked for Wilson Security raped a local woman who also worked at the centre'. *Guardian*, 6 August 2015

See *inappropriate*

appropriate financial envelope

Envelope from which Microsoft took 12,500 workers.

> 'Our device *strategy* must reflect Microsoft's *strategy* and must be accomplished within an *appropriate financial envelope*. Therefore we plan to make some *changes* . . . We plan to *right-size* our manufacturing operations to *align* to the new *strategy* and

take advantage of integration opportunities . . . We plan that this would result in an estimated reduction of 12,500 factory direct and professional employees over the next year. These decisions are difficult for the *team* . . .'

Stephen Elop, Microsoft VP, letter to employees, July 2014

architect

1. (n) An architect.
2. (v) Construct. Conceive. Create. Design. Come up with. As, 'Building on their years of successful *framework* development and *leveraging* the proliferation of WiFi enabled devices, engineers at Jargon have *architected* JargonTalk to simplify entertainment app creation.'

'We can *architect* a *strategy* to *drive* real business results through content, social media and a variety of other *tools*.'

www.focalpointcoaching.com

'*Architect* a *strategy* and set a trajectory to implement your long-term *vision*.'

www.theshapeofthings.com

'I *architected* it my way.'

architecture

High principles.

'Customer Experience Reference *Architecture* . . . In essence *architecture* principles translate business needs into IT mandates that the solution must meet. Because *architecture* principles span the entire solution, they are at a much higher level than functional requirements. Establishing *architecture* principles drives the overall technical solution . . .'

From Oracle's 'Customer Experience Reference *Architecture*'

artisan / artisanal

1. (n) One trained in manual dexterity; a craftsperson or mechanic.
2. (adj) Bread, eclairs and croissants, ice-cream, cheese, crisps, etc. 'hand-made' – often to a 'centuries-old' recipe or tradition.

As, 'In 1624, the first dairy cows were brought to the Boston area by the settlers from England, birthing *artisanal* cheese-making in America. Great cheeses are still made here, on our lands, between the stone walls and the sky.'

> 'Today's zeitgeist of mindfulness offers good will to the little guy. Smaller is more honest, *artisanal* and quality-minded.'
>
> Geoff Kruth, Champagne *Reality Check*, 30 April 2015

> 'It's a group (*millennials*) that has grown up during a time of rapid change, giving them a set of priorities and expectations sharply different from those of previous generations. Among these priorities is a desire to experience *brands* that are *authentic*, that offer hand-crafted or *artisanal* goods, specifically those with an appreciation for how things are made, for who makes them, and for health and wellness.'
>
> Allen Adamson, *Forbes*

Possibly related to *early onset nostalgia*. See also *authentic/ authenticate*; *millennials*

aspiration

Desire to *actualise* vanity.

> 'Our writings on the "*aspirational* gap" have *focused* more on how *lifestyle brands* should help *customers actualise* their *aspirations*.'
>
> *New York Times*

> 'Follow every rainbow,
> till you *achieve* your *aspirations*.'

aspirational

(adj) Characterised by desire or ambition. A political and *marketing* category.
(n) 1. An aspirer. One who *aspires*, has ambitions, wants, etc.
2. A class of people or political constituency – said to be new or 'of the future' – who want something better for themselves, want to 'get on'.
3. Working people who don't see themselves as working class. Ditto customers and companies that cater to them. As, '. . . *aspirational* companies like Virgin'.
4. People with 'higher-purpose *commitments*'; (adj) *aspirational* voters, shoppers / shopping (as, 'buying slightly above their true station in life'), *customers*. A person – or class of people – pursued by politicians and commercial interests for their votes and money.
5. Social climber; grasper; upstart; philistine; (adj) greedy; materialistic; meretricious; selfish.

> 'Estates like these are home to the *aspirationals* . . .'
>
> ABC Radio

> 'Australia is *aspirational* . . .'
>
> Consultancy to Australian Tourism Commission

'I had the opportunity to share with *Aspirant* Principal Leaders on Tuesday morning some information relevant to the improved data trend at Mont Albert Primary School over the last two years.'

Mont Albert Primary School Bulletin, 27 October 2011

'If You Want Your Brand To Succeed, Make It *Aspirational*, Not Inspirational. Companies that ditch tired celebrity personas and transform themselves into vehicles for realizing their *customers' aspirations* will transcend single transactions.'

www.fastcoexist.com

'. . . as he was *aspirational*, I slew him.'

Julius Caesar

attitude

1. Outlook, opinion, standpoint, manner, posture, etc.
As, 'He has a curious *attitude* to underwear.'
2. Character, personality; being. ('What *attitude*!')
3. Also *attitude* problem – bad *attitude*, poor *attitude*, wrong *attitude*; heretical *attitude*, reactionary *attitude*, enemy of the state sort of *attitude*; *attitude* that needs to be addressed by team-building exercises, large group awareness training, Neuro Linguistic Programming, *re-engineering*, downsizing, etc.

'The basic Chevron assessment test is a three part test which includes:

. . . Workplace *Attitude* and *Behavior* Inventory – this is your basic personality test which assesses whether your personality and *behavior* will *align* with the company ideals and workforce.'

www.testprep-online.com/chevron-assessment-test

'Thou shalt not bear false *attitude*.'

attrit

(v) From attrition – wearing down. As, 'war of attrition'. Confined to the military for now.

> 'It can *attrit* enemy capabilities and frustrate enemy movements on the ground.'
>
> Dakota L. Wood, *Daily Signal*

> '"They were *committed* to this and we could see fighters flooding in from Raqqa and we saw that as an opportunity to *attrit* their manpower," he said.'
>
> *Guardian*, 20 December 2014

> '"The more I *attrit* him there," Austin said . . . "the less I'll have to fight him on some other part of the battlefield."'
>
> CNN, 17 October 2014

> 'We shall *attrit* on the beaches, we shall *attrit* on the landing grounds, we shall *attrit* in the fields and in the streets . . .'
>
> Winston Churchill

Australian (un)

See *caffè latte*

Australian lifestyle

1. The style of life in Australia. Bushfire prone. Easygoing; fair go; she'll be right; slip, slap, slop; lucky country, etc. Not up yourself. Just like us. Not 'not the sort of people we want here'. Relaxed and comfortable. Democratic, tolerant, rich multicultural diversity, etc. Crocodile hunting. Mateship, stick together in adversity. Alert but not alarmed. Sport.

Anzac spirit. Greatest shareholding democracy in the world. Aussie! Aussie! Aussie!

2. A handful of clichés useful in politics, media, marketing, etc. *Enhanced Australian lifestyle* – what *aspirationals* seek; i.e. *achievement* of *envisioned* personal *goals*; *implementation* of *goals*: private school, share portfolio, etc. In real estate a house or flat is a '*Lifestyle* Opportunity'.

> '"With the introduction of The Grove Mall in Windhoek, it provided us an opportunity to introduce Cotton On to a new community and export our laidback, quintessential *Australian lifestyle* to Namibians," she said.'
>
> allAfrica.com

> '. . . it was a fresh and sporty range that epitomised the laid-back *Australian lifestyle* and – gasp – it was all machine washable.'
>
> *Sydney Morning Herald*

> 'Three tours of duty in Afghanistan have taught Chief Petty Officer Damian Pawlenko the value of family and the *Australian lifestyle*.'
>
> adf.farmonline.com.au

> 'To think they gave their lives to defend our *Australian lifestyle*.'
>
> Football commentator on Anzac Day

> '*Lifestyle* Funeral Services.'
>
> Geelong, Victoria

> 'I love a sunburnt *lifestyle*,
> A land of sweeping plains.'
>
> Dorothea MacKellar

author

(n) Writer. (v) To write. As, 'Tolstoy *authored War and Peace.*' Lincoln *authored* the Gettysburg Address. *Authors* of English curricula sometimes speak of '*authored* texts'. Political commentators speak of the authors of military campaigns and catastrophes. As, 'There's no question who *authored* latest Iraq collapse' (Charles Krauthammer).

> 'Devil's Bible claimed to have been *authored* by Satan himself discovered in Czech Republic.'
>
> Standard Digital

> 'It is *authored.*'

> 'The *authoring*'s on the wall.'

> 'It's *authored* all over your face.'

axis

Externally and internally facing *enabler* of *strategy.*

> 'Our new operating model is based on a *matrix* structure with an externally facing *axis* led by our *Partnership* and *Programme* Director and six portfolio leaders; and a predominately [sic] internally facing *axis* led by our Research Director and six Science Group Leaders. Together they enable us to *achieve* our business *strategy* of "Building *Partnerships* and *Delivering to Stakeholders*".'
>
> Job advertised by AgResearch

B

backcasting

Not forecasting.

> '*Backcasting* is similar to *visioning*, however *backcasts* are not intended to reveal what the future will be, but rather to weigh up a number of possible futures, and decide the implications and preferable options, then to map out steps along the way.'
>
> www.dse.vic.gov.au

backfilling

1. To fill an excavated area.
2. To fill a recently vacated staff position.
3. To fill holes dug by ill-considered policy. As, ' "There was a headlong rush to be best buddies with Abe," explains a minister, "and we have been *backfilling* ever since" ' (www.watoday.com).

Backwards Curriculum Design

As follows (follows as?):

> 'Design a rubric to assess this subject/program/unit. For more information on designing effective rubrics go to Assessment Professional *Learning* Module 2, Activity 2–5 Creating Rubrics.
>
> 1. Create a table like the one below
>
> 2. Criteria – develop criteria from the standards identified in Step 1, write/type them in the criteria row, one criteria for each cell.

3. Labels for level of quality – make up your own appropriate labels

4. Check how your rubric scores against the sample rubric on designing rubrics below – share the rubric with students at the beginning of the subject/program/unit, for their input and to assist in developing their understanding of expectations of their learning.'

Office of Learning and Teaching, DE&T, Victoria

baked in

1. Cooked in. As in, 'fillet steak *baked in* pastry', or 'cake *baked in* a moderate oven'.
2. *Embedded* in the organisational *culture*. Not layered on or sprinkled, etc. As, '*Baking SEO into* the company workflow and *culture*' (SEO Book).

'Filippelli's scheme "*baked in* a continuum of environments", where workers could tap into a wide range of possibilities.'

www.metropolismag.com

'Inclusion of people with differing abilities needs to be *baked in* across the enterprise, rather than layered on to a company's *culture*.'

Huffington Post

'Sing a song of sixpence, a pocket full of rye,
Four and twenty blackbirds, *baked in* a continuum of environments.'

balance

1. Poise, equilibrium, steadiness. Weighed.

2. Poise, equilibrium, steadiness, even-handedness, as epitomised by Andrew Bolt.
3. Whatever serves the status quo; the government, the board; mediocrity, dullness, timidity.
4. Not 'emotive', 'hyperbolic, inflammatory or derogatory'. What the average viewer would consider 'respectful'. Not Sarah Ferguson. Emma Alberici not. Tony Jones not. Leigh Sales definitely not. *The Drum*, Barrie Cassidy, Kerry O'Brien – no, no, no (nope, nope, nope).

> 'But I still ask why the ABC is so biased, with all its main current affairs shows hosted by the Left, despite the ABC's charter requiring *balance*.'
>
> Andrew Bolt, *Herald Sun*, 16 December 2013

> 'In the 2012–13 financial year, the "percentage of people who believe the ABC is *balanced* and even-handed when reporting news and current affairs" was 79%.'
>
> Newspoll quoted in *Guardian*, 6 February 2014

> '". . . *balance*", the BBC's crudely applied device for avoiding trouble . . .'
>
> Tim Llewellyn, January 2004

bandwidth

1. In Information Technology, the amount of *data* that a communications line can transmit.
2. In *Human Resources*, the amount of time that managers have; their capabilities. As, 'Increased Management *Bandwidth* – added capability and capacity, alongside restructured *team* management.'

> 'Not needing to keep those feelings bottled up provides your employees with greater emotional *bandwidth* when facing the conflict triggers that pop up during interpersonal interactions.'
>
> Scott Verette, Springboard, The HR Blog

> 'Can you help?' 'Sorry, I don't have the *bandwidth*.'

battler

1. Low-income earner. One who battles in life; struggles to make ends meet, but never gives up; an honest, down-to-earth *ordinary Australian* on low-to-average wages. Salt of the earth. Hard-up. Incarnation of Henry Lawson, Anzac, John Curtin, Slim Dusty, Delta Goodrem, etc. A worker. A socialist (archaic).
2. Loser. Honest no-hoper. Mug punter. Race-track emu. Leaner (not lifter). Not effectually self-interested; poor bastard, etc. Fails to aspire sufficiently.
3. Not a yuppie, not New Age, not a member of the chattering classes or *elite*. Drinks instant coffee. Not *politically correct*. Person who really needs a 4×4, but can't afford one. Person who used to vote for the Labor Party, but now votes for anybody. Voters of influence. Also known as 'Howard *battlers*'; As, 'the former prime minister says Tony Abbott is connecting with middle Australia, the "Howard *battlers*" vital to four Coalition victories, because he is more "authentic" than Mr Rudd' (*Australian*, 15 March 2010).

> 'Howard, by contrast, strikes a chord with traditional working people because he understands that *battlers* want a hand up, not a handout.'
>
> Tony Abbott

'Abbott's Budget backflip over $150,000 "*battlers*".'

Daily Telegraph, 12 May 2011

'Mick Malthouse a *battler* from Ballarat with a steely determination to succeed.'

Herald Sun

'*Battlers* engage negative gear.'

Australian

'Give me your tired, *battling* poor,
Your *battling battlers* yearning to breathe free,
The wretched *battlers* of your teeming shore.' (after Emma Lazarus)

bed down

1. Go to bed, settle down for the night, hit the hay, hit the sack, doss, crash, sleep on the floor, etc. Encamp as animals do: 'At night they *bed down* in the open away from trees and bushes.'
2. To put in place permanently, or at least until the next *consultancy*. To *set in concrete*. Organisations like their *values* and *behaviours* to be *bedded down*. Also their *strategies*, *goals*, technology, etc.

'The trend is expected to accelerate as banks *bed down* CRM as a *customer management* and *marketing tool* . . .'

Australian Financial Review

'Stability at a premium as Australia *bed down* a new Test team.'

Australian

'Now I *bed me down* my goals.'

behaviours

More than one behaviour. Applied values. *Behaviours* are often *key* and sometimes *core*. For instance, 'knowing the personal *drivers*' and 'evaluating content of work and *quality*' are *key behaviours*.

> 'As members of the Department of Treasury and Finance, it is important that we all demonstrate *behaviours* reflective of both the *organisational aspirations* of the Department, and the specific work *accountabilities, deliverables* and *outputs* for which we are individually responsible.'
>
> Victorian Department of Treasury and Finance

> 'The *issue* is that when we read about *accountability* or experience it in the workplace first hand the starting point is typically misplaced. In order to hold yourself and others *accountable* for a task, a *project*, a *deliverable* or a business unit you need to start with some *behaviors* which are an *input* not the *goals* or objective which are *outcomes*.'
>
> thought leadership leverage

> 'These *behaviours*, generally referred to within the organisation as "The Eight *Behaviours*", are as follows: 1. . . . Ruthlessly seeking to understand, through the use of *dialogue* . . .'
>
> Leadership@City of Port Phillip

> 'He will "*drive* the leadership, *drive* the *values*, *drive* the *behaviours*."'
>
> Channel 7 football commentator

> 'In addition to the belief statements, we have developed some core *behaviours* to help us apply our *values*.'
>
> Department of Treasury and Finance, Tasmania

'Team *Behavioural* Inventory (TBI)

Team *Behavioural* Inventory is an inventory or checklist of positive and negative *behaviours* associated with team high-performance and based on the *team* wheel.'

www.argospress.com

'Give them according to their Team *Behavioural* Inventory, and according to their negative *behaviours* . . .'

Psalm 28

'If your *behaviours* don't improve, Shane, your *punishments* will be severe.'

benchmarking

(n) A surveyor's mark for observing tides; hence, a standard by which the performance of an individual or organisation can be measured.
(v) 'Learning, sharing information and adopting *best practices* to bring about step changes in performance' (Public Sector Benchmarking Service, UK).
(adj) '*Benchmarked*, the state of an organisation, individual or activity after *benchmarking*; that is, more efficient, successful or competitive.'
Whatever is the best is called the *benchmark*: *Citizen Kane*, *The Wire*, Krug, Sherlock Holmes, Black Caviar, Beluga caviar, Usain Bolt, Placido Domingo, Heisenberg's Blue Meth, Domaine de la Romanée-Conti, Steel Cut oats, Lionel Messi, etc.

'I think it is a time where defence and civilians will look at Australia as a community and *benchmark* how far Australia has come in 100 years.'

ABC

'The suite of *deliverables* for Rail Trail Phase 2 includes:

A detailed plan for *benchmark* interpretive, wayfinding, stay/eat/do and safety signs, online information hubs, rail trail furniture (think seats and tables, bike racks, horse tie-ups and more) and detailed construction and installation specifics.'

Mansfield Shire Victoria

'You're the top. You're the Colosseum,
You're the top. A *benchmarked* Museum.'

best of breed / best in breed / best in class

1. The best example (of Angora rabbit, White Orpington hen, Jersey cow, etc.) in the show.
2. 'The *strategy* of selecting the best *product* of each type (and *integrating* them yourself), rather than selecting one large *integrated* solution from a single vendor.' Also applied to people, but so far only in their organisational contexts.

'Wherever appropriate, these "*best of breed*" products are *integrated* to provide a *seamless* legal office *utilising* industry standard, client/server infrastructures.'

Consultancy

'With a line of sight to their *end customers,* they are seeking leading-edge and *best-of-breed* practitioners with a *passion* for *driving change* and *innovation* and a demonstrated *track record delivering* major *projects* to join their dynamic team . . .'

Job advert for Queensland Health

best practice

> '*Best-in-class* organizations are *migrating* towards a more *strategic mindset* by emphasizing deep partnerships with *internal customers* and suppliers.'
>
> The Good Procurement Guide: Launch & Creating *Value* from Internal Business *Alignment Workshop*, run by the Government Reform Commission

best practice

The best or equal to the best; the *benchmark*; none finer; that to which all procedures should conform; what organisations seeking *continuous improvement* try to *achieve*. Commonly 'International *best practice*', 'World's *best practice*'.

> 'The project is referred to as "Sourcing – Building *talent pipelines* and supply chains" and the first phase involves the engagement of an external provider who will assist the department in researching and identifying *best practice* sourcing *strategies* that are *appropriate* and adaptable for the Department of Human Services.'
>
> An email to government employees

bite

1. Bite.
2. Not so much a *bite* as the physical result of being bitten in the ordinary course of *events*. As, 'The truth is my colleague Giorgio Chiellini suffered the physical result of a *bite* in the collision he suffered with me' (footballer Luis Suarez apologising for the suffering of his Italian rival).

black-armband history

As a *black armband* signifies mourning or at least respect for the dead, history that respects or mourns the dead. Excessive maudlin concentration on the victims of imperial wars, especially the Anzacs at Gallipoli, France, Belgium, Palestine, Vietnam, Iraq, etc. History that mourns too much. History that pays too much attention to these unpleasant facts and too little to the happier strands of the national story, to 'all the good things that have happened'. 'Miserable', 'unpatriotic', 'unAustralian' history, as if it were 'little more than a disgraceful story of imperialism,' etc (John Howard). As, '. . . we don't want to beat ourselves up every day' (Christopher Pyne, January 2014). As, 'It is because of our history that we are a confident and positive nation. We must not allow a confidence-sapping "*black armband*" view of our history to take hold' (C. Pyne, 2014).

bleeding edge of innovation

Untested, possibly unreliable new technology. Much riskier than *leading edge* or even cutting edge. Edgy. Don't buy one. As, 'What remained astounding is that the OI executives I spoke with described themselves as operating at the *bleeding edge of innovation*. In their words, by participating in Open *Innovation*, they are daily risking career-ending failures' (Innovation Excellence).

> 'Through the newly cemented *partnership* with USC School of Cinematic Arts, the World Building Institute is evolving into an unmatched connector between the next generation of young and undiscovered creators traversing the *bleeding edge of innovation* and companies who want to be at the front-lines of the new media landscape.'
>
> World Building Institute

blue ocean strategy

Coming up with a product to sell into a market your competitors have not dreamed of. Not *red ocean strategy*. Uncontested territory. Wonderful. Downright paradisiacal. With 3.5 million copies sold (catching up to *Lost Horizon*), *Blue Ocean Strategy* tells you how to get there. Think iPad, Cirque du Soleil, Ryanair.

Then again, not everyone has bought it. 'The book titled *Blue Ocean Strategy* is not helpful to management – don't buy it and if you already have it dump it. Management can and should be *visionary* in formulating *strategy* but should do so by thinking about market environment shifts, how these could *impact customer sets*, and whether those *customer sets* are the ones you wish to serve. In your *strategizing* do not take advice on *strategy* (or any other *mission critical function*) from management who are not qualified to give advice and do not treat *strategy* formulation as an exercise in management *team* compromise' (TRU Group Inc.).

See *red ocean strategy*

blue sky thinking

Thinking without clouds. Imagining your *product* in a world free of downers. As, 'That's a bit *blue sky* if you don't mind me saying so, Colin.' But it has advantages.

> 'Further *blue-sky thinking* from Rothamsted Research, exhibiting with the John Innes Centre, will present developments in BBSRC research including using GM technology to produce a sustainable source of omega-3 fish oil in oilseed.'
>
> www.fwi.co.uk

'"A lot of customers are *blue-sky thinking* about where they can take this technology," Katanas said.'

www.cso.com.au

boil the ocean

Attempt the impossible. Waste time trying to do what can't be done. Over-*scoping*. As, 'You're *boiling the ocean* again, Colin.' Will Rogers might have started it when, during World War II, he was asked how he would deal with the Nazi U-boats and replied, '*Boil the ocean.*'

'But how would you do that?' the reporter continued. Rogers replied, 'I'm just the idea man here. Get someone else to work out the details.'

'Consultants can run the risk of attempting to "*boil the ocean*" when *scoping* their projects and must work with their clients to set realistic expectations and successful and timely *delivery* of results.'

Institute of Management Consultants US

'I believe that efforts by *knowledge management* programs to change the *culture* of an organisation are an exercise in futility, tantamount to the "*boiling the ocean*" metaphor.'

www.glentworth.com

border protection

1. Protecting borders from weeds, pests, drugs, terrorists, crime, disease, etc.
2. Protecting borders from people smugglers. As, 'the absolute scum of the earth' (K. Rudd) with whom we are in a 'fierce contest' – and 'if we were at war, we wouldn't be giving out information that is of use to the enemy just

because we might have an idle curiosity about it ourselves' (T. Abbott).
3. Protecting borders from *queue jumpers*, *illegals*, *illegal maritime arrivals*, '*economic refugees*', people who are not real refugees.
4. Protecting those who protect the borders from all public scrutiny.
5. Xenophobia. Wedge politics. Scare campaign. Race to the bottom, etc.

> 'Nope, nope, nope.'
>
> Tony Abbott, PM

bottleneck

An impediment to *throughput*. A weak link in the *value chain*. A clot in the *process* flow. A constraint. Something requiring *debottlenecking*.

Sometimes a person is a *bottleneck*. As, 'Inventory = *Throughput* × Flow Time: Where *Throughput* is the *throughput* of the *process* and is the *throughput* of the slowest resource (Person B) and Flow Time is the average time that a typical flow unit spends within the *process* boundaries' (*Six Sigma*).

bottom line

1. An accounting term. The last figure on the balance sheet.
2. What matters. The only thing that matters. Don't ask me about anything else. As, 'But the *bottom line* is . . .'

'QUENTIN MCDERMOTT: Tell me about the *bottom line*.

JANELLE: Well, the *bottom line* is this, Quentin. You either pass your scorecard or you or we go onto the performance improvement path – that's the *bottom line*.'

Four Corners

'The *bottom line*, I have been saying it for years, Labor will never *deliver* a surplus.'

Joe Hockey press conference transcript

'The *bottom line* is, as we show in the documents, as a result of what we've done since being elected, taxes are lower under the Coalition than they would have been under Labor.'

Joe Hockey, ABC

'The *bottom line* is: if you can win a battle, you take that victory, but you never give up on the war.'

Joe Hockey, ABC

'Well, there's not enough money to do it, anyway. That's the *bottom line*.'

Joe Hockey, ABC

'The *bottom line* now is we need to recycle precious taxpayers' money from existing assets that the private sector wants to own, that your superannuation is desperate to own.'

Joe Hockey, *Sydney Morning Herald*

'All animals are equal, but the *bottom line* is some are more equal than others.'

Animal Farm

bottom-up

1. (i) Capsized; defunct, kaput. (ii) Face down.
2. *Bottom(s) up!* Drinking salutation or toast; Cheers! Here's to a long *lifestyle* and a happy one! etc.
3. Not top down. Not Taylorism. Change that does not *cascade* or *trickle down.* Trickle up. Not 'everyone has their face toward the CEO and their ass toward the customer' (Jack Welch), but the other way round. More meetings. More teams. More team leaders. More scope for petty tyrants. '[R]ather than limiting the potential abuses of managerial power, it cloaks such abuses in a cloying, false morality' (James Hoopes).

Bottom-up management creates a 'perspective transformation', which is not surprising in view of the following:

> 'The continuum from "*Top Down*" to "*BottomUp*" is circular. We are talking about turning the chart upside down hence it must be rotated. As we turn the chart we will find that it rotates on the axis of middle management. This is significant because the largest transformation of perspective will take place at the top and bottom of the organization. Middle management will feel less momentum and will be most inclined to identify with or understand the value of *BottomUp* Management™.'
>
> BottomUp Management™

> 'O'Neill's "crusade" was not based on top-down decrees, but on *bottom-up buy-in*.'
>
> smartcompany

> 'A spectre is haunting management – the spectre of *BottomUp* Management™.'
>
> *The BottomUp Management™ Manifesto*

brainstorming

Group ideation, especially popular in advertising. Let's get together, throw off our inhibitions, put our critical faculties on hold, and toss a few ideas around. See what we come up with. First, catch your brain.

> 'They have hosted two company-wide *events* based on the Open Space approach of loosely themed, self-organized *brainstorming* sessions, on audience growth and cross-*brand products*.'
>
> Lucia Moses, *Digiday*

> 'More than 100 Aussie business people wrap up a unique *brain-storming* session in Antarctica amid hopes the trip will help reinvigorate entrepreneurialism.'
>
> SBS (Note: some 'expressed disappointment at the program's structure and the inclusion of holistic personal development activities'.)

brand / branding

1. (n) Distinguishing name or trademark. To distinguish with a *brand*, as e.g. cowboys do with cows.
2. As advertising and *marketing* (speaking of cowboys) does with underwear and universities. Brands are built on big ideas, such as Deakin University – 'Worldly'; or Queensland – 'The Sunshine State'. Queensland's used to be 'Bold, Aye, and Faithful Too', which had a ring to it, but *brands* (or visual identities) need to be refreshed from time to time. *Brands* should be *agile*. (How else for *branding* people to make a living?)

Examples of *brands* built on big ideas include Coke Life, Toyota Kluger, Yogurberry, Golden Gaytime and Fcuk.

'Our *challenge* was to create a design that allowed passengers to easily navigate the system and perform various options whilst *ensuring* that the *brand* values of friendly, professional and *service-orientated clients* were clearly enunciated throughout the design.' It is a scandal that no brander has yet won the Nobel Prize.

Branding frequently means changing an impossibly mundane name into a marvellous new one: National Bank of Australia to National Australia Bank and Australian Opera to Opera Australia, for example.

Universities in pursuit of market share appoint *brand* managers and pay large sums to agencies for big ideas: as, the University of Western Australia's 'Pursue Impossible'.

> 'In a secret 86-page advertising pitch brief obtained by *Crikey*, the Australian arm of Rupert Murdoch's global empire – to be *rebranded* "News Australia" – reveals its plans for a local resurrection under the code name "Project Darwin" . . .
>
> "Research revealed some *misalignment* with espoused and enacted *values*. It also suggested that any existing *value* statements were often disconnected from the company or *brands* and were not well communicated." '
>
> Andrew Crook, *Crikey*, 21 September 2011

> '. . . tell the Jetstar story and empower employees to be *brand* ambassadors . . .'

> 'The *Brand* Tasmania Council is *committed* to the promotion and protection of the Tasmanian *Brand* and the values that constitute that *brand* in national and international markets . . . In order to join the *Brand* Tasmania organisations must demonstrate a *commitment* to the Tasmanian *brand values* and agree to meet the membership criteria.'
>
> *Brand* Tasmania

'The Entrepreneur *Brand* Accelerator

From how to better PITCH your business, right through to creating valuable *PRODUCTS* and establishing powerful *PARTNERSHIPS*, this conference presents the 5 essential soft skills for gaining influence, building a *brand* and doing what you love.'

keypersonofinfluence.com.au

'Thou shalt have no other *brands* before me!'

1st *Commitment*

brandactional

Brand advertising combined with direct marketing.
A trademark of Haggin Inc.

'We visualized information overload with "burden balls" to help demonstrate how the product worked, created rich media and contextually relevant online ad units, point-of-sale video, in-app iPad advertising and more. Our "*brandactional*" campaign featured more than 40 publishing partners and delivered nearly 250M online impressions, including more than 75M video impressions.'

www.t-3.com

brandgagement

Another *driver* of the 'purchase cycle': using social media to multiply word-of-mouth a million times over. Now everyone knows what you have bought or what you are thinking of buying. In the process you '*brandgage*'.

'Sam's *brandgagement* blog and accompanying social media channels will contain examples and insight gleaned from the latest trends in marketing and advertising, and thoughts on how marketers can redefine the *customer experience* to *drive brand* preference, loyalty and growth. We encourage you to visit the blog and post a comment.'

Publicis Healthcare Communications Group (PHCG)

'Denny's has the best *brandgagement* I've ever seen.'

Twitter

'Her *brandgagement* is through the roof.'

Twitter

brand (living the)

To be engaged, to such an extent that you 'outbehave' your competitors. What one wants from one's workforce.

'The only true employee-driven measure of whether the workforce is "*living the brand*" is the perspective of others in each work area. Use a company-wide assessment at least twice a year to understand and remind the team to outbehave the competition.'

Martin Zwilling, *Forbes*

brand story-telling

What you find on artisanal cereal packets: how Bruce and Eric were just sitting around the campfire one night and wondering why you couldn't get *authentic* pre-washed biodynamic quinoa and well, dammit, they went right out and did it, and now they're selling a whole range of stuff and they're so glad you've decided to join them on their *journey*. Big companies do it too: not just in words, but in pictures. Every *brand* has a story – who doesn't want to be part of it? Every *brand* has a personality – who doesn't want to be its friend?

> 'Marketing is no longer about the stuff that you make, but the *stories* you tell.'
>
> Seth Godin

> 'Hillsong is definitely Australia's modern *brand* success story. As an entertainment *brand* more than anything, they've been able to *leverage* and *monetise* Christian *stories* to create the perfect entertainment for young people, without any of the guilt or hassle of having to be held *accountable* to Christian *values*.'
>
> Mumbrella – comment

> 'Every *brand* has a story to tell. And telling it well can make the difference between passive and *passionate stakeholders*.'
>
> PRSA West Michigan Nonprofit Workshop

budget repair levy (temporary)

A tax, but don't call it that. C.f. with Mining Tax, Carbon Tax, etc.

> 'There will be a three-year *Temporary Budget Repair Levy*. From July, it will be payable by individuals with taxable income above $180,000 at a rate of two per cent.'
>
> jbh.ministers.treasury.gov.au

> 'The *Temporary Budget Repair Levy* will also be reflected in a number of other tax rates that are currently based on

calculations that include the top personal income tax rate, including fringe benefits tax.'

www.budget.gov.au

build capacity / capacity building

(v) Educate people so that they can create good communities and useful, lasting institutions. Give them the wherewithal to become self-reliant. (n) *capacity building*. Also, 'community *capacity building*'. As, 'The process by which individuals, organizations, institutions and societies develop abilities to perform functions, solve problems and set and achieve objectives' (United Nations Development Program). First popular with the UN and aid organisations to describe practically everything they do in underdeveloped countries and First Nations, now common in schools, local councils, aged care, child care, consumer directed care, etc. As, 'Consumer Directed Care *capacity building* service for aged and community care providers' (ACSA).

'*Build Capacity*: To support partner organizations by providing volunteer administrator training series, connecting them with: *strategies* for effective volunteer management, practice *utilizing outcomes-based* problem solving plans, opportunities for on-site coaching, and local peer interaction.'

United Way

'In the beginning God created the heaven and the earth. Thereafter he *built capacity*.'

Genesis

bullet points

The dots in *PowerPoint* presentations, corporate documents, etc, marking *key points* (•). *Bullets* are believed to make an argument easier to follow. An argument boiled down, the truth distilled. Child-like statements of the obvious, in combination often suggesting relationships that do not exist. 'Faux analytical'; may diminish the cognitive abilities of those who regularly use them. 'Sentences are smarter than the grunts of bullet points' (Edward R. Tufte).

How do I love thee? Let me count the ways
• depth
• breadth
• height

My soul can reach
• freely
• purely
• passionately (old griefs)
Etc.

Elizabeth Barrett Browning

Some *PowerPoint* users appear to have responded to Tufte's criticism and recommend writing their *bullet points* in sentences. Thus:

'*Action* Verbs in Action: Sample Job-Seeker Resume *Bullet Points* that Kick Off with Powerful Verbs:

- *Aligned* and trained management staff to *focus* on attaining *world-class* service *levels* through *quality feedback* to staff, *utilizing* Witness Monitoring System, top-level training programs, and *targeted* interviewing/hiring specifications.

- *Architected* operational and financial business cases for *outsourcing*. Assessed effectiveness of 16,000-employee Symantec's global payroll operations (APAC and EMEA).
- *Delighted* management and employees by redesigning job descriptions, using a "*Vision* for Success" statement to illustrate successful job performance.
- *Delivered* annual revenue of $1.5B annually across Europe/Middle East/Africa, accounting for 20 percent more revenue and profit than comparable operation in North America *delivered*.
- *Authored* paper for publication in New Jersey Association of School Business Officials magazine on implications of Sarbanes-Oxley Act to New Jersey School Districts' (Quintessential Careers. Empowering job seekers since 1996).

burning platform

Crisis. A situation from which there is no apparent escape, but in which the wise and well-*aligned* may see a *window of opportunity*. As, 'We poured gasoline on our own *burning platform*. I believe we have lacked *accountability* and *leadership* to *align* and direct the company through these disruptive times . . . We're not collaborating internally' (Nokia CEO).

> 'We have, if you like, a *burning platform* and as a result of that *burning platform*, increasingly, police and other crime fighting agencies are going blind.'
>
> Tony Abbott PM, 5 February 2015

'My criticism of Hegel's procedure is that when in his discussion he arrives at a contradiction, he construes it as a *burning platform* in the universe.'

Alfred North Whitehead

buy-in

(v) 1. Accept, support, declare allegiance, fealty, enthusiasm for shared goals, embrace, sign up, drink the Kool-Aid, etc. Join in making your organisation a cult.
2. Submit, comply, roll over, go through the motions, pay lip service, sell out, give up, resign oneself, go along with, whatever . . . etc.
(n) What is achieved by any of the above means.

'General Manager Performance and Talent

. . . Establish the performance and talent management unit as a collaborative business partner on performance and talent management initiatives to ensure the needs of the business are met and *buy-in* to *strategies* is established.'

Job at Queensland Rail

'Integral to achieving staff *buy-in* is involving staff in the development phase so they have a sense of *ownership* and connection to what the business stands for and where it is heading. If the *vision*, *strategy*, *goals* and *values* are determined without any staff *input* they are unlikely to receive full *buy-in*.'

www.smh.com.au

'But, as I've said, this is a *plan* that has *buy-in* from just about all the *stakeholders* . . .'

Tony Abbott PM, 21 March 2015

'Every Party member, every branch of work, every statement and every action must proceed from the interests of the whole Party; it is absolutely impermissible to violate this principle.'

'Rectify the Party's Style of Work' (1942),
Mao Tse Tung, *Selected Works*, Vol. III, p. 44

'The point on which the murky world of *Human Resources* turns; an illusion peddled by *management* to pretend they care what their *reports* think about changes forced upon them. A term to indicate compliance, but not whether it is genuine or why it is granted. Employees *buy in* to changed "*behaviours*": sometimes they also *buy in* to humiliation, demotion and the sack.' (See *anytime feedback tool*)

'All those who *buy in* say "Aye". To the contrary, "No". I think the "Ayes" have it. The "*buy-in*" is carried.'

C

caffè latte

1. Coffee made with steamed milk.
2. *Chattering class* or *elite* that drinks it, especially at tables on inner-suburban footpaths. Not commoners, nor yet people of much substance. A pretentious, lazy, parasitic, opinionated, left-liberal caste; flaneurs, poseurs, Green voters. 'Sneerers and . . . wreckers' who 'misrepresented Australia's history, misread its present, misjudged its people and projected a miserable vision of the future' (N. Cater quoted in M. Devine, *Daily Telegraph*, 23 April 2013). People never seen in your average chop house drinking Pablo Instant and milky tea with N. Cater and M. Devine. Modern incarnation of George Orwell's 'sandal wearers', a slight used by G. Orwell in 1936 and G. Henderson still.

> 'So those people who were paying for the middle class welfare that Labor was putting out there – for the champagne sippers and the *latte* set – with whom they hang around all the time *in terms of* making themselves feel good, but making the rest of Queenslanders pay for it.'
>
> *Brisbane Times*

> 'A new ruling class of university-educated "progressives", "sophisticates", "*elites*" and "*latte-sippers*" have emerged as an *un-Australian* clique trying to lord it over everyone else.'
>
> Miranda Devine, *Daily Telegraph*, April 2013

> '*Caffè latte* set save economy.'
>
> *Australian Financial Review*, October 2003

capability

1. The ability to do something. Being able. Able to be leveraged, negotiated, influenced and cross harnessed.

> 'Prominence of the need to *harness* cross-organisation *capability* (scale and assembly of complementary capabilities), *leveraging* the *significant strategic* differentiation from cross-discipline and cross-boundary activities in line with our chosen *strategic* direction, as articulated in our 03/07 *Strategic Plan*.'
>
> CSIRO

> 'We removed a declared enemy of America, who had the *capability* of producing *weapons of mass destruction* . . .'
>
> George W. Bush, July 2004

> 'Would you like to *leverage* your *capability* on a star?
> Carry moonbeams home in a jar?'

capability building

Training people to be able (see above) in such ways as the following: 'Business projects primarily *deliver capability building outcomes* and not direct *value*. Programme and project management with a strong *focus* on project *level delivery* (the *capability outcomes*) is necessary but often insufficient to *deliver* the final business benefits promised in the business cases' (Victoria University, New Zealand).

capacity

1. Power to contain, absorb, receive, etc., wine, ideas, watermelons, etc. As, mental *capacity*, cubic *capacity*, etc.
2. What is built to fill a *capacity gap* – or a *capability* gap.

'We are building the *capacity* of our *communities* so that *communities* can more effectively *manage change* and the only way *community capacity* building can be *sustainable* is if the people who live in the *community drive* it.'

Department of Human Services, South Australia

'No *capacity gap* at the inn.'

captain's pick / captain's call

Schoolyard method of unilaterally choosing teams, accomplices, etc., more recently used by fully grown politicians, Kevin Rudd, Julia Gillard and Tony Abbott. As, 'As Prime Minister, as Labor leader, I have decided on this occasion to engage in a *captain's pick*, and I think that Nova particularly has a *track record* . . .' As God made a *captain's pick* with David.

'It was a *captain's pick*. Just about every one of his [Tony Abbott's] picks has been a disaster for him, including paid parental leave, knighthoods and local government recognition.'

Peter Reith, *Age*, 3 August 2015

'The point is, the "*captain's pick*" is a leading indicator of the lack of control – the lack of authority – that our political leaders currently experience.'

Tim Dunlop, ABC, 28 Jan 2015

'And the Lord said, Arise, anoint him: for this is my *captain's pick*.'

Samuel 16:12

capture

1. To catch, imprison, confine, seize, trap, take captive, etc. To encapsulate, neatly define or express, etc. As 'Yeats *captures* the Irish temperament . . .'
2. To take possession of the ball; grab, grasp (Australian football).
3. To take captive information, including personal information, contact details, etc., for purposes of *networking*, sales, *leveraging*, data analysis, etc. As, *data capture*, *digital capture*. Also data mining. To study, learn, commit to memory.

> 'Operating in close concert with real-time ISR carried out from these remote *platforms* are other modes of digital data *capture*, not least the panoply of communications intercepts carried out by the National Security Agency. In many cases the targets Air Force crews are tasked to track and ultimately to kill by the CIA or the US military have been identified through SIGINT (signals intelligence) derived from "harvesting" e-mails, text messages and cell phone calls.'
>
> Geographical Imaginations. Posts about Edward Snowden by Derek Gregory

> 'This required a *level* of discipline and activity that was new to many of the group, including *capturing* data against measures for which they had taken *ownership*.'
>
> Westpac

> 'He has also steered numerous funding bids and managed grand *capture* at a faculty level.'
>
> Speaker at a seminar, University of Queensland

> 'What did you *capture* at school today?'

cascade

A fall of water over rocks, or something suggestive of this, such as a garden water feature; vomit, spew, throw a map (*vulgar*); the spread of viruses; a series of electrical circuits set up so the first powers the second and so on; similar methods or phenomena in physics, biochemistry, engineering and computer science. In social science an information *cascade* occurs when the ideas of a few people take hold among many. The same principle governs marketing campaigns and management *buy-in*. Related to the herd instinct. As migrating wildebeest, lynch mobs, etc.

> '*Achieving* workforce *commitment:*
>
> There is an obvious intensity to the *communication cascade*.'
>
> www.nbrii.com

> 'So, we're making these representations. We're making our position clear right around the world that this is a number one priority of the Australian Government: to protect the Barrier Reef and, of course, then at every level there are further representations, *cascading* representations, right through the system . . .'
>
> Tony Abbott PM, 21 March 2015

> ' "Well, as of July 1, if you went through the four thresholds, I think the high threshold kicks in at $175,000, then I think it *cascades* down the spectrum," Mr Rudd said.'
>
> *Sydney Morning Herald*, 20 September 2007

casual

(n) (adj) An employee; member of the *casual* workforce (35 per cent of the whole Australian workforce). As, 'Economists are warning an increase of *casual* and part-time work means Australia's unemployment rate is higher than we think' (ABC, 17 June 2015). A person affording *flexibility*, *agility* and *competitiveness* to employers. One affording cheap labour. People who do not in general receive annual leave, sick pay, carers' allowances, superannuation or other benefits to which permanent employees are entitled. Formerly c. labourer, a drifter or pauper. 'Casual Night Fill Assistant . . . In this casual role, you will be responsible for filling and replenishing shelves at night' (oneshift).

Also anything informal, indifferent, cursory, chance, laidback, offhand, etc. As, casual clothes (casual, smart-casual, etc.) c. lifestyle, c. dining, c. atmosphere, c. encounter, c. sex, c. fling, c. kind of guy. 'Perhaps the way we ought to look at it is that Queensland fashion describes a boho luxe *lifestyle*, as opposed to a *casual lifestyle*' (Alison Kubler, Fashion Archives).

catalyst

In chemistry a substance that triggers or accelerates a reaction. An agent of change. Necessary antecedent of an action or state. Whatever causes, ignites, incites, provokes, creates, makes happen, occasions, determines, motivates, begets, etc. Cause, reason. An *impactful* person or thing. As, 'The Australia Council has to *drive* improvements in the arts sector, by *building the capabilities* of artists and arts organisations . . . to *ensure* we are a *catalyst* for greater *impact* . . .' (Australia Council). As God was the *catalyst* in a forty days and forty nights rain *event* (*Genesis* vii, 4).

'Lev comes to this from a position of proactive *engagement* in the positioning of the university as an intellectual *catalyst* in a network of community organisations and public services.'

University of Queensland

'. . . even with dividend stability anticipated from here, we lack clarity on a *catalyst* to re-value shares higher.'

www.benzinga.com

'I'm sure many people agree a thing like this should be clipped – it may be a *catalyst* for a "domino effect" of worst things to follow.'

Twitter

'Look like th' innocent flower, but be the *catalyst* under 't.'

Macbeth

challenge

1. Call to fight; call into question; test of ability; object to a ruling or declaration or to authority; contest, compete, vie: As, 'Ministers and backbenchers have told the ABC they believed Communications Minister Malcolm Turnbull now has the numbers to win a *challenge* and should use them.'
2. Something you meet every day; humdrum; life itself. *Issue*, problem, task, hurdle, obstacle, water-jump, trial, injury, conundrum, paradox, poser, enigma, difficulty, question, job, things to do, etc.: peace in the Middle East, end world poverty, change human nature, find cure for cancer, solve crossword, deal with problem on the back line, *enhance* tea and coffee-making facilities.
3. To have some physical, mental or environmental shortcoming is to be *challenged*; as in: 'vertically *challenged*' (short); 'fiscally *challenged*' (short of money); 'mentally

challenged' (sandwich short of a picnic). *Problems* or *issues* of an *ongoing* kind.

> 'I would suggest that people stop looking back to what it was and focus on the *challenges* of today and the *challenges* of tomorrow.'
>
> Joe Hockey, *Sydney Morning Herald*
> (The people were Peter Costello)

> 'The Senior Management Summit's *agenda* followed on from the endorsement of the Monash Futures *Agenda* and the establishment of task forces on the themes of academic strengthening, campus *enhancement*, improved services, grand *challenges* and Passport Mark II. I trust that each Monash University staff member will make an important contribution to the ensuing *process* that will turn our *vision* into reality.'
>
> A message from the vice-chancellor of Monash University

> 'To be or not to be, that is the *challenge*.'
>
> *Hamlet*

change(s)

1. (v) Adjust, vary, modify, switch, transform.
2. Sack, lay off; dismiss, fire, let go, put out to pasture, downsize, right-size, give the heave-ho, trim the overall headcount, be offered a package, receive a 'workforce reduction notification', etc. As, 'Due to a *change* in business operations, the X department and every job in it will be eliminated. Your position will no longer exist and you won't be replaced.' (HR Specialist)
3. Increase fees, charges, etc., or impose new ones. As, 'Parks Victoria – *Changes* to camping and accommodation fees.'

See *appropriate financial envelope*

change agent

1. Person who *changes* things; a team that *changes* things; consultancy that *changes* things; anyone or anything that causes, facilitates or assists *change*, e.g. psychotherapist, God, Lenin, hair stylist, etc.
2. One who practises or does the bidding of *change management*. As, 'Working through the *Managed Change*™ model, *change agents* identify the potential for resistance, why that resistance may occur, who could potentially be resistant, and the severity of that resistance' (www.lamarsh.com).

> 'Lead creative sessions with senior management for *project* conceptualization and kickoffs.
>
> As a strong leader, act as a "creative" *change agent*, a vocal *team player*, and *passionate* communicator *driving* from conceptual ideas through to execution and ongoing maintenance and improvement.'
>
> HR job advert

> 'Ms Silverman said the main objective of the project is to raise awareness and knowledge around the use of telehealth consultations but also to increase the uptake of telehealth in general practices and healthcare settings using nurses and midwives as the *change agent*.'
>
> www.pulseitmagazine.com.au

> 'Death is very likely the single best invention of life. It is life's *change agent*. It clears out the old to make way for the new.'
>
> Steve Jobs

> 'The philosophers have only interpreted the world, in various ways; the point is to be a *change agent*.'
>
> K. Marx

change management

1. Managing change. *Change* that requires managing, including multi-tasking. As, 'The first and most obvious definition of "*change management*" is that the term refers to the task of managing change' (Fred Nickols).
2. A category of *consultant*. Money for jam, old rope, Magic Pudding, etc.

> 'Understand the process of *Change Management* and the skills required to successfully manage the *process*' (Trans. 'Learn the process of *change management* and learn the process of *change management*'?)
>
> Melbourne University Leadership & Professional Development Program

> '*Change management* is also useful *in terms of* one's personal *life-style*: "First realise that due to a combination of technology, travel and *communications* advances, most of us live fast-paced, urban-minded lives that require constant *multi-tasking*."'
>
> Stan Stalnaker, *GQ*

> '1.5 School *Change Management Plan*
>
> Details of each *impact* identified as having *significant* effect upon the school, will be summarised in the school's *Change Management Plan*. This will include a comparison of the current and future *practice*, as well as the *impact* upon the school and any activities that can or need to be undertaken to support the school and the school's staff. The *impacts* and activities are derived from the *Gap Analysis* and School Readiness Assessment.'
>
> Queensland Government

change manager

A *change management* manager. As, 'Interface and *Change Manager*. This role is responsible for interface management across multiple providers and owner-managed *scope*. Duties include maintaining *oversights* across overall program development via integration of layouts, planning and ensure interface activities *align* with objectives. Support *implementation* of program *strategies* and *prioritise* of *project* activities across overall program schedule. This may include *plans*, spread sheets and models to support the *program strategies* and to centrally manage all resource requirements for the *projects*. Manage interface and change management *processes* and systems across the program' (Job advert. Parsons Brinckerhoff).

> 'The *Change Manager* need not come from a procurement background. Your primary *focus* will be to shape the *innovative change strategies* essential to the success of a *transformational enterprise project*.'
>
> Job advert, Queensland Health

channel agnostic

Agnostic (from Greek *agnostos* – unknowing) and channel (from Latin *canalis* – canal). An unknowing canal, or a canal unknowing. Or a channel that cannot be known (agnostic – one who believes that, while God may exist, his existence or non-existence cannot be known). Hence, marketing decisions made without a bias to any one channel – television, radio, print, social media, direct mail, telephone bombardment at mealtimes, billboard, etc.

> 'Like It or Not, Your Content Marketing Is *Channel Agnostic*.'
>
> '*Channel agnostic* audience creation . . .'
>
> PowerPoint slide

churn

1. To agitate, stir, blend, roil. To produce by agitation, as with butter. To produce in a dull mechanical fashion ('The *churn* of stale words . . .' S. Beckett).
2. Joseph Schumpeter's 'creative destruction' in microcosm. As, 'We may lament the tragedies of the *churn*'s *downside*, but we shouldn't lose sight of its very powerful and important *upside*: it makes us better off. What's really going on is a healthy recycling' (W. Michael Cox, US Federal Reserve). Necessary, inevitable and desirable phenomenon produced by *competition*. Primitive religion of free enterprise. 'Paradox of progress.' Means by which everyone grows richer and happier. ('The Great American Growth Machine. At its *core* are *consumers* and their endless list of *needs*, *wants* . . . Unlimited wants clash with the fundamental fact of limited resources . . .' W. Michael Cox.) The view of the *churn* as creative destruction is not unrelated to 'this is the recession Australia had to have'.
3. *Product churn* – selling more than the *customer* needs (or wants). Or selling the basic *product* (e.g. razors, printers) at a low price, and associated products (razor blades, printer cartridges) at an exorbitant one.
4. Customer *churn* – *churning* of *customers* from one business to another. (*Consultants* will tell you how to deal with it.)
5. Job *churn* – *churning* (or 'recycling') of employees. (*Consultants* deal with job *churns*, too.)
6. Proactive *churn* prevention/management. As, 'Those companies who are doing proactive *churn management*, they have to understand customers respond differently to different actions.'
7. *Churn* and burn – subjecting workers to regular performance review, including by *anytime feedback tool*, and

throwing a percentage of them under a bus. Also known as 'rank and yank' (*New York Times*, 17 August 2015).

> 'The paper, "The Perils of Proactive Churn Prevention Using Plan Recommendations: Evidence from a Field Experiment," co-authored by Columbia Business School Ph.D. candidate Martin Schleicher and Wharton professor Raghuram Iyengar, will be published in the Journal of Marketing Research.'
>
> www.mediapost.com

> 'And thus they joined the Rio Grande Valley's eight thousand other former inseam, watch-pocket, and waistband experts in what economists call capitalism's necessary *churn*.'
>
> Katherine Boo, *New Yorker*, 18 July 2004

> 'To everything - *churn, churn, churn*
> There is a season - *churn, churn, churn*.'

circle back

To go back, get back to, revert, revisit, retrace one's steps, do again at a later date, etc. As, 'Can you *circle back* to me on that.' 'We'll need to *circle back* on action item number two.'

> 'City Manager Grabowski stated he would start with the Library *circle-back*, pg 193 10-03 Overtime Full Time . . . Alderman Levin stated he would not make an *issue* of Sunday overtime and stated he and Alderman York are satisfied with the answers they received on the *circle-back* items . . . Alderman Healy, pg 150 40-46 Salt, this is not a *circle back* item. He stated salt was discussed at tonight's meeting and stated there might be a fluctuation in cost.'
>
> www.elmhurst.org

citizen-centric

Centred on citizens; citizens at the core.

'The Citizen Experience Portfolio has an intimate knowledge of citizen expectations and emergent trends and *strategically* defines and *navigates* BDM's *service delivery model* to *ensure* a relevant and *sustainable citizen-centric offering* . . . The Portfolio initiates and enables the collaborative exploration and *dynamic* adaptation of BDM's *citizen-centric service delivery* model and citizen *value proposition* . . . The Citizen Experience *Development Team* is responsible for the development and *implementation* of business *transformation* and service *development initiatives* and accompanying *processes* and *tools*. This *Team* also leads the exploration, analysis and *development* of *citizen-centric* discretionary services' (job advert for a 'Citizen Services Ambassador' at Victorian Births, Deaths and Marriages Office).

class warfare

Common conservative riposte to left-wing critics of unfair budget measures, support for private schools, unequal distribution of income, etc. A blunt arrow in the neoliberal quiver.

> 'Criticism of our strategy has been political in nature and has drifted to 1970s *class warfare* lines, claiming the Budget is "unfair" or that the "rich don't contribute enough".'
>
> www.joehockey.com

> 'He [Joe Hockey] accuses Labor and critics of the unfair Budget of engaging in *class warfare*. Joe Hockey is committing open-warfare against the families of Australia . . .'
>
> Bill Shorten, 12 June 2014

client

1. Company or individual; *customer*, buyer, patron, etc.
2. Patient, inmate, student, drug-addict, convicted felon, *job seeker*; person, including child, held in a detention centre on Manus Island or Nauru; pretty well everyone. Companies value their *client bases*, especially *client-focused* companies. *Clients* are often addressed as *valued clients*. As, 'We *commit* to the *actions* we take to *achieve* the best possible *outcomes* for our *clients*' (*Core* DHS *Values*. Victorian Department of Human Services).

> '1. Placing integrity and honesty above all else.
> 2. Putting *clients* first.'
>
> CACI's mission statement revised after certain events in Iraq

> '*Innovative strategic client driven stakeholder framework*'
>
> Australasian College for Infection Prevention and Control: job advert for a national operations manager

> 'A former immigration department employee told the inquiry into children in detention he was conditioned to calling them "*clients*" to strip them of any hope . . . He told the inquiry that the language used by employees was designed to dehumanise those held in detention.'
>
> ABC, 31 July 2014

> '*Clients* all, let us rejoice . . .'

> 'Friends, Romans, *clients*!'

client service officers

Guards at Nauru refugee detention centre.

closure

1. Finish, conclusion, completing the circle.
2. Notion deriving from Gestalt theory that 'completion' is a primary human *need* (or '*want*' that has grown into a *need*) replacing paradox, doubt, enigma, vagaries of fate, the essential unknown, the existential dilemma, etc. As, 'Some therapists have gone so far to state that true *closure* is a "myth" and impossible to achieve. Indeed, many individuals experience unending loss that is ambiguous and open-ended' (Science of Relationships). Popular in *est* and other movements dedicated to *self-actualisation*.
3. What one needs to '*move on*' – from a relationship, a death, an argument, an insult, crime, folly, serial misfortune (see Book of Job), bad haircut, etc. A popular term among drama queens and the legal profession. C.f. get over it, live with it, etc.

> 'Individuals have a need for *closure* . . . The need for *closure* has interesting *implications* for *marketers*.'
>
> Marketing textbook

> 'A collaborative systems approach to Christian community development . . . Bringing ministries, leadership, services, congregations and sometimes churches to healthy *closure*.'
>
> johnmark.net.au

> 'I done one thing today and that was for my children and grandchildren . . . I am pleading for someone to come forward to give them *closure* . . .'
>
> Widow of murdered criminal Victor Peirce, March 2004

'To die, to sleep –
No more – and by a sleep to say we end
The heartache and the thousand natural shocks
That flesh is heir to – 'tis a *closure*
Devoutly to be wished!'

Hamlet

cluster deployment

Necessary in these troubled times.

'Roll-out milestones and *cluster deployment* at the UN.

I am writing to inform you that a decision has been taken to postpone the next two phases of Umoja (Foundation) deployment by 30 days. The Umoja Steering Committee met for an extra-ordinary session on 28 August 2013 and decided unanimously to revise the schedule for *Clusters* 1 and 2 *deployment*.

Cluster 1, consisting all Peacekeeping Missions, will now *deploy* Umoja Foundation on 1 November 2013 and *Cluster* 2, consisting all Special Political Missions, will *deploy* the new solution on 1 February 2014. All successive roll-out milestones remain unchanged; *Cluster* 3 on 1 July 2014, *Cluster* 4 on 1 July 2015, and *Cluster* 5 on 1 January 2016.

The main reason to adjust the *deployment* schedule was a need to reconcile Umoja readiness dependencies against an obligation to support the *core* mandates of the *missions* in these challenging times.

As it became evident during the pilot *implementation* in UNIFIL and UNSCOL, the readiness to *migrate* to the new, common solution was *impacted* by the disparity among *missions* in the *processes* and configuration of systems currently in use and the large volume of *data* to be gathered and cleansed.

I am confident that the measures taken as a result of the lessons learned in the pilot *implementation*, and continued commitment of the senior management and all staff involved to the timely completion of Umoja *deployment* work, will enable us to remain on the revised schedule to *implement* this ambitious and transformational *initiative*.'

Email from the Project Director, Enterprise Resource Planning, United Nations HQ

collateral damage

Damage to innocent people, and their homes, possessions etc. Unintended damage. The ratio of *collateral* (civilian) to combatant deaths has been as high as 6:1 in recent wars. Also colloquially in politics, business, sport, personal relationships.

'Jews are "*collateral damage*" in Ukip's newly declared opposition to the non-stun slaughter of animals for religious reasons . . . Agriculture spokesman Stuart Agnew . . . told *The Jewish Chronicle*: "This isn't aimed at you – it's aimed elsewhere – it's aimed at others. You've been caught in the crossfire; *collateral damage*. You know what I mean".'

Huffington Post, 7 July 2015

'There will be all sorts of *collateral damage* accompanying Tony Abbott's presumed demise, with Peta Credlin and Joe Hockey only the most obvious.'

Sydney Morning Herald, 15 March 2015

colourful

History, if it is worth mentioning at all, is always *colourful*. Many, often colourless people have a *colourful* past.

> 'Lithgow today is shaped by a *colourful history*, *challenged* by ongoing technological and cultural development and, most importantly, surrounded by nature.'
>
> Lithgow tourism website

> 'Previous to venturing on his long and successful career with CSIRO, Noel had a *colourful history*.'
>
> Stored Grain Research Laboratory, CSIRO

> '*Colourful* past of prince dubbed Randy Andy.'

> 'Australian judge's *colourful* past.'

> 'Sofia Hellqvist's *colourful* past.'

> 'Holy Day Closet at Hampton Court Palace detailing Catherine Howard's *colourful* past, and how she had "lived most corruptly and sensually".'

come to Jesus moment

An epiphany; a moment of deep insight; a moment of truth. As, 'Abbott said the cabinet members had a *"come to Jesus" moment* when they realised the implications of breaching protocol.'

> 'The cynical among us will always assume that, when a celebrity has his or her *come to Jesus moment*, that it's probably been orchestrated by a PR professional of some sort.'
>
> Pajiba

'"The Fappening" Perpetuators Have a J. Law *Come-to-Jesus Moment* and "Cower With Shame".'

Daily Beast, 10 August 2014

'The other charts point to the *"Come to Jesus" moment* for the bankers and those short Comex and LBMA Silver contracts once Silver breaks through the resistance lines in a strong manner.'

www.maxkeiser.com

comfortability

An ability for comfort? Affording comfort? Comfort? The comfort of a paradigm?

'It is a great decision making *framework*, and one that I will spend some time speaking to at our next *Team* Meeting to build a sense of *comfortability* in using/adopting/applying (often sophisticated and nuanced) decision making within a project management *paradigm*' (from a local government manager).

'*Comfortability*: Our *passion* for creating comfortable environments for home owners and businesses is loud and clear. It's very rewarding for us and our *customers* as well!'

Airplus

'Nursing Mother Told to Pump Breast Milk in Lavatory for "*Comfortability*" of Passengers. For the *comfortability* of other passengers could you go in the bathroom . . .'

Flyertalk

'Relaxability and *comfortability*.'

John Howard

commit / committed / commitment

1. (i) (v) To pledge, vow, dedicate, warrant, assure; believe; hold dear; swear fealty to; determine; say you'll do it; etc. More than an *aspiration*. As, 'an aspiration not a commitment' (Tony Abbott).
(ii) (n) Dedication, allegiance, loyalty, attachment, obligation, promise, vow, responsibility, determination, resolution, etc.
(iii) (adj) A person or organisation determined upon doing something or believing in something. ('Esso is *committed* to the environment.' 'I am *committed* to leaving my wife for you,' etc.) According to *marketing strategy*, most people have a *commitment* to a *lifestyle*.
2. Put off to another time, consigned to a murky sphere. As, For sure . . . not. Of course . . . maybe. In all likelihood. Can't see why not . . . probably, depending on the circumstance. Intend to passionately. I'll *circle back* on that one. *Non-core*.
3. *Aligned* with our *values*, *mission*, *vision*, *goals* etc., but not be *actioned* at *this point in time* or any point in the foreseeable future. (iii) Absolutely . . . in the present context.
4. A promise that is neither fulfilled nor broken.

> 'I will have to check on the date, but Caroline Springs obviously there are *commitments* there, and the timing of that I would have to double check on that.'
>
> Ted Baillieu, Premier of Victoria

> '*Commitment* to the use of existing and deployment of *appropriate* new technologies in the workplace', in an advanced *business enabler* in the New South Wales Public Service.'
>
> NSW Public Service Commission

> 'It is rather for us to be here *committed* to the great *commitment* remaining before us – that from these honoured dead we may take increased *commitment* to that *commitment* for which they gave the last full measure of *commitment* – that we here highly *commit* that these dead shall not have *committed* in vain – that this nation, under God, shall have a new *commitment* to freedom – and that government *committed* to the people, by the people, for the people, shall not perish from the earth.'
>
> Abraham Lincoln

> 'Do you, Jason Birdwhistle, *commit* to Shannon . . .?'
>
> Solemnisation of marriage *event*

commitment (re)

A renewal of vows – or to something you were not very *committe*d to in the first place; as love sometimes does, the *commitment* faded. As, 'a *re-commitment* to our clients and the primacy of their interests; a *re-commitment* to reputational excellence associated with everything the firm does; a *re-commitment* to *transparency* of our business performance and *risk management practices* . . .' (Goldman Sachs, after the US government *committed* to bailing them out).

> 'Do you, Jason Birdwhistle, *re-commit* to Shannon . . .?'

common sense

1. Sense, as opposed to folly of any kind. As, '*Common sense* will tell us, that the power which hath endeavoured to subdue us, is of all others, the most improper to defend us' (Thomas Paine, *Common Sense*, 1776).

2. 'Received wisdom or opinion'. '*Common sense* approach' – not theoretical or fanciful. *Battler philosophy*; *ordinary Australians*, true Australians, real Australians. Not *un-Australians*. Not exclusive thought or language. Not politically correct. Plain, unadorned, genuine. Not fancy or obscure. Unsophisticated but sound. Appropriate. 'Every man thinks he is well supplied with it' (Descartes).
3. Populism. Tyranny of the majority. Anti-intellectualism, slumming, appealing to prejudice, stupidity, etc. Common justification for cruelty. Glorified pragmatism.

communicated / communicating

1. Conveyed, imparted, passed on.
2. Ineffectively conveyed. *Communicated*, not.

> 'The arrangement of multiple initiators of warnings also negatively *impacted* on the effectiveness for *communicating* accurate information to the public and the consistency of the warnings.'
>
> Analysis of Command and Control Networks on Black Saturday, Dept. of Defence

> 'Our *commitment* to safe, reliable and responsible operations starts with the group chief executive Tony Hayward and his *leadership team*: a *commitment* that filters down through the organization and is regularly *communicated* to all staff. BP's *leadership* has continued to reinforce the importance of safety when undertaking regular site visits to BP facilities around the world and from all parts of the business.'
>
> BP Global website

> 'Vengeance is mine. I will repay, *communicates* the Lord.'

> '*Communicated* the raven, "Nevermore"'

communications

1. Passing and receiving of messages.
2. Means by which messages are passed and received.
3. The messages.
4. Common category of (influencing) *skills*.
5. An industry.
6. Subject of study.
7. Spin.

'Extreme *events* often trigger high density of *communication* and interaction among *actors* to stimulate coherent response.'

Analysis of Command and Control Networks on Black Saturday, Department of Defence

'Failures of internal *communication* and breakdowns in warning *development* contributed to a lack of situational awareness and decision uncertainties among responders. The account of emergency response problems to the Kilmore East fire highlights a coordination *issue* most probably brought about by ineffective *leadership* and deficient *communication* infrastructure.'

Analysis of Command and Control Networks on Black Saturday, Department of Defence

'This is the must-attend conference for all government *communications* practitioners. Amazing presenters pitched at a number of career levels: post-graduate; career builder; consolidator and influencer – so there is something for everyone!'

www.govcomms.com.au

'Organisations need to use plain English for all their *communications* with *stakeholders*.'

Department of Education, Employment and Workplace Relations: authors of 'Our *strategic framework* . . .' and '7 *Goals* and 24 *Strategies*'

'And he said unto them, What manner of *communications* are these that ye have one to another, as ye walk, and are sad? Be not deceived: Evil *communications* corrupt good manners.'

1 *Corinthians* 15.33

community expectations

1. What the community expects; e.g., that all politicians rort the system.
2. What politicians say the community expects in order to shed themselves of blame for rorting the system.

'Do I think it's wrong for a member of Parliament to go to a fundraiser and maybe use a Comcar to do it? Not necessarily. Should you use a helicopter to get there? Well plainly that's outside *community expectations*.'

Tony Abbott, *Age*, 6 August 2015

'While I am completely confident that the questions in particular relating to Uluru and Cairns have been 100 per cent within the rules, they have also been completely beyond *community expectations*, and that's been made clear.'

Tony Burke MP, *Age*, 6 August 2015

community values

Values said (esp. by politicians and real estate agents) to exist in *communities*, much as mushrooms do in forests. Sound, decent, *common sense*, charitable, all-pull-together *values*. Not unlike family *values*, and even Australian *values* (fair go, etc.). Great place to bring up children, etc. *Community values* should be 'embraced'. Being in touch with *community values* is often the same thing as getting *communities* into your particular tent. As, perhaps, '"Never doubt this, we are the political party out there in the community driven by *community values*, by Labor *values*," Ms Gillard said' (ABC, 25 May 2013).

> 'Secondly, by 2005, *community values* had become less friendly to egalitarian policies in the workplace – reflecting such changes as the fracturing of worker solidarity, the growing equity investment *culture* (which *aligned* workers' interests more closely with those of companies), the cumulative effects of globalization in encouraging competitive individualism and the increasing community hostility to government hand-outs for able-bodied people in the buoyant economic conditions.'
>
> Centre for Policy Development

> 'Coming from a 3rd generation family in the rural township of Thirlmere, Terry has a great understanding of *community values*.'
>
> Terry Digger, Gerringong Real Estate

> 'An agent with an in depth knowledge of the local area, its *lifestyle* benefits and *community values*.'
>
> Western Keys Real Estate

competencies

Capabilities, abilities, expertises, aptitudes, attainments, proficiencies, *skills*, smarts, nouses, ablenesses, adeptnesses, dexterities, facilities, prowesses, artistries, workmanships, endowments, finesses, flairs, etc. Many *competencies* are key, some are core.

> 'Re-energise your CV with powerful, action-oriented words to drive home your key *competencies*.'
>
> Alumni e-news, La Trobe University

> 'Collaboratively, we work with organisations to assist their Leaders to enhance core *competencies*, build on interpersonal skills, solidify role clarification and workplace boundaries and strengthen their managerial language, behaviours and actions.'
>
> Brad Lockwood Consultancy

> 'Thy *competencies* and thy glory.'
>
> *Psalm* 63

competitive advantage

1. Whatever – labour costs, technology, skills, *brand*, monopoly – gives a company an edge over its competitors. A large *competitive advantage* is called a *sustainable competitive advantage*. Cities, communities, sporting clubs, scout packs, etc., often refer in their *mission statements* to *competitive advantages* and their desire to *leverage* them. Applied to nations it is called a 'national *competitive advantage*'. Related to but not the same as '*comparative advantage*', which is an ingenious theory of international trade devised in the early nineteenth century by Ricardo and only understood by *economists*.
2. Throwing spitballs (baseball); sledging (cricket); uttering orgasmic screams (tennis); deflating footballs (US football); taking performance enhancing drugs (cycling, AFL, NRL,

athletics, etc.). Equivalent rank cheating in business is not called *competitive advantage*.

> 'Riverbed enables hybrid enterprises to *transform* application performance into a *competitive advantage* by maximizing employee productivity and *leveraging* IT to create new forms of operational *agility*.'
>
> www.cso.com.au

> 'We should have a massive *competitive advantage* in the world given the abundance of coal reserves, the abundance of gas reserves, the abundance of sunlight. We should have a massive *competitive advantage* that we really need to seize on better than we have in recent years.'
>
> Mathias Cormann, Minister for Finance, 2014

comprises of

Comprises. As, 'HealthPACT *comprises of* representatives from all State and Territory health departments . . .' (www.horizonscanning.gov.au). 'The home *comprises of* three double bedrooms all with spacious built in wardrobe . . .' '*Comprising of* 3 good sized bedrooms, a separate study . . .' 'The accommodation briefly *comprises of* entrance hall, lounge kitchen, two bedrooms and a shower . . .'.

concerted indiscipline

Riot-like. As, 'The term "riot" is not a category that is used to record incidents in prison. Incidents where two or more prisoners act together to defy a lawful instruction or against the requirements of the regime of the establishment are all recorded as *Concerted Indiscipline*' (Mr Selous, UK Minister for Prisons, prisonuk.blogspot.com.au).

concrete (set in, not)

Not fixed permanently; not enduring, ironclad, indelible, everlasting, unending, unchanging or unchangeable. Don't hold me to it. Might have to *circle back*. Good idea but . . . You don't like it? Have no fear, it's not set in concrete. Formerly not set in stone, i.e. not like The Ten Commandments. *Key* but not *core*.

> 'As a pre-emptive measure which recognises that this *issue* is not going to go away. We . . . believe that there are three ways we can go, but this is not *set in concrete*.'
>
> Consultancy

> 'This is *not set in concrete*. If it doesn't work, we are prepared to look at it because ultimately we are determined to try and get as many people into work as possible. That is our *goal*.'
>
> Joe Hockey, *Australian Financial Review*

> 'He that believeth on me hath life *set in concrete*.'

consciousness

1. See Descartes, Locke ('the perception of what passes in a man's own mind'), Kant, Husserl, William James, the primary visual cortex, Freud, James Joyce, hashish, etc.
2. Sub atomic particle of *culture*.

> '"Corporate Power" comes from *consciousness*, which is the sub atomic particle of *culture*. It is made up of thoughts, beliefs and emotions which are inherent in an organization. Corporate Power is the sum of the collective *consciousness* of

individuals in the organization, derived from organizational *CULTURE*.'

Corporate Power, a consultancy group and affiliate of Deakin University

conscious uncoupling

Separation, breakup, divorce while conscious.

'*Conscious Uncoupling* is a term coined and created by Katherine Woodward Thomas, M.A., MFT in 2010. Katherine is a licensed psychotherapist, and the author of the national bestseller *Calling in "The One": 7 Weeks to Attract the Love of Your Life*.'

'If we can recognize that our partners in our intimate relationships are our teachers, helping us evolve our internal, spiritual support structure, we can avoid the drama of divorce and experience what we call a *conscious uncoupling*.'

Dr. Habib Sadeghi and Dr. Sherry Sami, goop.com/conscious-uncoupling

'The Nationally Acclaimed *Conscious Uncoupling* 5-Week Course Is Now Available In A Digital Format!'

evolvingwisdom.com

consensus

1. Unanimity or general agreement, consent, accord. As, '*Consensus* of opinion.'
2. An excuse for doing nothing or very little. As, 'What great cause would have been fought and won under the banner: "I stand for *consensus*"?' (Margaret Thatcher). Hence '*consensus* politician'.

'The environment minister has defended the federal government's $4m contribution to establish a "*consensus* centre" headed by climate contrarian Bjørn Lomborg, saying it is getting "bang for your buck".'

Guardian

'The Productivity Commission's review should *drive* greater national *consensus* on the workplace relations *framework* of the future, with a *focus* on firstly removing unintended consequences within the current *framework* and then maximising the stability of the *framework* over time.'

BHP submission to Productivity Commission Inquiry

consult

To have a *consultation*, or engage in a *consultative process*, perhaps with a *consultant*; to seek advice, deliberate together, or cover your arse. As, 'INTERVIEWER: . . . will the Coalition keep the tobacco excise? JOE HOCKEY: We will *consult* with industry sectors . . . INTERVIEWER: What about the bank . . . [inaudible]? JOE HOCKEY: Same. We will *consult* with the industry sector, same as I have said previously.' *Stakeholders*, of which *communities* are often one, are regularly *consulted*.

'For God's sake let us sit upon the ground
And *consult* . . .'

Richard II

consultant(s)

One who provides advice and direction for a fee. An expert in the field. As, 'I am a vintage guitar pedal *consultant* and appraiser to many fellow guitarists . . .' Alternative to school-teaching and unemployment. What the *dejobbed*, *rightsized* and *decruited* become. Something to do after politics or sport. *Lifestyle* incorporated. The plague-rats of managerialism.

> 'So that said, you can get *consulting* work knowing very little, as long as you can do what the *client* is paying you to do, and do it well.'
>
> The Consultant's Consultant

> 'Operating with the speed of a *consultancy* and the rigor of a university, we work with our *clients* to develop tailored *programs* using our proven methods that quickly *deliver* performance *uplift*. We insist on measuring and validating the *impact* of all of our work and are constantly researching and finding new Neurological programs and tools that assist our clients in gaining and sustaining a *competitive advantage*.'
>
> mindpeakperformance.com

> 'Get thee to a *consultancy*.'

consultation

1. Meeting, *dialogue*, workshop, seminar, weekend retreat, *team-building* exercise, etc., with a *consultant* or firm of *consultants*.
2. Telephone call with same.
3. Redistribution of revenue.

> 'The symposium and internal *consultation* will inform the nature of the documentation and processes for the proposed external

consultation. The following are dates and times for internal *consultation* that will be facilitated by either Donna or I [sic].'

Consultant to the Queensland Studies Authority

'If you would like to get a Pilates insurance quote, or a *consultation* on what you need then just simply fill out the form below. Rest assured, you will not be receiving a high-pressure sales pitch to where you are bombarded with high-pressure sales tactics or trick questions. Our *goal* is to educate you on what you really need, because we believe once we educate you on what is best for you and your Pilates business you will become a great *client*.'

consultation (community)

1. Form of community *engagement*; providing information, assuring transparency, etc. Giving communities a voice, etc. As, 'The term "*Community Consultation*" covers the range of activities that the City *utilises* to support the involvement of residents, non-residents, business proprietors, *stakeholders*, general public and other members of the community in the decision-making process' (City of Vincent, WA).
2. Hoop to be jumped through. As, 'Architect Phillip Thalis has criticised successive NSW governments over their lack of *transparency* and "parody of *consultation*", accusing the government of deliberately constructing *processes* which were "meaningless" (altmedia, 16 April 2015). 'It just says that [James Packer] is able to hold sway with the government over what he wants in this respect, and part of it being a second casino for Sydney without any *consultation* from local people . . .' (Jack Mundey, altmedia, 16 April 2015).

'I *consult* therefore I am.'

consultative process

Consult – in a process. Toolkits are available.

consume content

Watch TV or other media. As, 'More Boomers prefer to *consume content* in the early and late morning (5:00 a.m. to noon) rather than any other time of day' (*Social Times*, 2015).

consumer

1. One who eats, uses, reads, drives, or in other ways *consumes* products. Shoppers, *customers*, home-buyers; users of services; taxpayers, ratepayers, subscribers; those who attend the arts and games; *clients*, depositors, readers, patients, students, recipients of charity and government benefits; the needy, etc. Citizens. You and me. A person of *choice*. People in all their many aspects, etc. As in: 'Each *consumer* has a unique *personality*' – *marketing* textbook. People with '*lifestyle* characteristics' that marketing can 'segment' and '*target*'. Humans.

Consumer confidence – willingness to spend as a measure of optimism or of well-being. Gratification, deferred or not. As, 'The Greek debt crisis and sensational coverage of the Chinese share market crash are being blamed for another fall in *consumer confidence*.'

Consumer durables. An oxymoron.

Consumer needs – human wants when marketing has finished with them. As, 'Human needs – *consumer* needs – are the basis of all modern marketing' (marketing textbook).

Consumer opinion – what a *consumer* believes about consuming; what opinions they are able to form while consuming.

Consumer trading down – whatever. As, 'Where it does – where it can make a difference is in terms of if there's any *consumer* trading down by price points through our category . . . (Fosters CEO, ABC, 17 February 2009).

Consumer strategy – what to do with them. As, 'Leading *development* and *implementation* of *consumer strategies* and *plans*' (Edith Cowan university), etc. See below.

> 'The government is *committed* to active *engagement* with the *social partners* on the future of the commercial semi-state sector on the basis of the government's *commitment* to its role in providing services of *world-class* quality at a competitive price to the *consumer* with a viable long-term future for individual companies based on the most *appropriate* form of ownership or structure for its particular needs.'
>
> 'Towards 2016: Ten-year Framework Social Partnership Agreement 2006–2015', Government of Ireland

> 'A rapid review conducted by Kelly et al. (2011) sought to address the lack of *best practice* guidelines for the *development* and *implementation* of shared care models for mental health *consumers*.'

> 'The *consumers* of mental health services have taken over the asylum.'

consumer decision journey (CDJ)

Not your traditional funnel.

> 'And when purchasing *products*, *consumers* now enter what Edelman refers to as the *consumer decision journey (CDJ)*: a more dynamic and fluid *process* than the linear journey that the traditional funnel implied.'
>
> *Content* 26, 2014

> 'To keep up with rapid technology cycles and improve their multiplatform marketing efforts, companies need to take a different approach to managing the *consumer decision journey* – one that embraces the speed that digitization brings and focuses on capabilities in three areas . . .'
>
> McKinsey & Company, 2014

consumer finance

1. Banking
2. Loan sharking. 'Keeping customers on the hook by repeatedly and expensively refinancing their loans . . .' Providing *consumers* with adjustable-rate mortgages that only adjust upwards; extending *consumers*' loans 'designed to be unaffordable, to force borrowers into a series of refinancings and the fat fees that went along with them.' (Chair of US Federal Deposit Insurance Corporation, in Andrew Cockburn, 'Saving the Whale Again', *Harpers*, April 2015.)

> 'A pound of that *consumer's* flesh is thine.'
>
> *The Merchant of Venice*

contestability

Making the public sector private in the interests of the public, usually with a *framework*. As, '*Contestability frameworks* involve . . . examining effective ways of introducing market forces to price, quality and improve productivity: seeking to *deliver* government service in a leaner and more efficient way for the benefit of the citizen' (KPMG).

An idea providing lucrative opportunities for companies offering professional services. As, 'KPMG is experienced in supporting *clients* undertaking *contestability* reviews . . . These activities are typically supported by a *robust project management*, *stakeholder engagement* and *governance framework*' (KPMG).

context

The larger or whole part without which the smaller cannot be properly understood. (As, 'My remarks must be understood in the *context* in which they were made'.) (i) The part ignored by people wishing to impugn or traduce other people. (As, to accuse an opponent of enjoying or justifying mass murder because he wrote, 'Stalin was a hero', when he wrote 'Stalin was a hero *to many people*'.) (ii) The part claimed to be essential by people wishing to excuse their own malice, stupidity, naiveté, etc. (I was young, in love, impetuous, impressionable, drunk, had a migraine, etc.). The part that *is* essential: As, 'In the lost childhood of Judas Christ was betrayed.' Where both truth and ambiguity reside.

The overall circumstances or conditions of time and place. (As, 'Most people will see these pictures in their proper *context* and time,' a Palace source said. 'This is a family playing and momentarily referencing a gesture [the Hitler salute] many would have seen from contemporary news reels.')

A nourishing thing. As, '. . . but all are nourished in the *context* of exceptional scholarship to grow as exceptional scholars in their learning . . .' (Brisbane Girls Grammar).

context marketing

Finding out everything you can about your *target* and *aligning* your sales pitch accordingly. C.f. spying.

> 'Think about it: If you know that our B2B lead from the previous section is getting new budget in January, she's downloaded a couple buying guides in the past two weeks, she's visited your *product* pages, and it's December, you're able to send her insanely *targeted content* that *addresses* her *needs* – like, say, an offer for a custom end of year demo of your *product* with a rep that specializes in the finance industry – *content* that she's pretty likely to convert on.'
>
> Cory Ebidon, Hubspot blogs

contextualise

Put in context. (As, 'Can you contextualise that for me, please?') Explain. As, 'Whatever might be said by way of explanation and *contextualization* – and I am sure that Senator Brandis wasn't actively seeking the support of bigots for the government's amendments – this was more than just a tactical error by the minister . . .' (Australian Policy Online)

contingent labour / contingents

'Nontraditional' labour/workforce. *Consultants*, freelancers, independent contractors, etc. Glorified *casuals*, temps, seasonals, etc. About a quarter of the workforce and growing. Another source of *agility*, *flexibility* and – because they come with fewer entitlements – cost savings.

Contingents create *challenges* – and opportunities – for *risk management* and *HR*.

'Companies must seek new ways to find the right talent, develop skills, and share expertise. One of those *strategic* approaches is the growing reliance on *consultants*, intermittent employees, or *contingent labor*.'

Forbes

'One *risk* can be legal and regulatory *challenges* when governments pursue companies that misclassify *contingent workers*. This can lead to *significant* penalties, fines, and legal costs. Another potential *downside* is when managers use the *contingent workforce* to work around headcount and labor *spend* controls, driving increases in baseline costs with no discernible increase in *value*.'

Deloitte

continuous improvement (CI)

Unbroken, uninterrupted, unending, ceaseless, incessant, unrelenting, uninterrupted, constant, non-stop, unremitting, 24/7, endless, unrelieved, perpetual, everlasting, permanent, week-in week-out, undying, interminable improvement.

'*Continuous improvement* is a systematic, ongoing effort to improve the quality of care and services and: takes into account the needs of your care recipients and may involve them in improvement activities, is part of an overall quality system to assess how well your systems are working and the standard of care and services *achieved*, and is a results-*focused* activity demonstrated through *outputs* and *outcomes*.'

Aged Care Quality Agency

'Responsibility for the *Continuous Improvement (CI)* framework rests with Service *Delivery*. There will be joint responsibility for the completion of *CI initiatives* between Service *Delivery*, UTAS *leaders* and champions across UTAS (to be identified) to *implement CI* opportunities under a defined methodology.'

University of Tasmania

'How we do our work:
• Adapting to both a changing world environment and evolving *customer needs*
• Accepting *accountability* for our actions
• *Continuous improvement* in all that we do.'

CIA mission statement

'. . . ford every stream,
Continuously improve, till you *achieve* your dream.'

conversation

1. Discussion, debate, discourse, talk, colloquy, oral interchange, etc.
2. What you have when you don't have a policy, beliefs or convictions; or convictions but not the courage of them. What you have when you're stalling for time, waiting to see which way public opinion will go.

'The Government started a *conversation* on this with the launch of the Intergenerational Report last month. And today I want to advance this *conversation* with you . . . so that all interested members of the wider community can listen to experts and participate in this *conversation*.'

Joe Hockey, 8 April 2015

> 'Again, I'm not going to get into specific *outcomes*. You're asking me to go five months ahead of where we are now, which is to open the *conversation* about all the issues and this 200-page report . . .'
>
> Joe Hockey, ABC, 31 March 2015

> '. . . there is some genuine *conversation* that needs to be had about the common purpose . . . And I am here today to make a further contribution to that national *conversation* by releasing the Federal Government's discussion paper on taxation reform . . . Today is the start of the *conversation* . . .'
>
> Joe Hockey, 30 March 2015

> '. . . because if you're having a fair dinkum *conversation* with the Australian people, everyone should be fully informed . . . And again, that involves a *conversation* with the nation.'
>
> Joe Hockey, ABC, 30 March 2015

> 'For God's sake let us sit upon the ground
> And have a *conversation* about the death of kings.'
>
> *Richard II*

See *consensus*

conversation ready

You'll have to ask HR.

> 'Are you *Conversation Ready*?
> In conjunction with lead RMIT *Conversation Ready* is a new program developed for managers and supervisors to practically apply the Behavioural Capability Framework into performance *conversations*.

This session is hands on and is about preparing for:

• Types of *conversations* that present itself [sic] during the performance cycle . . .

Learning outcomes: By the end of the program participants should be able to:

• Plan for and use appropriate conversational structure

• Create and maintain an emotional climate for openness and action

• Practically practice [sic] and apply your learning

Conversation Ready – workshops developed for managers and supervisors to practically apply RMIT Human Resources Consultancy's Behavioural Capability Framework into performance conversations. Perform Develop Aspire.'

RMIT University Workshop

cooperative subjective status

Willing to cooperate. No longer displaying 'resistive behaviour' after 'pain' and 'motor dysfunction' has been caused by guards' 'striking techniques'.

'Subdue the subject using reasonable force so that he/she is no longer in the assailant category,' it explains. 'If justified, necessary force is to be used to bring the subject to *cooperative subjective status* whereupon they respond favourably to verbalisation.'

Serco Training Manual for dealing with asylum seeker/detainees

'Now, will you accept your *cooperative subjective status*?!'

core

1. The centre, heart or truth of something. The innermost part. As, '*Core* of my heart, my country . . .' The bit containing the seeds (*core* policy, *core commitment*, *core strategy*, *core* beliefs, etc.). The essential things.
2. *Key*. As in: *key* policy, *key* commitment, *key* strategy, *key* beliefs, etc. As, 'Although he may not be the man some/ girls think of as handsome/To my heart he carries the *core*' (George and Ira Gershwin).
3. *Core* business.

> 'Central Intelligence Agency (CIA) *core* collectors, under the direction of the Clandestine Services department, collects intelligence that helps high-level government officials make decisions that affect the safety and security of the United States.'
>
> CIA website

> '. . . politicians must stick to the *core* business of government. That *core* business is not gay marriage, it's not tampons and it's not often on *Q&A*. It's all about strong and consistent economic management and the ability to get that *message* across to the electorate.'
>
> Peter Reith

> 'Despite widespread claims by the industry that companies have adopted *CSR* as a "*core* competence", we argue that the industry has yet to incorporate the CRD function as part of "*core* business" at the level of practice.'
>
> Centre for Social Responsibility in Mining, University of Queensland

core promise

1. The main promise, the big one, the heart of the matter, the non-negotiable promise, the deal-breaker, the one to which we are *absolutely committed. Key* promise. Not *non-core*. The one that might be kept.

> 'What won't you concede? What are your *core issues*? What are your *core promises*?'
>
> Journalist to Shadow Minister, Channel 7, June 2004

> 'The *commitment* I made not to introduce a GST was not a *core* promise, but a *non-core* promise.'
>
> After John Howard

> 'The wow factor is Gaga's *core promise*, and as long as she keeps it pumping at this pitch . . .'
>
> *Sydney Morning Herald*

> 'Do you promise to love, honour, cherish and protect her, forsaking all others and holding only to her for evermore?
>
> Groom: *Core promise* or *non-core promise*?'
>
> Traditional Christian wedding ceremony

core values

Refer to the company *mission statement* (usually located in the reception area). Excellence: in poultry, earth moving equipment, interrogation, etc. Deep respect for people, oxen, poultry, all living things, etc. Integrity, probity, profit, tolerance, diversity, etc. *Customer-focused*, etc. Often discovered when setting and aligning the *vision*. (Note: there is no record of bastardry, greed, end justifies the means, devil take the hindmost, etc. being discovered at such times, hence these are not *core values*.) Schools and hospitals now have *core values* – a great blessing for their customers.

> 'Titan is very proud of its reputation for excellence and *commitment* to upholding the highest ethical standards. As always, Titan's ultimate success in both of these areas begins and ends with our greatest resource: our team of highly qualified and talented employees. All of Titan employees share certain *core values*.'
>
> Titan Corporation, a corrupt company now defunct

> 'Our *vision* at Florey Primary School is to *empower* students to acquire, demonstrate, articulate and value knowledge and skills that will support them, as life-long learners, to participate in and contribute to the global world and practise the *core values* of the school: respect, tolerance and inclusion, and excellence.'
>
> Florey Primary School

> 'Q. How do you determine the *core values* of your employees?
>
> *Core value alignment*. Don't tell them your *core values*, but ask probing questions that will get them to talk about things that they've experienced. . . . If you told someone, "Here are the three *core values* of our company; does that *align* with you?" they'd be crazy not to nod their head and say yes.'
>
> Smart Business Online

corporate citizens

Limited liability citizens.

> 'As part of our *commitment* to create real *value* in a world that is constantly changing, we are determined to be good *corporate citizens* in every corner of our global community.'
>
> www.jll.com.au

'Monsanto named one of *CR Magazine*'s 100 best corporate citizens for 2014.'

www.monsanto.com

corporate communications

Influencing, *supporting*, *communicating*, *enhancing*, influencing, etc. Whatever one makes of this.

'The mission of the *Corporate Communications Unit* is: To influence and support our *internal clients* to *communicate* effectively about the services they provide in order to *enhance community* perceptions of the council's activities and positively influence *community behaviours*.'

City of Port Phillip, job description

'Our Professional values involve a specialised approach to shaping *communication strategies* for *clients* with a *focus* on *delivering innovative* ideas and business *outcomes* . . . Our *consultants* work in close partnership with *clients* to *deliver* positive business *outcomes*. Our *clients* benefit from our strategic advice, our strong media relationships . . . [etc.], our financial markets expertise, our market intelligence capabilities and our interaction with internal and external stakeholders.'

canningscorporatecommunications.com

cost-effective communication vehicle

1. Advertisement.
2. Alan Jones (according to Telstra).

'"By immersing residents in an environment that is all about conservation and making it fun and inviting," said

Armenta, "they are likely to invite their neighbors next year. Word-of-mouth can be a powerful and *cost-effective communication vehicle.*" '

www.calwaterassn.com

'I am the way, the truth and the *cost-effective communication vehicle.*'

cost factor

How much it's going to cost – factored.

'Tony Eastley: Mr Mansfield, what is it and how much is it going to cost?

Bob Mansfield: The *cost factor* hasn't been ascertained *at this point in time*, Tony.'

ABC radio, May 2004

'Prime Minister Tony Abbott's *vision* for armed forces faces *cost factor*.'

www.smh.com.au, June 2014

credible trajectory

Going the right way, but it's further than we thought.

'We are still on a *credible trajectory* back to surplus.'

Joe Hockey, Federal Treasurer, May 2015

crisis

See *emergency*.

critical thinker

A deep, clear, careful, aware, Socratic sort of thinker. A thinker who does not accept surface meanings, clichés etc.

'Mentions of *critical thinking* in job postings have doubled since 2009, according to an analysis by career-search site Indeed.com' (*Wall Street Journal*). Like most businesses Goldman Sachs wants to employ *critical thinkers*. 'Do they make use of information that's available in their *journey* to arrive at a conclusion or decision? How do they make use of that?' (Global head of recruiting, Goldman Sachs)

Examples of critical thinking include shorting the mortgage market before it collapsed in 2008; selling bundles of bad mortgages to *clients*, offloading them in the knowledge that the market was about to collapse; selling 'collateralized debt obligations' without telling the buyers that Goldman Sachs stood to benefit if they fell in value; misleading Congress; being too big to fail; etc.

cross functional collaboration

Something of the kind described here. Involves a shepherd. Be careful to harness properly.

> 'Innovate with *Cross-Functional Collaboration*
>
> Select a shepherd. I recommend engaging a third-party expert from the outside to *facilitate* (and participate in) the *conversation*. The interpersonal and multi-dimensional dynamics presented during a *cross-functional collaboration* are very complex. When *harnessed* properly, this complexity can make a session go extremely well or, conversely, horribly wrong. Choose your session shepherd wisely, and trust her to keep the energy and *productivity* moving in a positive direction.'
>
> expertenough.com

crystal ball

1. (n) Fortune-telling *tool* (risk analysis and conjecture).
2. (n) Management *tool* (risk analysis and conjecture).
3. (v) To extrapolate from the figures. (As in: 'I'll just *crystal ball* it.') Aka: stochastic optimisation.

> 'Day 1 of *Crystal Ball* for Six Sigma uses *hands-on* instruction and real-world case studies to teach students the basics of Monte Carlo simulation . . .'

See *customer relationship management*

crystal clear

Foggy, murky, obscure, prolix.

> 'I want to make this *crystal clear* . . . The president is desirous of trying to see how we can make our best efforts in order to find a way to *facilitate*.'
>
> John Kerry, US Secretary of State, April 2014

cultural fit

Some fit and some do not fit.

> '*Cultural fit* is best understood when you consider it within the *context* of your organization's *culture* and how your organization's *culture* was formed. A potential employee may express and exhibit the characteristics, language, and *values* that exist within the current organizational *culture* – or not.'
>
> About Money

culture

Some are fit and some are less fit.

> 'Don't you know right away when someone *fits* in your workplace *culture*? Your gut tells you instinctively when those around you stand for the same *values* you do – or they don't.'
>
> Glenn Lopis, *Forbes*, 9 December 2011

> 'When *cultures fit*, an organization can transcend problems, *innovate* and flourish. Without *culture fit*, an organization and its members will fail to thrive and will always be vulnerable in the face of *innovative* challengers.'
>
> TalentCulture

culture

1. The sum total of learned beliefs, *values*, and customs that serve to regulate the behaviour of members of a particular society.
2. 'The sum total of learned beliefs, *values*, and customs that serve to regulate the *consumer* behaviour of members of a particular society' (Leon G. Schiffman and Leslie Lazar Kanuk, *Consumer Behaviour*).
3. The foundation of an organisation, such as an international corporation, a taxation office or a football club.
4. The foundation *in terms of the values* of an organisation. As, 'My main job today: I work hard at helping to maintain the *culture*,' Mr Bezos said.

> 'The intent of the CIIP is to remodel and *address* the barriers and *enablers* that have been identified, demonstrating a clear commitment to *cultural* reform and compliance with continued, concentrated effort to achieve enduring *cultural change*, recognised as an organisation that embraces *diversity*.'
>
> Acting Commissioner, Queensland Fire and Emergency Services, 13 March 2015

'As an example of the type of support we provide, scheduled the third week of May is a knowledge sharing and collaboration workshop with 45 senior, like minded, executives from across the organisation coming together to explore and set the direction for the *cultural* journey the organisation will go through to support the *knowledge* sharing *agenda*.'

Efficiency Quality Service newsletter, May 2011

'The *Levers* of *Change* team will *deliver strategies* that enable a *customer focused culture* by *addressing* organisational *issues* identified in the *culture* survey results as requiring priority attention (to *address* gaps or pursue opportunities for excellence) and *designing leadership development* and support *strategies*.'

Child Support Agency Intranet

'Our *goal* is to help you *leverage culture* to *drive* your *strategy* and achieve new levels of performance. With deep research into *culture* fit to *strategy*, an array of *innovative* diagnostic approaches and a *team* of organizational *culture change* experts, we can help your organization leverage its unique *culture* for future success.'

www.culturestrategyfit.com

'When I hear the word *culture*, I reach for my gun.'

Hermann Goering (attrib.)

'When I hear the words popular *culture*, I reach for my popgun.'

Jim Davidson

customer

Supermarket attendee, hospital patient, resident of nursing home or mental asylum, university student, library user, airline passenger. *Consumer*, *client*. Satisfied *customer*. *Target customer*. Victim. Prisoner, enemy detainee, taxpayer (see *knowledge officer (chief)*), subject of interrogation by private contractor, recipient of social welfare services, recipient of intelligence, person on whom every excellent organisation is *focused*. Citizen.

> 'The *driving* principles of these forms of thinking are recognition of a *brand* as a commercial and value building *asset*; an in-depth understanding of the *brand's consumers*; and a market level *strategy* that is *aligned* with the *brand's core promise* and is consistent across all forms of *customer touch points*.'
>
> knowledge.insead.edu

> 'What we stand for:
>
> • Intelligence that adds substantial *value* to the management of crises, the conduct of war, and the *development* of policy.
>
> • Objectivity in the substance of intelligence, a deep *commitment* to the *customer* in its forms and timing.'
>
> CIA *Vision, Mission* and *Values*

> '"We're trying to create those moments for *customers* where we're solving a really practical need," Ms Landry said, "in this way that feels really futuristic and magical."'
>
> Amazon employee who found a way to get Elsa dolls to customers within an hour of ordering.
> *New York Times*, 17 August 2015

> 'Details of the *strategies* to be *implemented* to *ensure* that service *delivery* is *customer focused*, taking into account patient's rights and the nature of the *core services* of the hospital.'
>
> Victorian Department of Human Services, Performance Standards (cleaning)

> '. . . our courses are popular, *customer focussed, driven* by purchaser requirements and responsive to external demands.'
>
> Lecturer/Senior Lecturer job ad, University of Bedfordshire

> 'Create a positive work environment in a small *team* that supports *continual improvement* in service *delivery* and excellent *customer* service methodologies.'
>
> Job description for liaison officer in a Queensland government department

> 'Friends, Romans, *customers* . . .'

customer-centric

Copernican view of the commercial universe, with the *consumer* or *customer* (or, us, we the people, formerly citizens) in the role of Sun. As, 'Mr. Manning compared the flawed perspective in many of today's business practices to Copernicus' original view of the universe. The philosopher changed his perspective to include the sun at the center and was able to build a successful model' (*Luxury Daily*).

Focused on the *customer*; but with *strategy*, *commitment*, *alignment*, etc. Interchangeable with *client-centric* and *consumer-centric.*

> 'A dynamic opportunity exists for a results driven Manager to ingeniously lead a newly formed team of *Customer* Service Representatives to *deliver* a *seamless journey* that *focuses* on providing solutions to *customers* with various *needs* across multiple *products* under the MyWealth platform.
>
> Reporting to the Head of *Customer Engagement* your *core* responsibility will be to lead and *drive* a *sustainable* business nurturing a *customer centric* and *continuous improvement* philosophy

in a manner consistent with CBA's *leadership* capabilities. You will *drive* and develop a high *performance culture* through motivating, inspiring and *continuously improving* our service proposition along with *engaging* the Mywealth *Customer Experience team* as well as other *stakeholders*.'

Job advertisement, Seek

customer delight

Extreme satisfaction.

'The company considered raising service levels to the "*delight* breakpoint" or reducing them to just above the "patience threshold". *Customer*-lifetime-*value* economics pointed to the second option: relaxing service levels but guarding against crossing the patience threshold. The drop in *customer* satisfaction was negligible, but the savings in staffing were *significant*, and the company ended up saving more than $7 million annually.'

'Maintaining the Customer Experience' by Adam Braff and John C. DeVine, *McKinsey Quarterly*, December 2008

'*Customer delight* is a *core value* at Porch.com. We literally have this *value* painted on our walls. So how to develop a *culture* that places an emphasis on *customer delight*?'

Matt Ehrlichman, CEO Porch.com, November 2014

'Did we *delight* you today?'

Receipt from Icebreaker, Auckland Airport

'Have a delightful day.'

Staff refrain at Auckland hotel

customer experience

What one, as a *customer*, goes through. Life. See *consciousness* – 'the perception of what passes in a *customer's* own mind' (after Locke). The experience of *issues* with *products* and services; of phone calls at dinner time; of intolerable music or promotions or commercial radio while waiting for a *customer service representative*; of being touched at a *customer* touchpoint; of falling for a brand; of retail therapy; of dreams and disillusionment, etc.: everything between the *delight* breakpoint and the patience threshold and beyond. The mind as seen by *marketers* possessed of empathy and data. A *holistic*, non-*siloed* experience. Life-enriching, as, 'As a market leader in their service based industry, they are known for innovation, high quality products and services and they pride themselves on enriching people's lives through their *customer experience*' (job advert on www.mycareer.com.au). 'How's your day been so far?' experience.

> 'In order to deliver exceptional *customer experience*, an emphasis within the business must be put on *customer experience* specifically from the *customer's* perspective i.e. a *customer-centric* approach. This requires that the company take a *holistic* approach to address the total *customer experience* as opposed to a *siloed* approach. Thus, both the business and IT need to be organized and *incentivized* to *deliver* exceptional *customer experience*.'
>
> From Oracle's '*Customer Experience Reference Architecture*'

> 'A second source of strategic and tactical help is my book *Addicted Customers: How to Get Them Hooked on Your Company*. This book was written before the recession but what it provides is *actionable insights* into the psychological principles that lead to emotionally compelling *customer experiences*.'
>
> John I. Todor, 'The Perfect Customer Experience' blog, December 2008

customer experience (differentiated)

> 'Our *customer experience* approach encompasses a series of *customer* interactions – your *brand*, offerings and *touch points* – and draws upon a foundation of decades of *client* work and research. The goal is not simply *customer* satisfaction, but building a base of promoters. We deeply understand that positive *customer experience* and advocacy *drive competitive advantage*, leading to faster organic growth and lower cost. Our *customer-focused* approach to *brand management*, *channel strategy* and *marketing* mix can more than double a company's organic revenue growth rates.'
>
> Bain and Company

customer experience (differentiated)

There's a cup of tea, and there's a Starbucks cup of tea.

> 'Teavana's world-class tea authority, coupled with the romance and theater of the retail experience that is the heart and soul of Starbucks heritage, will create a *differentiated customer experience* and business opportunity that *delivers* immediate *value* to *shareholders*.'
>
> Howard Schultz, Starbucks, November 2012

customer lifecycle

Self-explanatory. As, 'With respect to the *customer lifecycle*, the *focus* for these components is on the Need and Recommend phases of the *customer lifecycle*' (Oracle's 'Customer Experience Reference Architecture'); '6 Steps to Customer Life Cycle Optimization with Content' (Lee Odden, Top Rank Online Marketing).

customer obsession

Ultimate customer-centricity. '*Customer Obsession*: Leaders start with the customer and work backwards. They work vigorously to earn and keep *customer* trust. Although leaders pay attention to competitors, they *obsess over customers*' (Amazon Leadership Principle No. 1).

customer service

1. Once *marketing* has got them into your tent, *customer service* is meant to keep them there. *Client* service. *Consumer* service. Punter service. Joe Six Pack service, etc.
2. Say it often enough and they might believe you mean it.

> 'Contribute to *team* function during *events* so procedures are adhered to and a high level of *customer service* is attained.'
>
> Personnel advertisement, Groundsperson: *key* duties

> 'Treat *customer experience* as a competence, not a function: *Customer service* is everyone's priority, not just that of the contact center. Call it "*customer experience*", "*customer* advocacy", "*customer* insight" – anything, Temkin pleaded, that avoids dumping it into a *siloed* department.'
>
> Jessica Tsai, 'The 5 Levels of Customer Experience Maturity'

> 'The award was presented as part of the inaugural Best *Customer Experience* Companies List in Sydney today. The list was developed and presented by *customer engagement strategy consultancy*, Fifth Quadrant, and supported by CMO and event sponsor, Oracle.'
>
> www.cmo.com.au

> 'There is a tide in the affairs of *customers*, which, taken at the flood, leads on to fortune.'

customer service representative

Will be with you shortly.

customer (valued)

A *customer* with a value put on her. A paying *customer*. Not a worthless *customer*. *Customer* presumed to be susceptible to smarmy condescension.

> 'Dear *Valued Customer*,
>
> During the year the *key* cost drivers of our industry – commercial property prices, transport and labour have continued to rise. Whilst we have absorbed some of the rising costs by way of operational *productivity* improvements, it has been necessary to review our pricing . . . We are confident that you will appreciate the responsible approach we have taken to the pricing review. Should you have any queries with regards to the new rates, please do not hesitate to call our *Customer* CARE team . . . Recall thank you for your continued support and recognition, and appreciate your understanding of this necessary price increase.'
>
> Recall

> 'As a *valued customer* of ANZ, we are always looking for ways to enable you to conduct your business in a faster, more *agile* fashion.'
>
> ANZ

> 'Dear *Valued Customer*
>
> We would like to welcome you to Café Va Bene and thank you for letting us be a part of your day.'
>
> www.cafevabene.com.au

customer value proposition (CVP)

A sales pitch. Why the 'target' *customer* should buy your *product* and not your competitors'.

> 'Leading *development* of integrated *customer value propositions* for identified *market segments* and channels.'
>
> 'So how do you go about ensuring that your *CVP* is up to scratch?
>
> A good starting point is to gather your team to *brainstorm* your business' *key* differentiators and areas of expertise, using a structured *process* to *drive* the discussions and allow their creativity to flow.'
>
> Macquarie Bank

cuts see *efficiency dividends*

cutting edge

(n & adj) Leading edge. Where innovation occurs.
The frontier. The absolute latest and most advanced.

> 'The further slashing of funds may cost Australia its reputation for conducting *cutting-edge* scientific and medical researches.'
>
> *Business Times*

> 'While we are a long way from the *cutting edge* gender reforms of Norway, which mandates 40 per cent female representation on all publicly listed companies, the progression of this bill will be an interesting one to watch.'
>
> Elizabeth Knight, *Sydney Morning Herald*, 2 July 2015

cutting edge

'Presented in a logical yet entertaining format the techniques of Neuro Linguistic Programming and Spiral Dynamics will integrate to produce *cutting edge* aspects of training design and *delivery*. Be able to layer and nest exercises for maximum instructional *impact*. Extend your stage anchoring and platform skills.'

Training Dynamics 2004

dangerous aquatic organisms (DAOs)

Sharks etc. As, Gold Coast waterways have the 'potential for *dangerous aquatic organisms*'.

> 'These waterways, a Bond University expert explained, could be "physically penetrated" by bull sharks. Other DAOs include stingrays, jellyfish, catfish, stonefish, sharks, algae and other micro-organisms.'
>
> www.goldcoast.qld.gov.au

> 'Help! Dangerous aquatic organism!'

dashboard

A *tool* that displays the current status of metrics and *key performance indicators*. Not a scorecard.

> 'The *business intelligence dashboard* is often confused with the performance scorecard. The main difference between the two, traditionally, is that a *business intelligence dashboard*, like the dashboard of a car, indicates the status at a specific *point in time*. A scorecard, on the other hand, displays progress over time towards specific *goals*. Dashboard and scorecard designs are increasingly converging.'
>
> searchbusinessanalytics.techtarget.com

> 'The center's quality of life *dashboard* tracks 15 economic and environmental indicators. Residential electricity consumption, air quality and venture capital funding were areas that improved from last year.'
>
> www.kpbs.org/news

data

'*Dashboard* allows News Corp journos to track readers. News Corp is set to roll out a real-time *dashboard* that will give its 2500 journalists unprecedented access to data on the size, demographics . . .'

Australian, 26 April 2015

data

What is known about you, and you, and you, and you . . .

'To prod employees, Amazon has a powerful *lever*: more *data* than any retail operation in history. Its perpetual flow of real-time, ultra-detailed *metrics* allows the company to *measure* nearly everything its *customers* do: what they put in their shopping carts, but do not buy; when readers reach the "abandon point" in a Kindle book; and what they will stream based on previous purchases. It can also tell when engineers are not building pages that load quickly enough, or when a vendor manager does not have enough gardening gloves in stock.'

New York Times, 17 August 2015

Data lakes: 'Clearly Accenture wants to grow its analytics business by encouraging enterprises to trawl through their *data lakes* looking for the – jargon alert – high-quality insights they can *action*. Chatelain thinks the time is ripe for a *mindset change* in the way business decisions are made' (www.theregister.co.uk).

'*Data* is incredibly liberating.'

Sean Boyle, Amazon Web Services

dedicated

1. Set apart for some purpose.
2. Committed to an action, creed, vocation, person, team, principle, proposition. As, '. . . a new nation, conceived in Liberty, and *dedicated* to the proposition that all men are created equal.' Organisations *commit* themselves to being *dedicated* to whatever it is they do, and to the processes, *strategic plans* and *implementation strategies* by which they do it. They are *dedicated* to their customers, their *stakeholders*, their *bottom line* and to *going forwards*. Sometimes they *dedicate* themselves to being *committed* to these things. Often they are *passionate* in their dedication.

> 'Engagement Consultant × 3
>
> This is an exciting opportunity to join this *passionate* and talented group that is genuinely *committed* to people investment and *development*. As a progressive and dynamic *leader*, our *client* is *dedicated* to continually build and *develop* people capital.'
>
> Seek.com

> 'Southcorp is *committed* to being a *dedicated* and leading premium winemaker with a portfolio of brands and wines that range from the contemporary to the *iconic* . . .'
>
> Southcorp media release, 2004

deep dive

1. Dive deep, into water for instance.
2. Dive deep into data. Like *drill down*, but deeper. Process that takes you into new dimensions.

> '. . . we introduce the concept of a *deep dive*, an intervention when top management seizes hold of the substantive content

of a *strategic initiative* and its *operational implementation* at the project level, as a way to *drive* new *behaviors* that enable an organization to shift its performance trajectory into new dimensions unreachable with any of the previously described forms of intervention.'

Howard H. Yu and Joseph L. Bower, 'Taking a "Deep Dive"',
Harvard Business School

'A clear *goal*, resources, expectations of success and *developing* that sense of *synergy* working towards Maslow's "*Self Actualisation*" for the team and all of its members. This is what the *Deep-Dive process* is designed to do – when run and integrated to the organisation as a whole.'

Rapidbi, '*Deep-dive brainstorming* technique – Ideo'

'Having selected one or more programmes to analyse in more detail – a *Deep Dive* pack would examine *pathways* in more detail to identify evidence of opportunities for improvements within specific *pathways* – together with other work to build the evidence and business case for *change* they *address* the second part of the Right Care approach – What to change.'

NHS UK

'Ability to *Deep Dive* and develop innovative ideas for process challenges.'

Amazon job advert

'20,000 Leagues under the Data.'

Jules Verne

de-escalate

Purpose of verbal reasoning.

> 'He states that he used force to prevent her escape, having used "verbal reasoning . . . to *de-escalate* the situation initially".'
>
> Melbourne Metro Ticket inspector after body slamming a 15-year-old girl. *Age*, 9 December 2013

deliver / delivery

1. To send successfully, take to, hand over; set free; assist at the birth; make good on an obligation or promise.
2. To teach or instruct (as in: *deliver training packages* or *trainings*), modify behaviour in another. To *implement*. Some people (and racehorses, greyhounds, ferrets, etc.) never *deliver* on their promise, talent, etc.

> '. . . her experience with direct investments enable [sic] her to *deliver* insight into this area.'
>
> Consultancy promotion

> 'Through this initiative we are working to *deliver* the evolution in how we interact with you.'
>
> Bank promotion

> 'With this in mind the Executive Management Committee has approved the creation of a new unit called Flexible *Delivery*. The *vision* is for this unit to provide students with opportunities to have their complete flexible *delivery* needs met in one place. The creation of Flexible *Delivery* Unit will see the combining of all RPL, Rapid Recognition, and Off Campus *delivery* functions across the Institute.'
>
> Email from a TAFE senior manager to employees

'Navigate a financially sustainable workforce by implementing a right size organisational structure to *deliver key outcomes* effectively and efficiently within agreed budget allocation and achieving necessary *targets* . . .'

Advert. for Deputy Director-General Service Delivery, Department of Natural Resources and Mines, Queensland

'And more, much more than this,
I *delivered* it my way.'

deliverables

(n) That which is to be *delivered. Key deliverables* are the most important ones.
(adj) Able to be *delivered.*

'*Communicating* major *deliverables* and activities to all *key stakeholders.*'

Victorian Department of Human Services

'The final *deliverable* is a recommendation for the future asset network, as well as a 3 time horizon executable transition plan.'

Du Pont worker Facebook page

'So there's a real *focus* on the funding is going to achieve *deliverable outcomes* that people are *accountable* for and there's been a move away from simply funding *process* and *input*.

So consistent with that approach, it would be good to see that the funding is going to achieve very specific and *deliverable outcomes* where you know they're sort of proven *track records* and so on of success.'

Andrew Penfold, www.abc.net.au, April 2015

'For unto every one that hath shall be *delivered*, and he shall have abundant *deliverables*; but from the one who does not have many *deliverables*, even the *deliverables* he does have shall be *delivered* away.'

Matthew 25:29

demotivated / demotivating

Suffering a loss of motivation. Jaded, crushed, stuffing knocked out, rug pulled from under, fit of the blues, etc. Depression, ennui. As, 'She was *demotivated* by the news that her *skill sets* needed *enhancing*.'

'We are *demotivated*.'

Sergeant Chris Grisham, military intelligence office, Iraq

'Many factors can *demotivate* your team. Mass layoffs, losing a valued team member or key client, or rumors of a shutdown all can lower morale and cause internal discord.'

smallbusiness.chron.com

'Even cowgirls get *demotivated*.'

deplane

Get off the plane (US). C.f. deboat, debus, debike, depot.

'We are waiting on Customs to provide us with authorisation to *deplane*.'

Pilot

'If you can't stand the heat, *dekitchen*.'

deranged

1. Crazy, cracked, mad, etc.
2. No longer available. As, 'The product in question would no longer be available for sale as they planned to "*derange*" it' (Kmart head office replying to an enquiry).

detention centre

Prison.

develop / development

1. Expand, amplify, improve, grow, enlarge, increase, intensify, strengthen, deepen, coach, mould, train, teach, change in various ways, etc.
2. Anything that moves, even slightly. As, 'This newly created role will have *accountability* for the *development* and *implementation* of Organisational Effectiveness and Talent *Development frameworks* and initiatives inclusive of *Customer-Centric Culture development*, *Leadership* & Management effectiveness, Talent & *Capability development* and *High Performance Teams*.'

> 'Let me not to the marriage of true minds
> Admit *developments*. Love is not love
> Which *develops* when it *development* finds,
> Or *develops* with the *development* to *develop* . . .'
>
> Shakespeare *Development* 116

dialogue

(n) Discussion, conversation, exchange of ideas, deliberation, etc. (As in: Plato's *Dialogues.*) *Dialogues* are 'cultivated' or 'entered into'. We 'open the way' to them. They are 'fruitful', 'constructive', 'creative' or 'useful'. *Strategic dialogues* are considered essential in some fields. Some dialogues are '*process* steps'.
(v) To talk, converse, discuss, chew the fat, parley, palaver, confer; phone, email, fax, text, etc. (As: 'Let's *dialogue* on Wednesday.' 'We should *dialogue* with Harold asap.' 'We've been *dialoging* for months but he hasn't *delivered*.') Shakespeare uses it as a verb, as do Pope, Coleridge, Carlyle and these people.

> 'Teaching Social Class through Alternative Media and by *Dialoging* across Disciplines and Boundaries.'
>
> '*Dialoging* with God through the Tabernacle Experience'

> 'What makes Yseop's NLG Smart is that we take this commenting on data one step further: we explain WHY a particular data point or *product* or service recommendation is relevant to you and HOW to apply it to your personal *context*. Doing this requires both reasoning and *dialoging* before the language generation begins.'
>
> YSEOP

> 'A mentoring moment is an intersubjective coming to know in *dialogue* that engages unitary humans in a *transformative* process, confirming beliefs and *values* in creatively imagining and launching projects . . .'
>
> *Nursing Science Quarterly*, April 2002

> 'You *dialogin'* to me?'
>
> Robert de Niro, *Change Driver*

direct reports

People. Underlings, folk of lower rank, privilege, status, intelligence, worth, etc. Need managing.

> 'A major goal of the program is to help managers to become emotional coaches for their *direct reports*.'
>
> Consortium for Research on Emotional Intelligence Organisations

> '25 tips for managing your first *direct reports*
>
> . . . Managing your first *direct reports* is one of the most challenging transitions a leader will ever have to navigate.'
>
> smartblogs.com

> 'Studdert's *direct reports* describe him as a restless explorer, constantly *pushing the envelope*, constantly thinking, "Are we doing it right?"'
>
> www.brw.com.au, April 2015

> 'The *direct reports* are hungry.'
> 'Then let them eat cake.'

> '*Direct reports* who need *direct reports*,
> Are the luckiest *direct reports* in the world.'

disclosure (poor)

Failure to tell the truth, the whole truth, etc., in a business context. Misstatements, lying, dissembling, deceiving, dodging, weaving, hiding, etc. As, 'The man is a pathological *poor discloser*!' A failure of *transparency*. *Unaccountable behaviours*.

'After a number of record corporate collapses, *poor disclosure practices* and some highly questionable *behaviour* by a few, who can blame them?'

Bank chairman

'We've also continued to make steps to improve the *disclosure* and *stakeholder engagement* regimes. And most importantly for me, we've filled most *key* roles and the new *leadership team* is shaping the business *going forward*.'

Gordon Davis, Australian Wheat Board CEO, ABC

disconnect

1. (v) To cut off; to break or end a connection.
2. (n) The state of being dissimilar, not the same. As in, 'There's a *disconnect* in the figures.' 'There's a *disconnect* between our *outcomes* and our *core goals*.' 'We need to do something about the *disconnect* – Nigel, can you *recontextualise* it?'

'What a *disconnect* a day makes.'

disincentivise

Deincentivise. Reverse *incentivisation/incentivation*.

'Werner said there are more elegant solutions to this transportation problem that do not require *disincentivising* hybrid and electric cars.'

Badger Herald, December 2014

'When the friction of authentication is eliminated and consumers can experience and enjoy new content from various locations and devices without restrictions, piracy will become *disincentivized*.'

GE Reports/Ideas, June 2015

'Even cowgirls get *disincentivised*.'

disposition matrix

Guide for *wet work* by drone. Matrix of (terrorist) targets for servicing. Kill list. '. . . a sophisticated grid, mounted upon a database that is said to have been more than two years in the development, containing biographies of individuals believed to pose a threat to US interests, and their known or suspected locations, as well as a range of options for their disposal' (*Guardian*, July 2013).

'Nicknamed the "*disposition matrix*" and coordinated by presidential counterterrorism adviser John O. Brennan in conjunction with the National Counterterrorism Center (NCTC), this new system integrates drone technology, satellite surveillance, massive databases and presumed congressional authorization to target and kill persons of interest globally.'

Wired.com

diversity / diverse

1. Variety, assortment, mixture, polyglot, disparate, varied, mixed, etc. Not uniform or homogenous.
2. Universal good. As, 'rich multicultural diversity'.

'In order to *leverage diversity*, she said the first step is to build an inclusive *culture* by instituting protocols which will assist moving beyond unconscious bias.'

HC Online, 25 September 2011

'Our mission is to *enhance* people's understanding of how a *diverse* work place; which includes *diversity* of thought, experience and people – *impacts* an organization's *bottom line* and stimulates innovative business *practices*.'

Culture Coach International

'*Diversity* is at the very *core* of our ability to serve our *clients* well and to maximize return for our shareholders. *Diversity* supports and strengthens the firm's *culture*, and it reinforces our reputation as the employer of choice in our industry and beyond.'

Lloyd C. Blankfein, CEO Goldman Sachs

dogfooding

Testing products within the company, esp. software products.

'As a part of our *dogfooding* deployment efforts, we must keep upper management and other concerned groups (for example, *product teams*, tactical deployment teams, and *Marketing*) up to date with regular, predictable, and consistent reports. The reporting *deliverables* vary by audience.'

Microsoft

dog whistling

As dogs respond to whistles pitched so high that humans cannot hear them, in politics a *dog whistle* is a message pitched in a way that only some voters recognise it. Racist voters, for instance. Form of wedge politics.

'Federal Labor accused the Prime Minister of "retreating to the *dog whistle*" – on one hand rejecting [Pauline Hanson's] views, on the other saying he understood why some people would agree with her.'

Sydney Morning Herald, August 2003

'So it is back to *dog whistle* politics again: *dog whistle* and wedge. This is the only feasible explanation for Howard's extraordinary attack on state schools as too "politically correct" and "values neutral". It was a not-so-coded message to his constituency of former Hansonistas . . .'

Mike Carlton, *Sydney Morning Herald*, January 2004

down in the weeds

1. In the detail, especially excessive or irrelevant detail. As, 'Don't get too *down in the weeds* when talking to reporters' (Kristin Weitel on Twitter). Don't stray too far from the main game, the substance, the message, etc. An expression common among policy wonks, managers, media etc. Also 'getting into the weeds' – getting into the detail, the finer points. Possibly derived from Acadian French 'Dans la rhubarbe', for someone who has lost sight of what really matters.
2. *In the weeds* – overworked and overwhelmed, common among restaurant staff (US). As, Waiter 1. 'How goes it? Waiter 2 (sighing), 'In the weeds.'

downside

1. Bottom, lower, under side. Not the higher side.
2. What comes with an upside, and often as a consequence of it; the depressing bit that you have to put up with. Disadvantage, drawback, shortcoming, flaw, flipside, bad side, bad part, part to be regretted, hitch, snag, deficiency,

defect, imperfection, weakness, impediment, encumbrance, hindrance, fly in the ointment, sting in the tail, bummer, bad news, downer, etc. (NB. Some things are all *downside.*)

> 'We may lament the tragedies of the *churn*'s *downside*, but we shouldn't lose sight of its very powerful and important upside: it makes us better off. What's really going on is a healthy recycling.'
>
> W. Michael Cox, Federal Reserve Bank, Dallas

> 'Polygamy has a big *downside*.'
>
> www.timeslive.co.za

> 'From a technical perspective the energy complex remains in a *downside* correction with the peak of the upside move that began in mid-March still in place for about the last week or so as the pricing formation is now more of a consolidation pattern with a drifting to the downside.'
>
> www.resourceinvestor.com, April 2015

> 'In our base case simulation there is an upside case that, er, corresponds on the flipside of the *downside* case in kind of an adverse direction.'
>
> A World Bank economist, 2008

> 'What do you want to hear first, the upside or the *downside*?'

> 'The *downside* is – you'll have to pay tax on the upside.'

downsize / downsizing / down balance

To make smaller, diminish, reduce, especially the number of your employees.

'This is not an evacuation, just a further *downsizing*, and the security situation in the country remains under constant review.'

UN spokesman

'As I said we're studying that now but we believe that the personnel implications of the *down balance* will be in the region of 300 to 350 employees.'

Sinead McAlary, Ford Australia spokeswoman, ABC radio

'Ukraine Shoppers *Downsize* Buying Habits to Counter Hryvnia, War

Drifting through the aisles of a Kontynent supermarket in Kiev, Mykhaylo Ilchuk was learning what it takes to *downsize* his personal life.'

www.bloomberg.com

'Following the meeting, Mayor Geoff Kettle attributed the move to a "*downsize*". "They have *downsized* the regional office and they were discussing whether they would stay in Clinton St or centralise as a lot of other NSW Government offices in Goulburn have done," Cr Kettle said.'

www.goulburnpost.com.au

'As the just-completed reporting season demonstrated, you can't keep *downsizing* your way to executive bonuses indefinitely.'

Michael Pascoe, *Age*, 31 August 2015

'So she swallowed one of the cakes, and was delighted to find that she began *downsizing* directly.'

Alice in Wonderland

drill down

Analyse. To 'focus in'. One *drills down* through a data base to find the information one needs. As, 'But we are going to *drill down* beyond that to provide some options' (*Australian Financial Review*). More generally, to seek and sometimes find more information or knowledge; as for example, Newton *drilled down* to discover gravity, Bach the fugue, etc. Analyse. Get to the bottom of whatever. A *deep dive*, but not as deep. Never drill up.

> 'Nevertheless, when the group came together for a first *Strategy Review* meeting, they were able to assess the progress that had been made toward objectives, identify and *drill down* on road blocks and develop *short to medium term* solutions.'
>
> Westpac

> 'The *enablers* revolve around the creation of a fund level data store at a level of detail that will support the sort of *drill downs* specified in the data *framework* referred to above, including individual details. Above this will be a datamart derived from the data store and aggregated to a level that supports the types of analyses the client requires to identify trends or segregate segments and *clusters*. The use of aggregated data to establish segments and *clusters* and to identify trends will offer favourable response times by narrowing the amount of data to be *churned* in the interrogation and filtering *process*.'
>
> Memorandum from a superannuation administration company

> 'Users can also *drill down* into the *KPIs* to see their deeper workings and what exactly is generating the numbers.'
>
> www.zdnet.com

drive

Steer, impel, induce, make go, etc., as with a car, tram, herd of cattle, etc. All of these and many more. As, '*Drive* the execution of product development initiatives that meet *customer* needs' (SEEK job advert for position in Mental Health Services).

> 'On reflection, I think I ended up *driving* the desire for change too quickly and became less open to advice and compassion about the *impacts* on individuals.'
>
> Port Phillip Council CEO, after paying a change-management consultant $600,000

> '. . . Is to *impact* business growth and development through *implementation* of learning and development solutions that identify Executive *Values*, *Align Values* to *Drive* Motivation and Change, and so provide all *stakeholders* in the Enterprise, a *transparent* competitive edge.'
>
> www.tmoa.com.au

> 'Many *HR processes* tend to treat all employees the same way, but in our observation, 22% of the people in a business *drive* 98% of the impact.'
>
> *Harvard Business Review*, July–August 2015

> 'But, there you go, that is the level of mentality which *drives* the drivel from the left.'
>
> 'Hairyback', Twitter

> 'Baby, you can *drive* my execution of product development.'
>
> Beatles

driver – key, core, critical, etc.

1. Someone or something that drives; or, as with a golf club, is used for driving.
2. The most important forces or factors for *change* or growth in a business, department, economy, school, hospital, football team, etc. Hence also *change drivers*. Talent, effort, *productivity improvements*, *enhanced skill sets*, teamwork, *international benchmarking*, loyalty and accounting processes that focus on *outcomes*, are all *key* (or *core*) *drivers* at various times. Blind faith, greed, jealousy, favouritism, luck, bribery, covetousness, sociopathy, fawning, social aspirations, the primitive urge to win at all costs and performance-based salary packages including allocations of shares are not called *key drivers*. Nor are sabotage, murder, etc.

> 'Commitment and discretionary effort as *key drivers* of *competitive advantage*.'
>
> Corporate document

> 'It is your own reflection affected by your own career *drivers* (i.e. what *drives* you to satisfaction).'
>
> Memo sent to participants in a development program

> 'This perception study, based on the internationally recognised RepTrak™ model tracks mass market and *Key* Opinion Leaders' views about Origin against seven *drivers* of reputation.'
>
> Letter to a *key* opinion leader from Origin Energy

> '*Key driver* is to have a physical and organisational infrastructure in place that can best support student *centric outcomes*.'
>
> Internal document, Weasel Words website

'Infirm of purpose! Give me the *drivers*!'

'May the *key drivers* be with you.'

dynamic

1. Pertaining to power; energy; force; change. Producing an effect.
2. Pertaining to pretty well anything.

'Demystifying the Informational Interview: How to Utilize this *Dynamic* Process to Advance your Job Search.'

Columbia University

'The *dynamic*, entrepreneurial and pioneering values which drive UL's mission and strategy ensures that we capitalise on local, national and international engagement and connectivity.'

Job advertisement, University of Limerick

'*Dynamic* Hair Salon, Limerick'

'The market is also supported [sic] a *dynamic* business community with a shared vision and willingness to collaborate through the Greville Village Market Working Group . . .'

'This is a great opportunity to hear from one of the most *dynamic* Ministers of the Abbott Government. Julie Bishop was sworn as Cabinet Minister for Foreign Affairs . . .

Alex Hawke MP, Mitchell Community Newsletter, May 2015

E

early onset nostalgia

An affliction, especially acute in *millennials*, identified by marketers. '"We call this '*early-onset nostalgia*,' where there is such an information overload that it has compressed their sense of time," said Deep Focus' Gutfreund' (Digiday).

Long before the *millennials* were born, Don Draper remarked on nostalgia's usefulness in *Mad Men:* 'Nostalgia is delicate but potent . . . It's a twinge in your heart more powerful than memory alone. It's not a spaceship, it's a time machine.'

> 'Appealing to nostalgia – that yearning for yesteryear – has emerged as a *strategic* and effective marketing technique in recent years, spilling into not only *brands*, but also entertainment, fashion, food and more. The Proustian madeleine of nostalgia marketing can take an array of forms and flavors: Last month, fast-food giant KFC brought back its brand mascot, antebellum oldster Colonel Sanders, just as McDonald's rebooted the Hamburglar as a hipster dad.'
>
> *Digiday*, June 2015

See *authenticity*, *millennials*.

economic refugees

Second order refugees arriving on leaky boats; ones without a legitimate claim on our sympathy or generosity; ones with enough money to pay for airline tickets to Indonesia and a 'people smuggler' for a berth on a boat; refugees who have made a *lifestyle decision* to leave Iraq, Iran, Afghanistan, Sri Lanka etc.; refugees who are not fit. Refugees for whom Australia has a 'very generous' migration program.

> 'Yeah, so just to clarify what I said. I said that in recent boat arrivals 100 per cent appeared to be *economic refugees* . . . if someone pays money in Iran to a people smuggler involving a flight to Malaysia and or Indonesia, and then the trip on the leaky boat, they're certainly not people down on their luck in a refugee camp . . .'
>
> Bob Carr, Foreign Minister, 2GB, 3 July 2013

> 'They're not people fleeing persecution. They're coming from majority religious or ethnic groups in the countries they're fleeing, they're coming here as *economic migrants*.'
>
> Bob Carr, Foreign Minister, *Lateline*, 26 June 2013

> 'The Immigration Department's most recent quarterly data combining those assessed by the department and those dealt with by the tribunal shows that 90.5 per cent of people who arrived by boat were found to be refugees in the first three months of 2013.'
>
> *ABC Fact Check*, 15 August 2013

economic upgrade

What resettlement of people arriving 'illegally' in Australia is not meant to be.

> 'CHRIS UHLMANN: Cambodia has a GDP of $15 billion a year. Fifteen million people live there. Don't you think that it will look somewhat odd that Australia is sending its problems there?
>
> SCOTT MORRISON: Well, a refugee resettlement is not an *economic upgrade* package: it's a safe haven package . . . refugee resettlement should not be just limited to first-world economies to provide *economic upgrades*.'
>
> ABC, 19 August 2014

efficiency

'Efficiency is why you'll hear managers saying "actioning" instead of "putting into action", "progressing" instead of "making progress", and "less" instead of "fewer". Less syllables = more efficient' (neurotaylor.com).

efficiency dividend

1. More for less
2. Budget cuts

> 'Well, they're not cuts . . . Well, the ABC has been exempted from *efficiency dividends* for the last 20 years, *efficiency dividends* which apply to every other department in government, every other agency of government that is funded by the taxpayer.'
>
> Mathias Cormann, *Age*, 19 November 2014

efforting

Striving, toiling, making an effort (to get) As, 'Group *efforting* signature to repeal transgender law', or just trying, as, 'We are *efforting* to get an interview with General Tommy Franks.' Popular with US television reporters or sports broadcasters.

> 'We are *efforting* her report.'
>
> Brian Williams, NBC

> '. . . can now report a CNN freelancer was abducted in Ukraine. Taken 2 days ago, still detained. We'd held reporting while *efforting* his release.'
>
> CNN reporter tweet

> 'If at first you don't succeed, *effort*, *effort* and *effort* again.'

elephant in the room

A dead elephant now.

elite

1. Small privileged group; socially superior, by virtue of birth, accomplishment or other means. Elevated in rank, status, power, wealth, celebrity, education, skill, etc. Pick of the crop, crème de la crème, the best, esp. in sport. As, 'The Toyota Extreme Superbull Bullriding Series will . . . continue the great tradition of *elite* Bullriding and rodeo events being showcased in Central Queensland' (*HatTown Herald*, July 2004). People at the pointy end.
2. A select interwoven group exercising great power in politics, society, commerce, the military, etc. Power *elites*. Artistic elites. Elite athletes, etc. As, 'The email demonstrates just how close Brooks and Rupert Murdoch were to Britain's *elite*, a relationship critics said allowed him to use his powerful stable of British newspapers to influence politicians for the benefit of his business interests' (ABC, 20 February 2014).
3. Powerful liberal-minded, *politically correct* people. Chattering classes. Liberal *elites*. Not battlers, bogans, yobbos, dinkum Aussies; effete, not fair dinkum. As, 'Much fuss and publicity in UK as horrible *elites* yak on about Page 3. Worry not, The Sun will always have great looking women – and men!' (Rupert Murdoch, Twitter, 25 January 2015)
4. Powerful people not aligned to or supported by Rupert Murdoch. As, '*Elites*' policies crushing poor, printing money etc, uneconomic climate investments, all causing higher costs, more inequality. Backlash near' (Rupert Murdoch, Twitter, 28 September 2014).

'Much of what passes for quality on British television is no more than a reflection of the narrow *elite* which controls it and has always thought that its tastes were synonymous with quality.'

Rupert Murdoch, 1990

'There is perhaps no more curious and blatant moment of newspeak than that which had Rupert Murdoch describing his media competitors as "*elites*".'

Helen Razer, July 2015

embrace

1. To hug, hold, cuddle, squeeze, clasp to one's breast, As in: '*Embrace* me, my sweet embraceable you / *Embrace* me, you irreplaceable you'. Live with, accept. As, 'Let me *embrace* thee, sour adversity.'
2. To include; take on, take up. As, 'The Vatican's dangerous *embrace* of climate-change theory' (Phil Lawlor, CatholicCulture.org, 29 April 2015).
3. A metaphysical, quasi-religious act of submission to abstract principles, mundane tasks, *core values*, diversity, *key behaviours*, *mission statements*, *consultants*, whatever you're told to do. *Embrace* change, technology, culture, etc. Related to *buy-in*, which is related to sheep, dolts, cannon fodder, etc.

'The Most Successful Companies *Embrace* the Promise of their *Culture*.'

Glenn Lopis, *Forbes*, 9 December 2011

'America Is Losing Religion: Why More and More Women Are *Embracing* Non-Belief.'

www.alternet.org, 14 May 2015

'Fostering and *facilitating innovation*, the intelligent use of knowledge and an internal enterprise *culture* which *embraces change* are critical *issues* for universities and their libraries.'

Paper, International Association of Technological University Libraries, Brisbane

'*Embrace* this remarkable opportunity to create your dream home on a premier 923sqm land parcel in an established location.'

Real estate advert

'Final embrace – mortuary cot covers'

emergency

1. crisis, freefall, out of control, etc.
2. not a crisis.
3. not an emergency.
4. challenging.
5. sunny

'I would just like to reflect on this issue of what Labor has sought to do, to deal, in a structural sense, with what is now clearly a Budget *emergency*' (Andrew Robb, Shadow Minister for Finance 2013) '. . . they're faced with an *emergency*' (Andrew Robb) '. . . it is out of control' (Andrew Robb).

'JOURNALIST: Mr Robb, you characterise this as a Budget *emergency*. Do you think the ratings agencies have got it wrong giving Australia a AAA credit rating?

ANDREW ROBB: No. We see this clearly as a breakdown of $3 billion a week. The ratings agencies will make their own assessment.'

'We are facing a budget *emergency* as a country, we are facing a very *challenging* fiscal situation but the government is dealing with it.'

Mathias Cormann, Minister for Finance, Sky News

'BARRIE CASSIDY: In what way is the Australian economy in *crisis*, what justifies the use of the term budget *emergency*?

JOE HOCKEY (Treasurer 2014): Well we didn't say the economy is in *crisis*, we said the budget is facing huge *challenges*. We used the term budget *emergency* because this Government keeps promising surpluses but it actually never delivers.'

ABC

'Let's fix our roof while the sun is shining because we're on a course to hit the rocks and we have to fix it.'

Amanda Vanstone, the Australian National Commission of Audit member

empathy (deep)

Understanding of others; to put oneself in another's shoes. Sublimated ego. 'I forget myself entirely because I live in her' (Keats). In psychology, history and social sciences, to know what it's like to be somebody else: poor, grieving, exhausted etc. Often used where 'sympathy' is called for. In 'design thinking' (think of Steve Jobs) to know what it's like to be a stakeholder, a customer, a potential (end) user.

'Start off with a *deep empathy* for something. You start off with a *deep empathy* for an end user and you try to solve their problem . . . "*Deep empathy*", "ideate a solution", "rapid

> prototyping": are these the words that will revolutionise entrepreneurship? You may doubt it, but stay with me.'
>
> *Australian Financial Review*, 9 April 2014

employee engagement

'Willingness to invest discretionary effort at work.' Engaged employees being more productive, *employee engagement* is holy grail to managers. As, 'Driving higher employee engagement' (email from Gail Kelly, Westpac CEO). Stakhanovite capitalism (after the venerated Stakhanov, the ultimate engaged employee who exceeded by 1400 per cent average per person mining productivity in the Soviet Union). As, 'Is there a company of any *significant* size that doesn't seek and venerate "*employee engagement*"'? (*Australian Financial Review*, 15 March 2015.)

Engagement by all sorts of means – from financial bonuses to meditation classes, and all sorts of incentives in between, including treating employees like human beings with human needs – if you're of the school that counts company productivity as an essential human need.

(See *sustainable engagement*, which is the kind that is less likely to work them to death or neurosis.)

> '*Employee engagement* will improve within the *strategic context* of assisting your managers to *lead* their people against the engagement *framework*.'
>
> Mission Statement, Human Resources team, private health insurer

C.f. people 'surpassing the existing designed capacities, surpassing the existing production plans and estimates . . . who have completely mastered the technique of their jobs, have harnessed it and driven ahead' (J. Stalin, 1936). C.f. 'Maria Demchenko, the well-known "five-hundreder" in sugar beet. She achieved a harvest of over 500 centners of sugar beet per hectare' (J. Stalin).

> 'Greetings are shouted to . . . the leader . . . from all parts of the hall. The three thousand members of the conference join in singing the proletarian hymn, the "Internationale".'

empower, empowered, empowering, empowerment

Key goal of all organisations. Employees are *empowered* when they *take ownership*, usually by becoming *competent*. Customers are *empowered* by *choice*, *shareholders* by profit, dividends etc. Thus is the *triple bottom line empowered*. We are all *empowered* by employment, education, a win at the races, a new set of spectacles or teeth, etc. Some are *empowered* by God; others are *disempowered* by Him. Faith *empowers*: the loss of it can *empower* equally. Ditto reason. Hitler and Stalin were both *empowered* by 'transforming unwanted beliefs into beliefs that *empowered* them'. An *est* word.

> 'I've actually worked with a lot of great male actors, like Tom Cruise for example. He is very *empowering* to females in a huge way.'
>
> Emily Blunt, May 2015

> 'To reach and influence the world by building a large Bible-based church, changing *mindsets* and *empowering* people to lead and *impact* in every sphere of life.'
>
> Hillsong Church Mission Statement

'I can't even begin to tell you how *empowered* I am now after our coaching. I'm spending two-thirds of my week *building relationships*.'

Professor Jeanette Ward, former area director, NSW Health

'*Empower* thy sheep.'

enabler

Whoever or whatever enables . . . better outcomes, innovation, transformation, the delivery of deliverables, etc. A deliverer.

'Development of *processes* for incident *management* should be matched with qualified people responsible for responding to crises, while technology is considered the major *enabler* for spanning *processes* over functional and organisational boundaries.'

Analysis of Command and Control Networks on Black Saturday, Dept. of Defence

'*Business enablers* are like internal entrepreneurs, they are hugely important to the effective functioning of the organisation, but more importantly they provide an *innovation* mindset. A true *business enabler* is someone who is able to identify, and instigate, opportunities for *key* business improvement.'

Simon Feary, a judge in the UK Business Enabler of the Year Awards

'The Queensland Government has undergone *significant transformation* and ICT is an effective *enabler* of continuing *change* and *innovation*, as well as *delivering* better services to Queenslanders.'

Ian Walker, Minister for Science etc., Queensland, 2014

> 'Thus saith the *Enabler* of Israel, I *enabled* you up from Egypt, and *enabled* you out of the house of bondage . . .'
>
> *Judges* 6:8

endeavour, endeavoured, endeavouring

Never say 'try'. As in: 'We shall *endeavour* to answer your call as soon as possible.' 'Just bear with me, and I'll *endeavour* to find out.' A kind of *efforting*.

> 'This Statement *aligns* to Council's *core values*, primarily through the *value* of "Openness and *Accountability*". In keeping with this value, Council will *endeavour* to behave with integrity, impartiality, *transparency* and fairness at all times.'
>
> Nambucca Shire Council

> 'By working over the period of a full day with a select group of the target audience . . . we are able to cut through to the essence of required organisational imperatives to take their talent management *endeavours* to new heights of effectiveness.'
>
> Stephenson Partnership Pty Ltd

> 'If at first you don't succeed, *endeavour*, *endeavour* and *endeavour* again.'

end of the day (at the)

1. Dusk, evening, nightfall.
2. When all's said and done; after all; in the end. The gist of it; what really matters; the nub of it. When you boil it down, separate the wheat from the chaff, the sheep from the goats, etc. The truth, however unpalatable. As, 'At *the end of the day* our little life is rounded with a sleep'.

'*Look, at the end of the day* I know that they had [weapons] programs, there's no doubt about that.'

Alexander Downer, ABC radio, January 2004

'Now *look, at the end of the day, look,* people can make up their own minds about this, but John Howard and I are as one in our *passionate* concern . . .'

Alexander Downer, 3AW, June 2004

'And look, *at the end of the day* . . .'

Alexander Downer, 2GB, March 2004

'I think, *at the end of the day* . . .'

Alexander Downer, *Australian*, June 2004

'But look, *at the end of the day* . . .'

Alexander Downer, *Sydney Morning Herald*, July 2004

'It was suggested as a very good idea at the time and, because it was an election *commitment*, we implemented it, but *at the end of the day*, the market is the test in these things and, you know, the market has not supported it in a way which is viable, *going forward*.'

John Brumby, Premier of Victoria

'I know that state governments are looking to try and find ways of separating out their psychiatric wards but, *at the end of the day*, that's not going to happen overnight . . .'

Mark Butler, Minister for Mental Health and Ageing, etc., ABC, 29 April 2013

end-to-end

A form of business *process* review that 'simplifies, standardises and consolidates a company's *processes* and practices'. Front to back? Back to front? *Back-ended going forwards*.

> 'The intent of the *End-to-End (E2E) framework* is to serve as the foundation for *business process reengineering* (BPR), which *drives* business improvement and encourages interoperability, *ensuring* defense business systems support and *enabling* cross functional Business Mission Area *processes*. This *framework* provides a common point of reference for E2E efforts throughout all levels of the DoD.'
>
> Dep. Chief Management Officer, US Department of Defense

> 'Let Amadeus lead you straight to a *seamless*, efficient, *end-to-end* travel *management process* that will help you controls costs and *empowers* travellers [sic].'
>
> Amadeus

> 'NAB has appointed Mr Weiser as a general manager in the HomeSide arm to drive "*end-to-end customer experience*" and improve the bank's relationships with mortgage brokers.'
>
> *Herald Sun*, 17 June 2010

> 'You took the part that once was my heart
> So why not take me end to end.'

end-to-end delivery

Delivered at both ends. From one end to the other. Here to there.

> 'Work in collaboration with Science Group Leaders, *Stakeholder Relationship Managers* and other Portfolio Leaders to develop and manage *strategic relationships* for a portfolio of *stakeholders*, working closely to identify their research requirements and ensure *end to end delivery*. To develop and deliver on the *end-to-end programme delivery* from initial *stakeholder* contact to final *delivery* on contract, ensuring *stakeholder* needs are met or exceeded within operating budgets.'
>
> Job advertisement, AgResearch NZ

end-user experience

The experience of a user at or in the end?

> 'To support the "*end-user experience*" by *continual improvement* in the Centre's policies, procedures and service *delivery* in response to the University's needs.'
>
> *Key Result* Area 4, *Strategic Plan* 2005–2008, Centre for *Flexible* Learning (*Building Partnerships* for Success), Macquarie University

> 'From an *end-user* perspective, initially, there should be little change in the service. Moving forward Facilities and Services will be developing a more user focussed and performance-driven cleaning regime across the campus.'
>
> Monash University's 'New Cleaning Structure'

> 'Waiter! There's a fly in my *end-user* experience!'

end user perspective

As seen by the last person to use it.

> 'Asthma and ageing: an *end user's perspective* – the perception and problems with the management of asthma in the elderly.'
>
> uow.edu.au

> 'Airwave Network suffers "intermittent" London area disruptions. "The decision to cut over was taken due to the unpredictable (from an *end user perspective*) nature of the incident," Airwave said.'
>
> blue-light.governmentcomputing.com

engage

To *engage* in *dialogue* (discuss); *engage* with ideas (think); *engage* the enemy (fight); *engage* with another country (trade); *engage* the reader, student, audience, client, etc.; *engage* people (interest, entertain, amuse, occupy, get involved, absorb, engross, divert, charm, persuade, enlist, employ, captivate, fascinate, intrigue, excite, involve, seduce, please, delight, satisfy, get onside, keep onside, *capture*, rope in, bring over, intimidate, con, fool, trick, win, flatter, deceive, bamboozle, fob, inveigle into, dupe, hoodwink, gull, beguile, bluff, play for a sucker, cozen, gouge, swindle, dazzle, mesmerise, sign up, get on board, get in the tent/bag, etc.; get onside, *buy-in*, make one of the *ducks in a row*, etc. Get singing to the same tune, attending workshops, speaking the same language, on the same page, etc.) *Engage* employees in these ways. *Engage* in these *behaviours*.

Gregg Lederman, *ENGAGED!: Outbehave Your Competition to Create Customers for Life*.

'[Our] approach to *change* management consultancy is underpinned by Appreciative Inquiry that is an inclusive method to *engage* people *impacted* by *change* (*stakeholders, clients* and staff) in the process of *strategic planning* so as to achieve socially *sustainable outcomes*.'

Consultancy document

'Also to Champion preventative maintenance and housekeeping, ensuring we set high standards consistent across all operations and that we *engage buy-in* from all staff . . . To strictly adhere to the Absolutes issued by the Operations Director . . .'

Continuous improvement/quality manager, Harrison Scott Europe Ltd

engagement leader

One charged with the great task of *employee engagement*.

'[The company's] project manager and *engagement leader* will work with the *project team* in the creation of a *development plan* to enumerate the set of tasks needed to develop the Member Directory and coordinate the creation of content from the member organizations.'

'A good *leader* values employee happiness. A great *leader* values the *employee engagement* that results from that happiness.'

www.entrepreneur.com

See *employee engagement*

engagement marketing

In which *customers* feel like they own the product before they buy it. Participatory purchasing, especially through customer reviews, referrals, etc. on social media (viz. Amazon, eBay).

> '*Engagement marketing* begins when an interested person takes an action to begin an interaction with you.'
>
> www.pmzmarketing.com.au, June 2014

enhance / enhanced / enhancement

To improve, increase, grow, streamline, beautify, strengthen, lengthen, tighten, loosen where necessary or desirable; make go faster; *implement* an *efficiency-gain*; brighten, whiten, lighten; make hairier, scarier, lairier, etc. Make more violent or serene. There is nothing that cannot be *enhanced. Enhance* your garden, your prospects, your penis, your retirement, breasts, *lifestyle*, chances, medical cover, relationships, froth with a 'froth enhancer' (Qantas Inflight advertisement), life itself. As, 'Our *vision* – *Enhancing* Life and Liveability.' 'Our Strategic Direction formalises our vision of "*enhancing* life and liveability" for our region. It establishes our commitment to achieve this by working with others to overcome the challenges we face' (Melbourne Water).

> 'To *enhance* the performance of the vertical transportation at 222, Exhibition St, we wish to advise that the lifts are going through a re-adjustment program. Please excuse any inconvenience that the process may contribute to the lift services during this period.'
>
> Otis

> 'AusAid explored design and *implement* models for project design to *enhance* recipient government involvement in project preparation. This model [sic] proved to be expensive and inefficient.'
>
> Company document

> 'Be *enhanced* and *enhance*, and *enhance* the earth, and *enhance* it.'
>
> *Genesis* 1.28

> 'Go ahead, *enhance* my day.'
>
> Clint Eastwood

enjoy

1. To be pleased, amused, gratified, made merry.
2. To not be pleased, etc. As in: 'We hope you've *enjoyed* receiving your Telstra bills via email. We'd like to continue sending your bill by email so from your next bill . . .' (Telstra email to customers).
3. A need. As in: '"Companies often forget that their customers have needs and they need to *enjoy* something," Mr. Manning said' (Luxury Daily).
4. A command or recommendation. As, Enjoy! 'Enjoy your day!'

entrepreneur

A business person of sainted ambition and, every now and then, achievement. *Innovative* and energetic. One who invents the future. People who do start-ups. As, 'Master of Applied *Innovation* and *Entrepreneurship*' (University of Adelaide).

> 'Learn how great *entrepreneurs* and *innovators achieve* uncharted success.'
>
> University of Adelaide

'If suddenly all these people are yakking about their feels on the meeja rather than leaning over the back fence and having a natter while Bex dissolves their kidneys, it's because selfhood itself has been transformed by the *entrepreneurial model*.'

Guy Rundle, *Crikey*, 18 August 2015

'The trouble with the French is they don't have a word for *entrepreneur*.'

George W. Bush (attrib.)

envelope (push)

Tom Wolfe borrowed the term from test pilots whose 'flight envelopes' defined the limits of the new planes they flew. To 'push the outside of the envelope' was to see how far the limits could be extended (Wolfe, *The Right Stuff*). In business it is used to describe the same sort of daredevil thinking and behaviour.

'And God saw the light, that it was good: and God *pushed the envelope* . . .'

envision / envisioning / re-envisioning

1. To imagine, picture, conceive, conjure, dream up, think up, visualise, fancy, see in the mind's eye.
2. *Envision* structurally: to see beneath the surface in your *vision*.
3. Future *envisioning*: to have a *vision going forwards*.
4. *Re-envisioning*: when it is no longer a clear or agreed *vision*; when *focus* has been lost and must be regained, etc.
5. *Envisioning* process: the way it is done.

> 'Coming together to *re-envision* the Ph.D. to meet the societal needs of the 21st Century.'
>
> University of Washington, Graduate School

> 'VisionLink is a consulting firm located in Irvine, CA dedicated to helping companies *envision*, create and sustain compensation *strategies* that will be *key drivers* of results and increase the *productivity* of employees.'
>
> The VisionLink Advisory Group

> '*Envision* there's no heaven,
> it's easy if you try . . .
> *Envision* all the people . . .'
>
> John Lennon

envisioned future

Scenario, but sounds grander; and *much* grander than a guess.

> 'A well-conceived *vision* consists of two major components – *CORE IDEOLOGY* and an *ENVISIONED FUTURE*. Notice the direct parallel to the fundamental "preserve the *core*/stimulate *progress*" *dynamic*. A good *vision* builds on the interplay between these two complementary Yin-and-Yang forces; it defines "what we stand for and why we exist" that does not change (the *core ideology*) and sets forth "what we aspire to become, to *achieve*, to create" that will require *significant change* and progress to attain (the *envisioned future*).'
>
> Jim Collins

escalate

1. Ascend, for instance by an escalator.
2. To take to a new, higher level, esp. to *escalate* a conflict. Increase in intensity, extent or severity. As, 'In a *passionate* speech which could *escalate* conflict between the ABC and the Abbott government, Mr Scott responded by saying the ABC's independence from government must be jealously guarded' (*Age*, 26 June 2015).
3. Something to be done with concerns. As, 'How to raise and *escalate* a concern.' Put in a higher pigeon hole. Bring up in a meeting. Suggest *actioning*.

> 'This flow chart covers the process for both raising and *escalating* concerns within your workplace, and the process for formal whistleblowing. This flow chart should be read alongside the whole advice on raising concerns and whistleblowing.'
>
> www.hpc-uk.org

> 'The Senior Ministerial Writer/Editor is responsible for the provision of an accurate and timely correspondence and *customer feedback escalation* service at a senior level.'
>
> Seek.com

> 'Kalminios and Shea were sacked in 2010 for failing to *escalate* concerns about what would happen after the payroll system went live.'
>
> www.itnews.com.au

ethic / ethical

1. Relating to moral action, motive or character. Treating of moral codes and behaviour. Guiding principles. As, 'work *ethic*', 'Protestant *ethic*'.

2. Boilerplate for *mission* and *vision* and *value* statements. As, Enron's Code of *Ethics* 2000 – 'dedicated to conducting business according to . . . the highest professional and *ethical* standards.' (Ken Lay, Enron's Code of *Ethics*. NB. Lay died before sentencing in 2006. He had been found guilty on 10 counts of corruption.)

> 'We don't expect him to win the game off his own boot but we know he is going to give strong *ethic*. He will stand up based on the *values* we stand for.'
>
> Carlton AFL coach referring to a ruckman

evaluate

Appraise, measure value or amount, assess, weigh, calculate, add up, judge, value, review, examine, take stock, express numerically. C.f. Descartes: '. . . make everywhere enumerations so complete and reviews so general as to be sure of leaving nothing out' (*Discourse on Method*).

> 'The reasoning for this reflective summary is for you to *evaluate* your *alignment* with job enrichment (*achieving* high satisfaction in your place of work).'
>
> Memo sent to participants in a development program

> 'Is it possible to *evaluate dynamic*, complex, unpredictable, multifaceted, emergent *processes* where there is a shift from highly structured and linear professional learning and *development* to *embedding enablers* that support confident, capable, connected, curious and *committed* learners?'
>
> NSW Department of Education and Training

event

What happened. Happening. As, weather *event*, severe weather *event*, rain *event*, environmental *event*; hiring *event* ('*Strategies* for responding to hiring *events*'), literary *event*, publishing *event*, debris *event*, etc. Taxable *event* – *event* with a tax consequence. Macrosuede Sofa *Event* – furniture sale *event*. When thirteen Chinese inmates at Villawood detention centre slashed their wrists in June 2005, it was called 'an organised self-harm *event*'.

> 'Because if there is one thing that could damage the rich and strong social fabric of our country, it would be a mass casualty *event*.'
>
> Tony Abbott, PM, 18 August 2014

> '*Pandemic* . . . a hard-hitting docudrama on the nightmare scenario of a bird flu mass-dying *event*.'
>
> Fairfax TV guide

> 'In fact we had four *events* of thunderstorms compared to our normal one *event* in January.'
>
> Adelaide Weather Bureau spokesman, ABC, February 2005

> 'Earlier this month, Hastie's shares were suspended due to a "review *event*" prompted by the company's banking syndicate. The review *event* was set aside.'
>
> *Smart Company*, 28 May 2012

> 'The 6th of March 2010 will probably go down in Melbourne's weather history as a day in which a significant severe *thunderstorm event* affected the metropolitan area.'
>
> Melbourne Bureau of Meteorology

event (adverse medicine)

'In 70 per cent of adverse *events* [usually harmful and preventable errors], communication was a *key issue* in that *event* occurring.'

Australian Commission on Safety and Quality in Health, *Age*, 1 February 2013

'. . . an absurd amount of bulkhead door *events* . . .'

Overworked UPS driver

'And God said, let there be a light *event*; and there was a light *event*.'

'Singing in the rain *event*', etc.

event (adverse medicine)

Golden staph, amputation of a good limb, clinical error causing death, etc.

'Reducing the incidence of *adverse medicine events* (AMEs) has been difficult as there was no official channel for Australian *consumers* to document such *events*.'

Australian Commission on Safety and Quality in Health Care

event (birth)

Birth.

'Midwives must notify the Department of Health of the outcomes of all birth *events* (cases) attended, regardless of the *outcome* . . .'

WA Department of Health

event (death)

Death and other adverse outcomes.

> 'An adverse *event* is any undesirable experience associated with the use of a medical product in a patient. The *event* is serious and should be reported to FDA when the patient outcome is:
>
> Death
> Report if you suspect that the death was an *outcome* of the adverse *event*, and include the date if known . . .
>
> Life-threatening
> Report if suspected that the patient was at substantial risk of dying at the time of the adverse *event*.' (etc.)
>
> US FDA

> 'Cowards die many times before their death *events* . . .'
>
> *Julius Caesar*

event (plowable)

> '"It looks like it could be a plowable *event*," he said.'
>
> Snow report, bangordailynews.com

event (wind)

Wind.

> 'State Emergency Service crews are mopping up this morning after icy winds blasted the state overnight, with gusts of 135km/h tearing through the alpine region in what meteorologists have called the *wind event* of the year.'
>
> *Age*, 21 June 2011

'Blow, *wind events*, and crack your cheeks.'

King Lear

event – potentially avoidable

Events that might have been avoided, measures of which are a subset of *outcome* measures.

'*Potentially avoidable event* measures are a subset of *outcome* measures used in the HH QRP. *Potentially avoidable events* serve as markers for potential problems in care because of their negative nature and relatively low frequency. The *potentially avoidable events* reported are *outcome* measures, in the sense that they represent a change in health status between start or resumption of care and discharge or transfer to inpatient facility.'

CMS.gov

eventising

Making *events*?

'Fox's emphasis next season is on "eventizing", entertainment chief Kevin Reilly said at the network's upfront presentation to advertisers Monday.'

evolve

1. Develop or unfold through evolution. As in, The Origin of Species.
2. Change of direction occasioned by political expediency or influence. As, 'The Andrews Labor Government's commitment to Catholic and Independent schools has

evolved . . .' (into permanent lavish support). (Victorian Minister for Education spokesman, 3 May 2015.)
3. Develop through retrograde evolution. As in, sea squirt (Ascidacea) and above.

excellence

1. Possessed of superior qualities. Whatever excels in kind or degree – though inferior to 'awesome'. As, 'How's your day been so far?' 'Excellent.' 'Sorry to hear it.' Popular aspiration in *mission statements* and mottos (where 'awesome' is strangely absent). Tends to be concentrated in Centres. Often conjoined with arts (as opposed to dairying or panel beating, for instance); as, Abbott government's 'National Program for *Excellence* in the Arts.'
2. What we are all *committed* to *achieving*. Goes with innovation. As, 'Collaborating for research *excellence*. Improving Australia's mining industry, accelerating canola breeding and reforming healthcare are just some of the research *outcomes* identified through 251 new collaborative research projects that will inspire *innovation*' (C. Pyne, Minister for Education, Press Release).

> 'Incorporate a *quality improvement culture* within the *framework* for Pillars of *Excellence* and ACHSE expectations.'
>
> Work appraisal form for a nurse

> 'The course is open to any manager at any level in any function who leads *teams*, who wishes to learn more about team behaviour and is looking for an approach to this difficult but *challenging* art of *Team* Behaviour Management in the pursuit of relentless *excellence*.'
>
> www.coolavenues.com.au

> 'The *energy* and enthusiasm that our employees bring to the workplace creates an *exciting* place to work with a constant striving for *excellence*.'
>
> Titan Corporation: Abu Ghraib and Guantanamo Bay interrogation contractors

exciting

Causing excitement. Stimulating, stirring, inspiring, exhilarating, titillating, thrilling, etc. As in: '*exciting* new knitting patterns'; '*exciting* investment opportunity'; 'Victorian classic in *exciting* location'. Whatever is new is also *exciting* – *exciting* new era; *exciting* new offer; *exciting* new discovery; *exciting* new business opportunity, new development, new housing development, new retail development; *exciting* new *lifestyle*; new photos; new recipes; new competitions; *exciting* future, *exciting* past; *exciting* gardens; *exciting* possibility; 'a more *exciting* animated you', etc.

> 'Here is a taste of some of the *exciting* events we have planned for the first few months of this year . . . Exemptions and Preferred Service Provided *Processes*, Master Agreements . . . Conducting Tender *Evaluations* . . . Tendering for *Outcomes Workshop*.'
>
> FaCS Bulletin, 2014

> 'Please enter our website and choose from the *exciting* New Zealand bed & breakfast properties available throughout New Zealand.'
>
> Selections NZ

> 'Since the *focus* of the Australian Flexible Learning *Framework* for this year is *embedding* e-learning and *engaging clients*, here's

an *exciting* opportunity to re-energise the *change process* by *focusing* on what is working well and then amplifying it.'

Staff Training & Development Officer at a NSW TAFE

'Exciting was it in that dawn to be alive,
But to be young was very exciting'

Wordsworth

execute

To carry out, put into effect (e.g. execute a will); make valid (e.g. a deed) by signing; to put to death; in computers – to run a program (EXE). To put a vision into effect. As, '*execute* on the *vision*'. To execute against something – or something. As, 'Q: What advantage does the Project team see in rushing ahead with this change? A: . . . The board sees enormous *growth* opportunities on which Yahoo! can capitalize, and our primary objective is to *leverage* the Company's *leadership* and current business *assets* and *platforms* to *execute* against these opportunities' (Roy Bostock, chairman Yahoo, *Telegraph*, 7 September 2011).

'Everyone *impacted* by this reduction deserves our thanks and respect for their contributions to the company . . . This *realignment* will allow us to increase investment in high-growth areas of the company . . . [We] look forward to a bright future as a company if we can *execute on this vision*.'

AOL email to staff

'Welcome to Sense. We are a confident, creative agency, where *strategic planning* and meticulous evaluation lead to faultlessly *executed brand* experiences.'

Sense London

exit

1. To leave, depart, egress, flit. As, 'Now the government is facing a new controversy about a eurozone *exit plan*, creating uncertainty for this uneasy alliance' (*New York Times*, 27 July 2015).
2. To sell off assets; cash out an investment; get out from under. To in secret sell off worthless bonds that you have been selling to investors as triple A rated; *do a runner*; commit fraud. Also known as 'harvest strategy' or 'liquidity event'.
3. To do the same from a war. Cut and run.

> 'For investment banks such as Goldman [Sachs], the trick was knowing when to *exit* the high-stakes subprime game before getting burned.'
>
> McClatchy DC, 1 November 2009

> 'There is no certainty of *outcomes*, but if one follows criteria that have a statistically defined probability of occurring, then when those criteria mesh to create an alert they learn to trust the alert knowing that if they are right, they will enjoy the benefits and if they are wrong they will cut their losses when their *exit* criteria is alerted.'
>
> Sharesender, an investment company's media release

> 'Love me, or *exit* me.'

exiting employee

An employee who is leaving. A fleeing employee. A *migrating* employee. One who can bear it no longer. One who has been driven out by boredom, poor wages, oppressive or incompetent managers, insufferable jargon or a new vocational calling such as politics or religion. One attracted to viticulture or free range poultry. One who is entering the *churn* or becoming *vanilla*. One who has been headhunted. One who has been encouraged to go, or given no choice. An employee with a bad *attitude* or an inappropriate *mindset*: one for whom the company *culture* is not a good fit. An employee who was not prepared to do the company thing, who did not *grow* with the company, who did not *embrace* its *core values*, did not *sign off* on them or did not *buy-in*. One who did not sign the *Personal Business Commitment* (*PBC*). One who cannot stand the *mission statement* any longer. One who has been asked to write a new *mission statement*. One who has decided to get a life. A redundant employee. A *downsized* or *re-engineered in terms of business process* person. Etc.

> 'It is company policy to conduct an *Exit* Interview with all staff *exiting* [the company]. The purpose of the *Exit* Interview is to provide the *exiting employee* with an opportunity to pass on suggestions for improvement in company policies and practices, those of their department and managerial practices, to enable the company to consider and *implement* improvements.'

> '*Exit* thee to a nunnery!'

exit strategy

1. Plan for leaving. To cut your losses. Fly the coop. Get out while you still can. Midnight flit. Leave town. Leave by the fire escape. Discretion the better part of valour, etc.
2. *Cut and run*. Leave in the lurch.

'General John R. Allen . . . told the Foreign Affairs Committee that "there's no exit strategy" for dealing with ISIS . . .'

Business Insider, 27 March 2015

'Love me, or *implement* an *exit strategy*.'

expand

To enlarge, stretch, etc., especially footprints. Can be substituted for both *enhance* and *grow*. As in: 'In line with our *enhanced operational footprint* we are *committed* to *expand* pickling operations by 15 per cent.' Or: 'We are *committed* to *expanding* our operational *footprint* in line with a forecast 15 per cent *growth outcome* in our pickling operations,' etc. *Expand* is preferred to *increase*.

'When it comes to survival in a down economy, the answer is always the same: "*Expand* the Footprint."'

'Dr Switkowski also hopes to *expand* Telstra's *footprint* in Asia over the next four years . . .'

Age, January 2004

'Delegates will be engaged in small group *workshops* to consider how each *tool* will support and potentially *expand* their capacity to develop an integrated approach.'

NSW Department of Environment and Climate Change

expensed

Means by which costs of travel can be *evaluated*.

> 'Your journey to and from work is not *expensed*.'
>
> Private email

> 'The $1000 in charges by Mrs Bishop that Saturday were *expensed* in two amounts, both classified as "taxi".'
>
> reddit.com, 21 July 2015

experience

1. What happens to one in life.
2. What happens to one when shopping.

> 'As soon as the customer is identified, sales associates should be supported with real-time *customer* information and analytics that enable them to tailor the *experience* to each *customer*'s personal preferences, recent purchases and online browsing history.'
>
> *Luxury Daily*

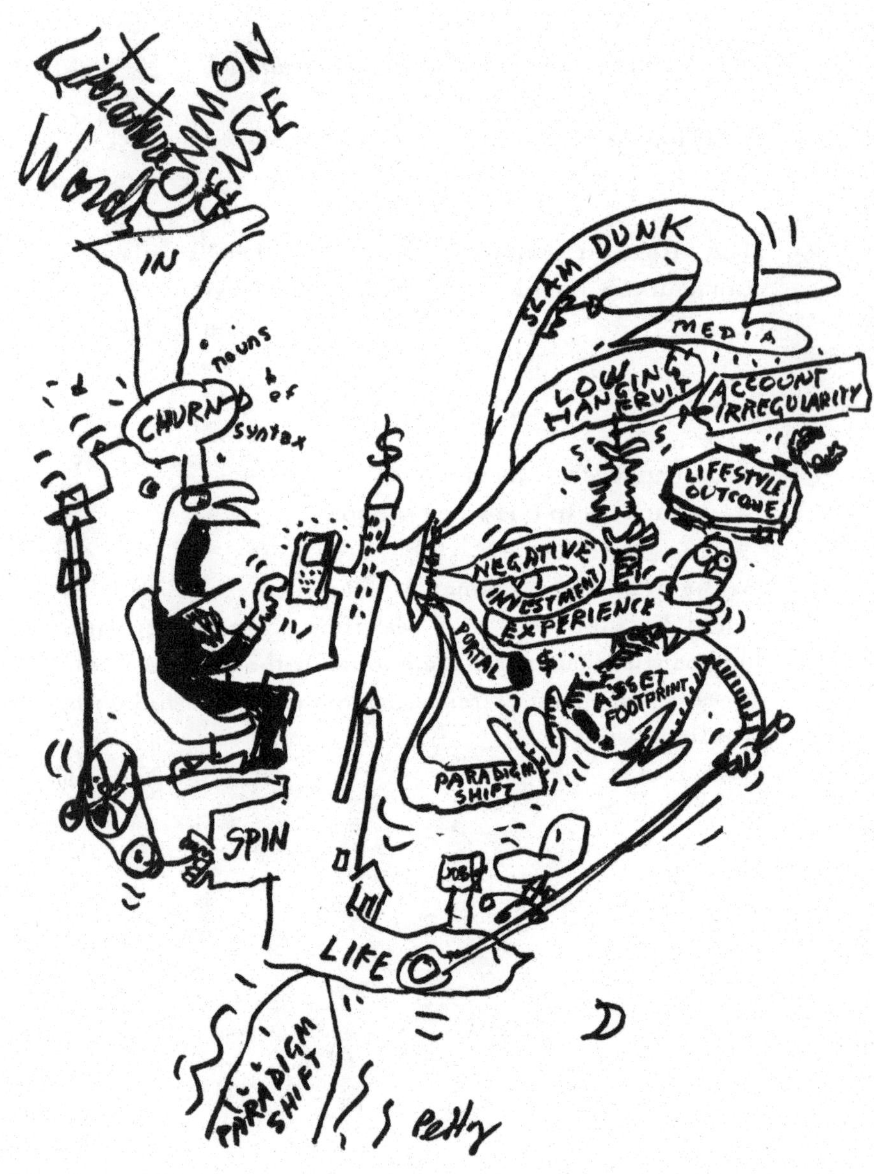

IN
nouns
of
syntax
CHURN
SLAM DUNK
MEDIA
LOW HANGING FRUIT
ACCOUNT IRREGULARITY
LIFESTYLE OUTCOME
NEGATIVE INVESTMENT EXPERIENCE
PORTAL
ASSET FOOTPRINT
PARADIGM SHIFT
SPIN
LIFE
PARADIGM SHIFT
Petty

F

face time

Time spent with others. Not alone. A creative breakthrough.

> 'Sir David Higgins, chairman of project promoter HS2 Ltd, said the rapid rail link from London to the North would allow more people to get together to spark profitable ideas . . . He said that quicker journeys between major cities would ramp up the amount of business that could be done in the UK. "In a knowledge economy, what matters is *face time*," he said.'
>
> *New Civil Engineer*, UK, June 2015

> 'No one has had more *face time* in Iowa than Rick Perry.'
>
> *USA Today*, May 2015

> 'Here's *face time* with you, kid.'
>
> *Casablanca*

facilitate / facilitator

(v) To make possible, easy or convenient; make happen; help, assist, lend a hand, grease the wheels; organise, marshall, direct, encourage, conduct, etc.
(n) Master of ceremonies, *catalyst*, group leader, discussion leader, teacher, *team* builder, *consensus* builder, problem solver, supervisor, adviser, instructor, guide, trainer, salesperson, motivator, coach, *refocuser*, *empowering* agent, mediator, guru, poobah, Rasputin, Svengali, *change manager*, *process re-engineer*, *process* improver, spruiker, carpetbagger, evangelist ('Veriditas Labyrinth *Facilitator* Training: *facilitating* the labyrinth is a spiritual path'); undercover agent, diplomat, linkman, go between, Machiavel, *consultant*, etc.

'*Facilitate* the creation of mission, vision and value statements.'

'High Country Collective will *facilitate* the delivery of *world class* Interpretation, Identity and Wayfinding *enabling proactive* interaction with users and potential users of the trail and its interconnection . . .'

Mansfield Shire, Victoria

'Dale is a *facilitator* of energetic exchanges in self-acceptance, belief identification, meditation, dreams / dream interpretation, trans-focal exchanges . . .'

intuitivefacilitating.com

'May God facilitate.'

From the conversation between Osama bin Laden's courier, Abu Ahmed al-Kuwaiti, and a friend, overheard by US intelligence

'When other *facilitators* fail,
and comforts flee,
facilitate of the facilitatorless,
O abide with me.'

fair go

Mythical. (Aust.) C.f. bunyip.

family values / family

Universal political mantra. Hitler recommended *family values* to the German people. *Family values* are 'simple' and 'enduring' values, such as love, togetherness, harmony, security, etc. Families provide 'secure nurturing environments'. Family *trusts* are for nurturing family assets.

George W. Bush comes from the Bush *family* which nurtured him into great wealth and the US Presidency after he gave up drinking. The Bin Laden *family* nurtured Osama. Other *families* include the Suharto *family*, the Holy Family, the Typical *family* and the Corleone *family*.

> '. . . the simple, enduring *values* – love, *family* togetherness, sharing and *mateship*.'
>
> John Howard PM, Christmas Message

> 'Kevin Andrews named "Natural Family Man of the Year" by Christian group
>
> The organisation says it aims to "affirm, defend and promote the natural *family* as the lifelong union of man and woman through marriage, bound by faith and tradition, for the purposes of sharing love and joy [and] having children".'

> 'I suppose three important things certainly come to my mind that we want to say thank you. The first would be our *family*. Your *family*, my *family* – which is composed of an immediate *family* of a wife and three children, a larger *family* with grandparents and aunts and uncles. We all have our *family*, whichever that may be . . . The very beginnings of civilisation, the very beginnings of this country, goes back to the *family*.'
>
> US Vice President Dan Quayle

fast track

Short cut to *achievement* of *agreed outcomes*.

feedback

Response; calls, cards and letters. Talk, abuse, boos, barracking, cat-calls, back-turning, pants-dropping, walkouts. Praise, tributes, congratulations, acclaim, commendations, applause. Information, criticism, analysis. *Feedback* is always welcome, wanted, useful – especially constructive or positive *feedback*. As, 'We welcome your *feedback*.'

Feedback tends to form loops. As, 'The purpose is to equip us better to *achieve* the "ambition inspired by *achievement*" which underpins our new *strategic plan* . . . It is now imperative that we define the *pathways*, the priorities and the *performance indicators* that will make a reality . . . This position is intended to optimise the *feedback loop* in which energy and *initiative* at the "*cutting edge*" is encouraged and also shapes and is influenced by *corporate strategies*' (University of Sydney).

> 'Many unexpected difficulties have been uncovered and corrected at this stage because of the *knowledge assets* of *stake-holders* . . . Once the *dialogue* has taken place and *feedback* has been considered, any adaptations to the design should be made. *Feedback* should be provided to *stakeholders* on the *dialogue process*, particularly about what has been incorporated and what has not. An outline of the rationale behind what *feedback* was not included in the approach is particularly useful to ensure a totally *transparent process*.'
>
> publicsector.wa.gov.au

> 'Ms. Chipman, I have *escalated* your concerns to the relevant department for a *feedback*. Please be assured that you will be contacted at the soonest possible time when a *feedback* is received.'
>
> Nokia

'Student priorities are *issues* arising from the contributing *feedback processes* and are generally underlying causal *issues* being different from specific *issues* identified and *addressed* within the contributing *feedback process*.'

University Student Priorities Policy and Process, Edith Cowan University

'I called upon the LORD in distress: the LORD gave me *feedback*, and set me in a large place.'

Psalm 18

flexible / flexibility

1. Supple, malleable, bendy, tractable, plastic, pliable, amenable; plenty of whip in it; movable, adjustable, adaptable, *agile*, embraceable, changeable; whatever you want to make it, bob each way; open to interpretation, ad hoc; not *set in concrete*; offering *customer choice*. What every company must *enhance*. *Flexible* working hours, employment practices, goals, *product* offerings, etc. Labour market *flexibility*.
2. No job security. Organisations must *achieve flexibility* without losing *focus* or *commitment*. They do this through *focusing* on a *commitment* to *flexibility*.

'With the collective decision to put the integration efforts on hold today we aim to contribute to Air India's flexibility to concentrate on its ongoing strategic orientation.'

Sydney Morning Herald, 7 August 2011

'Passion for entertainment *products* and a *flexible work ethic* is required.'

Advertisement for National Promotions Manager

'You'll experience a culture of flexibility, opportunity, equality and diversity.'

McDonald's Ireland

focus

(v) To concentrate on. Not to be distracted. Purposefully attend to in the appropriate way: e.g. *focus* on the soufflé: cooking it; *focus* on the garden: weeding, fertilising, cultivating; *focus* on the children: feeding, comforting, educating, clothing, reading to, etc. In business the *focus* is on *goals*, *core issues*, *key objectives*, *main game*, etc.
(n) That on which one *focuses* ('maintaining a strong *focus* on *core* business is the *key* to success' . . . etc.).
(adj) *Focused* – single-minded, resisting all distraction, switched-on, fired-up, pumped, come to play, etc. ('I was really *focused* today' – swimming, netball, high jumping, etc.)

'An *output* management *focus* by departments.'

Victorian Department of Treasury and Finance

'NEIL MITCHELL: The Government is not in strife? What?

TREASURER: You can make whatever comments you want, mate, I'm *focused* on my country. I am more positive about Australia than I have ever been.'

3AW, January 2015

'This presentation *focuses* on the communicative framing of intractable environmental conflicts. It reviews the different approaches to framing and focuses on framing as a communicative process in which the disputants reveal their sense-making about five aspects of conflicts.'

A Professor of Communication speaking at a Griffith University seminar

'We must *focus* on our garden.'

Voltaire

'*Focus* on the lilies, how they grow.'

for your convenience

It's very good of us when you think about it. We didn't have to put a toilet in the bus. We didn't even have to run the bus. '. . . *for your convenience*, the Westpac Bank and ATM are located next to Cafe Spice.' We did it for you and you alone, and it was for you that we have closed half our branches.

foreseeable future

Depends who is looking, where they are standing at the time and how far they wish to see. As, 'Treasurer Joe Hockey has announced an extension to the government's tax white paper consultation, while pledging not to make any major changes to super in the *foreseeable future*.'

forward leaning

Leaning forward – to look at something more closely perhaps? The future?

'. . . we have reorganized the *team* and work that we do around three *focus* areas – donor diversification, country-*customer*, and *excellence* – so that the division can be *forward leaning* and responsive to Pact's *communications* and business *development* needs throughout the business life cycle.'

PACT

forward-looking

Looking forward. *Focused* on the future, *focused* going forwards. Distinguishes an individual or organisation from backward-looking rivals.

> 'Statements contained in this news release that are not historical facts are *forward-looking* statements within the meaning of Section 27A of the Securities Act of 1933 and Section 21E of the Securities Exchange Act of 1934. Examples of such forward-looking statements include, but are not limited to, the statements by Gene Ray [CEO]. These statements are subject to risks and uncertainties that could cause actual results to differ materially from those set forth in or implied by *forward-looking* statements.'
>
> Titan Corporation, statement by CEO, 7 May 2004

framework

1. A skeletal structure to support the likes of a ship or a house. A system or form to support an organisation, a plan, an idea, behaviour, etc. As, Learning *Framework*, Performance *Framework*, Foreign Investment *Framework*.
2. A word that should appear at least once in every paragraph, every sentence if possible. As, 'workshops developed for managers and supervisors to practically apply RMIT Human Resources Consultancy's Behavioural Capability *Framework* into performance conversations.'

> 'Narendra Modi and Tony Abbott quietly signed a sensitive and potentially transformative new *framework* agreement.'
>
> *Sydney Morning Herald*, 18 November 2014

'The Reform Council has established an *Outcomes* Working Group to support opportunities for the co-design and trial of an agreed *outcomes framework*. Initially, this work will focus on identifying existing *frameworks* that we might draw on to form a view about the high level *outcome* domains. Further work will then *focus* on the design or integration of indicators and measures, and on *issues* relating to the *implementation* of the agreed *framework*.'

www.dhs.vic.gov.au

'Human-oriented workflow is the next frontier for *portal* frameworks. The year 2004 will be "the *year of* the *process portal*" for *portal* frameworks, whereas 2001 was the year of the content *portal*, 2002 application access, and 2003 collaboration – with each year adding to the *capabilities* of those before it. This pattern of feature creep will end with composite applications in 2007, after which *portal* and composite application *frameworks* will merge and become indistinguishable.'

International Association for Human Resource
Information Management

fulcrum of a strategic plan

A changing, unstable, irregular, arrhythmic thing.

'The reality is that the *fulcrum* of any *strategic plan*, not just this one, constantly changes. If you're aiming to achieve rhythmic harmony with the *strategic plan* as a *fulcrum* for the future, you may simply be setting yourself up to fail.

The unsavoury reality is that the *fulcrum* for this *strategic plan*, and many others, never really stabilise, entering an arrhythmic harmony; a harmony, with an irregular beat that is governed by the tides of the environment in which we work. Not quite right, but close enough, to work with the constantly moving tides.'

Reply to a blog which outlined the '*Strategic Plan – Mission, Vision and Culture*' on the Department of Agriculture, Fisheries and Forestry site

full plate review

The kind of review that supports a focus.

'. . . 6 . The *Leadership Team* has done a "*Full Plate Review*" to support a greater *focus* on truly critical activities at enterprise level, and reprioritise activities that aren't as important.'

fully job network eligible job seekers

Unemployed persons.

'This table refers only to *Fully Job Network Eligible Job Seekers* aged between 18–49 years in receipt of Youth or Newstart Allowance.'

Department of Employment and Workplace Relations

'A *fully job network eligible job seeker*, at last!'

Joseph Furphy, *Such Is Life*

functionality

Able to serve the purpose for which it was designed, e.g. lawnmower, pliers, staff members. As, e.g., 'The Speaker of the House has done an awesome job *in terms of* her *functionality*.'

'Over 2000 users from "early adopter" areas have already been *migrated*, with many expressing high levels of satisfaction with their newly gained *functionality*.'

Melbourne University Staff News

'Hence a key threshold activity of the project was to determine what *functionality* suite would be appropriate to the needs of Victoria and could also be financially justified.'

Impaq Consulting in Metering International

funnel (sales)

1. vessel, flue, chimney for the passage of liquids, smoke, vapour, etc.
2. 'the visual representation of the *customer life-cycle* . . .'

'In order to structure the right call-to-action, you need to understand the next logical step along the sales *funnel* for your attendees.'

Blog, 'How to Create a Compelling Webinar Call-to-Action that Converts'

future directions

Common name for conference, seminar, retreat, *brainstorming*, networking session, PowerPoint presentation, etc. Strategic planning. As, 'Property Council: Future Directions. One on One with Mr Clive Palmer.' 'Fair Work Commission: Future Directions: Continuing the Change Program.'

An opportunity to be *forward-looking*, or even *forward leaning*; to reflect on where we've been and where we're going, where we are *at this point in time*, *time period*, *journey*, etc., and where we want to be at a future *point in time*, *time period*, etc. The directions we should take *going forward*, etc.

futuring

1. Envisioning, imagining, predicting the future – in a systematic way, using tools. As, 'Offers examples of companies that used futuring and *visioning tools* to prepare *product scenarios* that anticipated the future, unarticulated voice of the customer' (Emerald Insight).
2. A type of action. As, 'This hothouse will ask how do we create a rhetoric of sustainment and specifically, how do we present new ways of thinking informing design as *futuring action*' (Queensland College of Art).

> 'CAESAR: The ides of March are come.
> FUTURER: Ay, Caesar, but not gone.'

game changer

A *catalyst* that will *transform* a frog into a prince or vice-versa. Example: 'Getting indicted for fraud was a *game changer* for Bernie Madoff.'

> 'The contribution of Australia, while always welcome, isn't a *game changer* one way or the other.'
>
> Defence Force Chief of Joint Operations, ABC, 21 August 2015

game plan

Plan. Essential in games, business, war, politics, love and other branches of human life. What one must stick to if one is to succeed. From American football, now also Australian football. (Likewise flooding, zoning off, zone defence, etc.)

> 'Well, I think when it comes to nasty surprises he made really clear last night his *game plan* is all about nasty surprises.'
>
> Senator Penny Wong, ABC, 17 May 2015

> 'The fusillade came as there are tentative signs that Tony Abbott's *game plan* for survival might just be working.'
>
> Paul Bongiorno, *Saturday Paper*, 18 April 2015

> 'Don't be a loser – stick to God's *game plan*.'
>
> Sign, Catholic Church, Terang, Victoria

> '. . . to love, cherish and to stick to the *game plan*, till death us do part.'

gifting

1. Giving with a view to profiting, marketing or reducing tax.
2. A kind of pyramid scheme. (Note: *Re-gifting* is the practice of giving to others unwanted gifts one has received.)
3. Giving, alternative to.

> 'It is better to *gift* than to receive.'

> '*Gift* it to me, baby.'

give birth and move on

> 'Taking at times a "*give birth and move on*" approach to projects and underestimating the need for additional handover and benefits tracking activities . . .'
>
> ABC new Information Communication and Technology (ICT) Strategy

globalisation

1. International economic integration through liberalised trade and technology that allows rapid flow of information and goods.
2. An unstoppable force already of inestimable benefit to billions of people and with the potential to enrich everyone.
3. '. . . the imposition on the entire world of the neo-liberal tyranny of the market and undisputed rule of the economy and of economic powers, within which the United States occupies a dominant position' (Pierre Bourdieu).
4. An ideal of shared wealth, limitless *innovation*, world government and no more war.

5. Another word for corporate greed, exploitation and destruction (particularly of the environment). Depends on your *end user perspective*, but also on where you live.

global village

The half of the globe that is on the phone. As, 'The new electronic interdependence recreates the world in the image of a global village' (Marshall McLuhan, 1962). More commonly now, a village in which the elders are powerful corporations, their lawyers and compliant governments. As, 'Globalist forces hope to use the same process of "regionalism" around the globe to finish smashing national sovereignty on the road to what top officials regularly refer to as a "New World Order"' (*New American*, 20 April 2015).

> 'The *Global Village* for Future Leaders of Business and Industry is a five-week intensive program . . .'
>
> Iacocca Institute

> 'Having trouble deciding what to pack for your upcoming *Global Village* build?'
>
> Habitat.org.au

goal setting

Setting goals (c.f. hen setting, trap setting, etc.). Comes with most *action plans*. Improves *focus* and *motivation*. In every consultant's toolkit – and should be in yours.

> 'Our school will be *implementing* an age appropriate structured career education program that will support the development of a positive self-concept, deep understandings of the world

of work and a positive attitude to learning through integrated learning, *feedback*, reflection and *goal setting*.'

Letter to parents from the principal of Kurri Kurri Primary School

'The morning exercise explores the character of Macbeth, the shadow potentials of the Warrior archetype, and the dangers of unbounded *goal setting*.'

Olivier mythodrama: Ethical leadership

'Come, you spirits
That tend on mortal thoughts, unsex me here,
And fill me from the crown to the toe topful
Of direst *goal setting*!'

Lady Macbeth

going forward(s) / moving forward(s)

1. Advancing, progressing, moving onwards, pressing on.
2. In future, the future, *at this point in time* in the future (As in: 'Excuse me, can you tell me the time *going forwards*?'); going on (ongoing). In the existential or evolutionary moment; not going backwards. A cousin of *continuous improvement*.
3. Now; in the future; *at this point / moment in time* between where you are and where you are going, between the past and the *agreed outcomes*. (As in: 'Romeo Romeo, wherefore art thou, *going forwards*, Romeo?')
4. Not looking backwards; not mired in the past; not regressive; *forward-looking*; progressively speaking; on the curve, *in terms of the strategy / game plan*, etc. Aware of life's unpredictability and the relentless passage of time.
5. Gillard ALP campaign slogan in the 2010 election

'And what is completely clear now is all of us need to unite behind Julia Gillard *going forward* and I do think that if we can do that, if we can take the division out of the equation . . .'

Richard Marles, Shadow Minister for Immigration, ABC, 21 March 2013

'What is very clear in terms of the best interests of the Labor Party now, what is very clear *going forward* is that everybody unites behind Julia Gillard.'

(ibid)

'And as such, the right thing to do now is to draw a line under the events of today and under the events of this week and indeed the past and to *move forward* . . .'

(ibid)

'In terms of *going forward* we are utterly committed to the fact that we need to make sure . . .'

Richard Marles, *Sydney Morning Herald*, 26 October 2014

golden parachute

But will it compensate for the hurt they feel inside?

'DEPARTING Orica chief Ian Smith will receive a $2.5 million golden parachute after being shown the door less than a week after he admitted to an unacceptable outburst against a female executive.'

www.couriermail.com.au

'FORMER Treasury Wine Estates chief David Dearie was handed a $1.3 million golden parachute after being ousted from the company on the back of a disastrous performance in the group's US division.'

www.heraldsun.com.au, September 2014

go live

(v, n) To begin, start, commence, launch, instigate, press the switch, ignite, make it happen, *implement* the *action plan*, *implement* anything, etc. (As in: 'Ready, set, *go live*!')

> 'DEAL – manufacturer certificates *go live* for registrable and listable therapeutic device applications.'
>
> Department of Health and Ageing

> 'At *Go-Live* the final transfer of knowledge and *ownership* will occur between the consultants and the *internal resources*.'
>
> SAP consultants

> 'And the Spirit of God moved upon the face of the waters. And God said, *Go live*.'

Good to great

A book by Jim Collins published in 2001, sold 4 million copies. Recommended reading for CEOs and managers for a decade, and foist on employees at countless very expensive retreats and seminars. Boon to consultants, resorts and conference centres and PowerPoint. Less popular since several of the companies Collins held up as paradigms – Fannie Mae, Wells Fargo, Circuit City, etc. – have taken spectacular dives, and few of the others have outperformed their competitors. This, despite his great passion, and such ingenious metaphors as the Hedgehog Concept and the Flywheel. [Note: By observing his principles not only can a good company *transition to greatness*, but so also can a church or a sports club, or even a person.]

> 'Indeed, the real question is not, "Why greatness?" but "What work makes you feel compelled to try to create greatness?" If you have to ask the question, "Why should we try to make it great? Isn't success enough?" then you're probably engaged in the wrong line of work.'
>
> Jim Collins

gospel truth

1. The infallible truth, the word of God, as many Christians hold the gospels of the *New Testament* to be.
2. 'Carefully prepared and scripted remarks.' As, 'Tony Abbott has told voters not to believe everything he says . . . [He] said his only utterances that should be regarded as "gospel truth" were carefully prepared and scripted remarks such as those made during speeches or policy pronouncements. Otherwise, he indicated that statements he made during the "heat of discussion" such as radio interviews or under questioning at press conferences, were not necessarily reliable' (*Sydney Morning Herald*, 18 May 2010). C.f. 'What is truth?' Pontius Pilate.

See *absolute fact*, *absolute principle*, *absolute crap*.

> 'The carefully prepared and scripted remarks according to St John . . . In the beginning was the Word . . .'

go the extra mile

To try harder, make a special effort, go out of one's way to help, work weekends, extend credit, offer discount, don't make a bastard of yourself, Good Samaritan, etc. Also trousers and shirts. As, '82% of Americans

Looking for Hassle-Free Clothes That *Go the Extra Mile*' (Nanotechnology information site).

> 'Will instinctively know when and how to "*go the extra mile*".'
> Advert for Relationship Development Manager

> 'But despite all that, the two-party swing in South Australia, as recorded by the poll aggregate, is nothing out of the ordinary – enough to cost the Liberals the always precarious seat of Hindmarsh, but not to *go the extra mile* and unseat Christopher Pyne from his losable seat of Sturt.'
> *Crikey*, 9 April 2015

governance

1. The manner and means by which one is governed; the method and conduct of it.
2. Corporate *governance*, 'the framework of rules, relationships, systems and processes within and by which authority is exercised and controlled in corporations . . . the mechanisms by which companies, and those in control, are held to account' (Justice Owen, HIH Royal Commission Report). Often involves ethics, the relationship between various *stakeholder* interests, *risk management* and *innovation*. As, 'To remain competitive in a changing world, corporations must *innovate* and adapt their *corporate governance* practices so that they can meet new demands and grasp new *opportunities*' (OECD). A guarantee of standards; as, trade union governance should have 'the same integrity that we've long had in corporate governance' (Tony Abbott, *Sydney Morning Herald*, 13 July 2015).

> 'The report recommends that the current TAFE *governance* model be retained but that the *governance* practices within

the *framework* as a whole and within individual Institutions could be *enhanced*. Therefore, to enable participants within the TAFE *framework* to fully *embrace best practice corporate governance* . . .'

TAFE Governance Review

'The presentation will discuss the *key issues*, barriers, *challenges* and implications that can be drawn out of the conference for *capacity* development for Indigenous *governance* in the NT as well as *key* principles for *best practice* that have been identified. These should inform the way in which *capacity building* for *governance* is carried out.'

NT Building Effective Indigenous Governance Conference

granular / granularity

Grain-like, having a high level of detail. *Drill down* to get it but not *down in the weeds*. As, 'The *key* concept is that of *risk assessment*, and this is becoming more *granular* by nature as the market matures. The question is, does the industry have the datasets required to *drill down* into to get the level of *granularity* required for this and, more importantly, are the data accessible to the industry' (Wallis Advisory Committee). Often the grains are you and me: as, 'Twitter Just Made Mobile Ad *Targeting* More *Granular*. Specific device *targeting* helps advertisers break down user demographics at an even more *granular* level, allowing them to launch a more specific *targeted* campaign' (www.businessinsider.com.au). To be told one needs more *granularity* is to be told that one's analysis is crap. (To be told it is not *robust* is to be told something similar.)

'To optimize these supply chains, enterprises will not only need to *harmonize* the point of view of their partner with their point of view (through the blending of underlying data that is being generated on both ends) but also share the insights that they are generating with their partners at the right *granularity* level without losing their intellectual property. This mode of collaboration will need to be *granular* yet *flexible* and grounded in real, *harmonized* data and analytics.'

www.cio.com

great / greatness

Excellent, better than good, what one transitions from good to; pleasing, profitable, internationally competitive, whatever. Anything or anyone exceptional (Winston Churchill, Stephen Hawking, hairdo, spring roll). Anything one likes. Any improvement. Anyone or anything it suits to flatter or inflate. As, 'Prince Philip has been a *great* servant of Australia, he's been a *great* servant of all the countries of the Commonwealth' (Tony Abbott, PM).

'Give me the opportunity to develop *greatness*.'

Advert for a Principal Marketing Strategist

'. . . all past and present Olympic representatives of our *great* nation . . . So there is *great* symbolism about this event in this building . . . how magnificently generous you have again been in a *great* national cause . . . We are, as everybody knows, *great* lovers of sport . . . this nation arguably has had its *greatest* sporting successes . . . And all of it is, in a sense, but a *great* national preparation . . . to see his *great* enthusiasm to do *great* things for his country . . . and the *great* decency of all of the Australian people . . . I want to wish every one of them the *greatest* of success . . . It will be our *greatest* sporting event ever. It will be a *great* world event. It will

> do *great* credit to our nation and the support that you are demonstrating tonight will deliver a *great* deal of that reality.'
>
> John Howard, September 2002

See *good to great*

greenwashing

Like whitewashing only green. Making your company look more responsible than it really is. Use words like sustainable, eco friendly, dolphin friendly, environment friendly; use 'Nature' pictures (dolphins, waterfalls, frogs, etc.). Deceptive or fraudulent advertising. A response to the *stakeholder challenge*. Alleging a concern for the environment for the sake of your share price.

> 'The Victorian Hazelwood power plant produces 8% of Australia's national electricity and 25% of Victoria's electricity. A brown coal fired plant, it also produces 3% of Australia's carbon emissions. Hazelwood is owned by International Power. International Power is owned by global giant GDF Suez. GDF Suez has a series of promotional and advertising products that boast its clean energy credentials while at the same time "*greenwashing*" over its ownership of plants like Hazelwood.'
>
> The Conversation, 12 July 2011

> 'The same companies that are being *targeted* by NGOs and indigenous *communities* for their negative environmental and social *impacts* are the leaders in espousing *triple bottom line* principles and it remains to be seen whether this approach can *deliver* real benefits to *communities* or becomes a more sophisticated form of *greenwashing*.'
>
> Subhabrata Bobby Banerjee,
> Contesting Corporate Citizenship

grocery code of conduct

1. How grocers should behave.
2. How China and Greece should behave.

> 'Journalist: Prime Minister, how concerned are you about the problems in Greece and China, these economic problems spreading to Australia . . .?
>
> Prime Minister: Michael, look, the important thing is to do whatever we can to build a strong and prosperous economy locally, and again I get back to the *Grocery Code of Conduct*. We have a *great* supermarket system. That rests on the shoulders of *great* local suppliers and this is about ensuring that we continue to have very strong local suppliers, best possible product at the best possible price so that we get the best possible deal for *consumers* – and if we do that, we will avoid the problems that we see overseas.'
>
> Tony Abbott, PM, 7 July 2015

grow

Enlarge, expand, increase, augment, multiply, add to, improve, *develop*, etc.

Businesses *grow*. As, '*Grow* the business'. Sometimes they *grow* by *growing* (increasing, swelling, enlarging, expanding, multiplying, adding to) the number of their *customers* or *clients* (punters, mugs, aspirational lifestyle seekers, segments, etc.) or their *customer* or *client bases*: 'Due to company *growth* this *dynamic* IT company is looking for a Business Development Manager to join them and help in *growing their client base*.' Economies *grow*.

'Andrew leads a talented and highly *focused* management *team* who will aggressively *grow* Chimes wholesale business.'

iiNet media release

'Financial security is essential to *grow* our influence and build an even stronger organisation for all Australians.'

South Australian Liberal Party

'Be fruitful,
and *grow* thy *client base*.'

growth (positive)

Outcome of growing something: daffodil, economy, business, market share, etc. As, 'For 2014, Australia will again be among the leading advanced nations for economic *growth*.'

'. . . in the long run, there is a tendency for the rate of return of capital to exceed the economy's *growth* rate, and this tends to lead to high concentration of wealth.'

Thomas Piketty

'One of the arguments against [Thomas Piketty's] point of view is that economic inequality is not only a feature of capitalism but is actually one of its engines. So we take measures to lower inequality, and at the same time we lower *growth*, potentially.'

Bruno Giussani, www.ted.com

'We will be modeling various sensitivities [to?] determine the best *strategies* to *optimize* our strong originations forecast and manage *asset growth* and capital. In addition, we will prioritize the launch of new *growth initiatives*, as well as the timing of these investments in comparison to the revenue projections.'

In a corporate memo from a US-owned Canadian company

growth (negative)

1. Not growing. *Growth* in negative territory. As, 'After many years of *negative* or very modest *growth* rates since the financial crisis erupted in 2008 . . . the euro zone is continuing to gain traction and is likely to attain pre-2008-09 crisis *growth* rates again next year . . .' 'In other words, had I subtracted the deficit spending times the current M2 velocity of 1.5, the *negative GDP growth* rate would be much greater than the chart reflects' (Joseph Stuber, Seeking Alpha, 30 July 2015). Two quarters of *negative growth* = recession.
2. View that *positive* economic *growth* is *negative*, because the planet's resources are not inexhaustible. As, 'there is a fundamental conflict between economic *growth* and conservation of natural resources. Growing the economy means shrinking the ecosystem' (Casse). 'Aristotle knew of insatiability only as a personal vice; he had no inkling of the collective, politically orchestrated insatiability that we call economic *growth*' (Robert Skidelsky, *Guardian*, 22 June 2012).

growth space

A space in which to grow? But grow what? Where is it?

'[If] we continue to do so, we are going to have rock star status in the *growth space* internationally at some stage in the next four years.'

ANZ Chief Economist

H

hands on

(adj) Human supervision, the personal touch, *implementation* with a human face. (As in: 'Brian is very *hands on in terms of* his approach.)
(n) The condition of being *hands on*. An operation conducted in this way. Some religions are very *hands on* in their approach.

> 'SMEDB's support and assistance for the emerging mineral sands industry will be clearly demonstrated by leading the mineral sands Murray Basin delegation to meet with Federal Ministers and Heads of Department in Canberra in late August, as well as through the continued *hands on*, across industry, government and education providers working relationship provided by SMEDB *dedicated* mineral sands project officer.'
>
> Sunraysia Mallee Economic Development Board

> 'After spending some *hands on* time with the Proactive Multi-Channel Customer Service Version, I found it to be a good *tool* for enabling *customer* self-service features and managing interactions.'
>
> IDG News Service

> 'He is *hands on* and there are things he gets involved with.'
>
> Joe Flint on Rupert Murdoch, KPCC, 12 June 2015

hardwiring excellence

Excellent hardwiring. Superior, first rate, top notch, top shelf, best possible hardwiring. As, 'Participation in the formulation of unit based Operational *Plans* that maximise the *focus* on patient and family centred care, including the principles of *Hardwiring Excellence . . .*' (Work appraisal form for a nurse).

> 'In *Hardwiring Excellence*, Quint Studer helps health care professionals to rekindle the flame and offers a *road map* to creating and sustaining a *Culture* of Service and Operational *Excellence* that *drives bottom*-line results.'
>
> Publicity screed

hard yards

Hard work. As, 'Tony Abbott says billionaire Clive Palmer will have to put in the "*hard yards*" and accept that being an MP is a full-time job if he wants to stand as a coalition candidate for federal parliament' (*Advertiser*, 1 August 2012).

> 'I've been out doing the *hard yards* at the bus stops and door-knocking. It's pleasing Tony Abbott sees the importance of that.'
>
> Clive Palmer, 4 July 2012

> 'People that are doing the *hard yards* and done the *hard yards* for the nation, upset, scared, worried sick about where they will be able to find the money so they can meet the co-payments and continue going to work.'
>
> Graham Perrett, MP, 12 June 2014

> 'And the suggestion that Australia, having done the *hard yards*, can now take a rest is wrong. We have to continue to do the *hard yards*.'
>
> Peter Costello, Federal Treasurer

> 'All *hard yards* and no play makes Jack a dull boy.'

> 'The Fair *Hard Yards* Commission.'

harmonisation

1. Uniformity of legislation relating to trade and industry in the 'global village'; the commercial world subject to a new *lex mercatoria*.
2. Lockstep. Tightening the corporate grip; loss of culture, personal independence and national sovereignty; loss of jobs and stifling domestic economies; 'allowing unelected and unaccountable transnational bureaucrats to develop "harmonised" regulatory regimes'.

> 'The Zambian government should immediately withdraw its signature from the COMESA and SADC seed trade *harmonisation* Act to ensure food security, says Kasisi Agricultural Training Centre executive director Paul Desmarias. Desmarias, in an interview, warned that once enacted, the seed trade and *harmonisation* Act which targets eastern and southern African countries would make it illegal for farmers to sell or barter their seed with neighbors or family members.'
>
> GMWatch

harness

(v) make ready for work, or some other convenient purpose, with suitable gear, esp. a horse, buffalo, mule or goat. By some apparatus generate power from, e.g. water, wind or sun. Also *harness* one's mind, one's strength, ambition, resources, competitive advantage, etc., or that of others. As, '25 Clever Ways To *Harness* The Power Of The Sun.' Use, *utilise*, exploit, employ, take advantage of, make use of, put to work, husband, avail oneself, mobilise, apply, adopt, adapt, capitalise on, leverage by squirrel grip, etc.

'While he took the orthodox approach of presenting a petition to the prime minister, Senator Lazarus told an anti-CSG rally in Sydney he could *harness* some of his experience from league in his lobbying. "I'm prepared to go and squirrel grip the prime minister," Senator Lazarus said.'

West Australian, 7 July 2015

'Easy HR can help you to *harness* the power of your people by assisting you *manage* your team more effectively.'

Easy HR

headcount reductions

Sackings, lay-offs, *downsizing* of *hires* – sometimes *synergy*-related.

'With the successful completion of these *plans*, we will have the vast majority of the *synergy-related headcount reductions* completed and we can then start to put this chapter of our *history* behind us and *focus* on creating a *world-class* company.'

Nokia Siemens Webwire, November 2008

heads up

Forewarning (forearming), warning, advance warning. As, 'Beware the ides of March', soothsayer's *heads up* for Julius Caesar. Update, alert, caution, tip-off, lowdown, latest, news, background, truth, etc.

'With the launch of Windows 10 less than a month away, Microsoft is giving users a *heads up* on how upgrades will work.'

ARNnet, 3 July 2015

high level

High level meetings, forums (*fora*), symposiums, gatherings, discussions are restricted to people occupying high level positions: prime ministers, presidents, general secretaries, CEOs, etc. Important people. Note: the level of written reports, communiques, recommendations, etc., issuing from high level meetings is no higher than those from meetings at a lower level.

> 'The European Commission set up a *High Level* Forum for a Better Functioning Food Supply Chain to *implement* a *roadmap* of *initiatives* to improve the *competitiveness* of the agro-food industry in cooperation with the *stakeholders*.'

> '84. We decide to establish a universal intergovernmental *high level* political forum, building on the strengths, experiences, resources and inclusive participation modalities of the Commission on *Sustainable Development*, and subsequently replacing the Commission. The *high level* political forum shall follow up on the *implementation* of *sustainable development* and should avoid overlap with existing structures, bodies and entities in a cost-effective manner.'
>
> Rio+20 'Future we Want' draft text, *Guardian*, 20 June 2012

> 'You're the top
> You're *high level*', etc.

high level / order thinking

Skills of analysis and evaluation, as opposed to memorising facts. An education philosophy.

> '1. Assessment will be *holistic*.

> Just as the *skills* and *processes* are not compartmentalised in the creation *process*, the evaluation of *outcomes* will occur against

a background of understanding that separation of *outcomes* into discrete components is subordinate to the evaluation of the total *process* as a comprehensive *outcome*. Put simply, "As a whole, what happened?"'

Greenwood Senior High School, WA

'In the Tasmanian *framework*, *higher order thinking* is situated in the broader *context* of higher order learning with the five 'essential *learnings*' listed as: communicating, personal futures, social responsibility, world futures, and thinking.'

research.acer.edu.au

high net worth individuals

Wealthy individuals. Rich, rich as Croesus, rich as, well-heeled, well off, well fixed, well to do, flush, loaded, filthy rich, pecunious, affluent people. People who are not short of a dollar, who are on the rich list, who are rolling in it. Nabobs, richlings, arrivistes, plutocrats, parvenus, magnates, tycoons, moguls, etc.

'Investec seek to improve financial services for *high net worth individuals*.'

www.treasuryinsider.com

'The investment by these *high net worth individuals* in Actinogen was a pittance compared to what is being spent by international pharmaceutical companies.'

Australian Financial Review

'Who wants to be a *high net worth individual*?
I don't.
Who wants to wallow in champagne,' etc.

high trust leader

Not a low price leader, but not necessarily a high price leader. A person you can trust; an honest, open, straight talking, transparent, just, decent person.

> 'To lead in the Connection Economy, Seth identifies the need for "*high trust leaders*". He notes, "It no longer works to be the 'low price leader' and focus on productivity. Today, it is necessary to transform to a '*high trust leader*'." '

> 'Trust is established through action and over time, and it is a leader's responsibility to demonstrate what it means to keep your word and earn a reputation for trustworthiness.'
>
> Hank Paulson, former US Secretary of the Treasury, former CEO of Goldman Sachs, author of the bailout of companies too big to fail, inc. Goldman Sachs. Named in *Time* Magazine as one of the '25 People to Blame for the Financial Crisis'. In Stephen M.R. Covey, 'The 13 Behaviors of a *High Trust Leader*'

> 'To further improve its effectiveness, the School *Leadership Team* worked with a *leadership* coach to develop a *mission statement* and to explore the roles and *behaviours of high trust leaders*.'
>
> St Thomas More School, Belgrave

high value

1. Valuable. More valuable. Extremely valuable.
2. Value added: *customers*, *consumers*, crops, jobs, *managers*, *products*, *knowledge objects*, purchase orders, insurance, fluorine compounds, people, talent, etc.

'Without efficient and *Lean process* designs your organisation risks *bottlenecks* and unproductive behavior in every phase of the recruiting *lifecycle*. What good is an expensive and efficient applicant tracking system that no one uses or cares to use or if *high value* candidates fall out of the *process* at the very last minute?'

4HR Consulting Group

'Seize the opportunity to *grow* your top line and beat your competitors through delivering *high value* to *customers* . . .'

PA Consulting Group

'The women, however, are kept in another part of the prison, cell block 1A, together with nineteen *high value* male detainees.'

Guardian, 20 May 2004

high value target

1. Killing your worst enemies.
2. 'We define *high-value targeting* as *focused* operations against specific individuals or networks whose removal or marginalization should disproportionately *degrade* an insurgent group's effectiveness. The criteria for designating *high-value targets* will vary according to factors such as the insurgent group's capabilities, structure and *leadership dynamics* and the government's desired *outcome* (CIA, '*Best Practice* in Counter Insurgency. Making *High-Value Targeting* Operations an Effective Counterinsurgency *Tool*', July 2009, WikiLeaks).

'The intelligence source said Anzac Day at Gallipoli would be a "*high value target*" for Islamic State terrorists . . .'

Daily Telegraph, 20 April 2015

hire

1. (v) To employ, obtain a service for money.
2. (n) A person hired. As, '*On-boarding* accelerates a *hire's* progress by reducing the *transition* time between his or her starting date and full *productivity*' (Development Dimensions International).

> 'It is critical NIMS baseline training becomes an integral part of the organization's training program. Organizational changes as a result of new *hires,* promotions or mission changes amplify this training requirement.'
>
> FEMA, US

> 'Decruit those *hires!*'

> '*Hires* of the world, unite!'

history

1. Story of events. Study and interpretation of past events. '. . . a tableau of crimes' (Voltaire); '. . . a nightmare from which I am trying to awake' (Joyce). Whatever is past, gone, obsolete, dead and buried. (As in: 'She's *history.*' 'He's in "the dustbin of *history*".')
2. A weapon for defending oneself and attacking others. A movable feast. Whatever it suits one to make of it. Calling of pedants. Rubbish, humbug, baloney, '. . . a distillation of rumour' (Carlyle); '. . . more or less bunk' (Ford).
3. Story that repeats itself: '. . . the first time as tragedy, the second as farce' (Marx).
4. Story which, if we do not learn it, we are 'condemned to relive' (Santayana).

5. Story of which all citizens should be proud, etc. *Colourful* story. Heritage. That which made us, inspires us, enriches, informs and guides us.
6. Judge. '*History* will judge me kindly'; '. . . stand before the bar of *history*', etc.
7. Second refuge of the scoundrel.

> 'Now there are some who like to re-write *history* – revisionist historians is what I like to call them.'
>
> George W. Bush, June 2003

> '. . . *history* is on our side. We will bury you.'
>
> Nikita Khrushchev, 1958

See *black-armband history*.

holism / holistic approach

1. Thesis that wholes in general are more than the sums of their parts (Gk. *Holos* – whole, complete); and the parts being interconnected, none can be explained without reference to the whole. Organicism.
2. Taking account of more than one part. Not partial or fragmentary, therefore yielding superior *outcomes*. Not inadequate. As *holistic* medicine might treat the liver to cure a sore ankle, a *holistic approach* in business will try to cure declining sales by overhauling the *communications department*.
3. In financial planning, anyone's guess: for example: 'The immediate establishment of a financial planner education-working group (FPEWG) to develop a considered, *strategic* and *holistic* financial planner education *framework*.' (Point 3 in Financial Planning Association's 10 Point Plan for raising standards in the financial planning profession.)

Point 9 suggests that a *framework* might not be enough (if syntax is a part of the education *framework* as a whole), viz., 'Once the Federal Budget position has been improved, that the government commence consultation with industry to determine the benefit to have the preparation of an initial financial plan be expressly stated to be tax deductible.'

Pretty well anything can be called *holistic*: 'There is no legal definition for the term "*Holistic*" so companies can use it as they wish. What you need to do is read into the label and past the title to find out what *holistic* means for that particular product' (*Holistic* pet food supplier).

Holistic products include education, soup, ice cream, dentistry, health, shirts. *Holistic* approaches may be taken to virtually everything, from personal hygiene to warfare.

> 'Our practice is *holistic* and is based on the integration of theories and practices related to human development, psychology, system psychodynamics, systems theory, organisational *development* and learning, neuroscience and adult and *transformational* learning. [But, note, for some reason, not horticulture, phobias, soil science, genetics, meteorology, etc.] We examine the mental, emotional, physical, spiritual and energetic dimensions of leadership and organisational life.'
>
> The Global Leadership Practice

> 'All of me, why not take me *holistically*?
> Can't you see, I'm no good without you.'

holocracy / holacracy

'[S]imultaneously a whole and its parts' (Allen Holub, Dr Dobb's bloggers, 14 March 2014). From Arthur Koestler's book about the human brain, *The Ghost in the Machine* (1967). A theory of non-hierarchical organisation.

'*Holacracy* is a distributed authority system – a set of "rules of the game" that bake empowerment into the core of the organization.'

holacracy.org/how-it-works

'Please follow Earth *Holocracy* to keep up on the upcoming Northern Rivers Regional Peoples Assembly and Activation of Real Democracy throughout Australia in our Australian Spring.'

www.earthholocracy.org

hopefully

1. Buoyantly, optimistically, rosily; prospectively, expectantly.
2. I/we/they hope. I hope so. With hope. In the hope that. With luck. With a bit of luck. Here's luck. If we're lucky. God willing. With every confident expectation. With hope in our hearts. Here's looking up your kilt. Here's mud in your eye. Touch wood, etc. Barring accident. Hope, hoping, hopeful. (As in: I hope we can meet – *hopefully* we can *dialogue*. Hoping to hear from you – *hopefully* we can *touch base*. I am hopeful – *hopefully*.)

'He was really good and *hopefully going forward* that can really help the team, and for us to play some key forwards around Pav to help him out when he is there.'

Fremantle Dockers' coach

'Whilst his work will *hopefully* result in a profoundly improved foundation for the master planning, the expression "reverse brief" merely describes the process of communication for now.'

'*Hopefully*, hope springs eternal.'

horizon scanning

Searching for issues *going forward*. Don't *go forward* without it. As, 'The Jon Day review defined *horizon scanning* as: A systematic examination of information to identify potential threats, risks, emerging *issues* and opportunities, beyond the Parliamentary term, allowing for better preparedness and the incorporation of mitigation and exploitation into the policy making *process*' (www.gov.uk/government/news/*horizon-scanning*-programme-a-new-approach-for-policy-making).

> 'Welcome to the Australia and New Zealand *Horizon Scanning* Network (ANZHSN).'
>
> www.*horizonscanning*.gov.au

hot desking

Cost-cutting management ploy. Open plan office with fewer desks than people. Reduce costs by saving office space. Encourage collaboration. Break down *silos*. Abandon privacy. Reduce *productivity*; as, 'They [Gensler US] found that the most significant factor in workplace effectiveness is not collaboration – the stated justification for most of the office changes – but individual focus work. Whoever would have thought being able to concentrate on your work could be so important?' (Ross Gittins, 'How *hot-desking* offices can wreck *productivity*', *Sydney Morning Herald*, 30 December 2013)

How's your day been so far?

1. How's your day been so far?
2. As if I care.

SHOP ASSISTANT: 'G'day, mate.'

CUSTOMER: 'I would like to buy a ripe pineapple.'

SHOP ASSISTANT: 'Awesome. *How's your day been so far?*'

CUSTOMER: 'Hello. I want to complain about the telephone service.'

CALL CENTRE: 'Jolly good, sir. *How's your day been so far*, sir?'

human centric

Working with staff.

> 'Deloitte and the *Customer Experience* Company (CEC) will begin working with the Department on Monday to work with the Department to *implement* the next phase of the Corporate Services *Transformation Program* . . .
>
> For the next six months, the Deloitte and CEC *partnership* will work alongside the Corporate Services Management Office to deliver the required *outputs* of the two-year *Transformation Program*. The main approach of the next six months will be "*human-centric*", whereby the CSMO and Deloitte/CEC will work with staff, namely frontline staff, to understand and co-design our future state of Corporate Services.'

human resources (HR) management (HRM)

1. People. '*Human resources* are like natural resources; they're often buried deep. You have to go looking for them, they're not just lying around on the surface. You have to create the circumstances where they show themselves' (Ken Robinson). Personnel. Human capital. People working in the *knowledge economy*, i.e. more people than not.

2. Human resources management (HRM). Managing workers, inc. recruiting and *decruiting* them. Getting the most out of them for as little as possible. Making them *effort*. *Enhancing* their *skills*, *competencies* etc. *Harvesting* their minds for *value adding* in the organisation. Coercing, manipulating and controlling their thought and behaviour. *Downsizing tool*. '. . . a management vehicle to shape and configure malleable human resources in the interests of the firm (Knights and Willmott, 1990). '. . . a tool of managerial control to repress opposition and resistance of employees [that uses] . . . emancipatory rhetoric to cultivate illusory feelings of unity between management and employees [and] colourful and emotive imagery of unprecedented managerial concern for employee welfare to minimise opposition and tighten the "reigns of control" ' (Sewell, 1998). (Timothy Bartram, Employee management systems and organizational contexts: A population ecology approach. highered.mheducation.com)

> 'The university is reviewing *human resource* policies to *ensure* that such policies are updated to be consistent and appropriately linked, unambiguous, written in plain English and do not contain unnecessary detail. A clear *strategy* for *communication* of the policies will form an integral part of the *implementation* process.'
>
> University of New England

> 'Mercer's new *HR* Effectiveness Monitor survey can show the degree to which your *HR* function is *transforming* from a task oriented, administrative back office to a front-line, *strategic* powerhouse for today's *leading-edge* organisations.'
>
> HR consultant

hydration option (zero kilojoule)

Water.

> 'People willingly pay for the convenience of a zero-kilojoule *hydration option* when they're out and about.'
>
> CEO, Australasian Bottled Water Institute

> 'Plain water is always a good *hydration option*.'
>
> In motion

> '*Hydration options* everywhere, And all the boards did shrink; *Hydration options* everywhere, Nor any drop to drink.'
>
> S.T. Coleridge

I

icon

1. Image or representation, usually of a saint or other sacred Christian personage. As, '. . . the Holy Father communicated to the patriarch of Moscow his wish to give to the Russian Orthodox Church the sacred *icon* of the Lady of Kazan.' Communism tried to ban icons. Capitalism, the more inventive system, deprived them of meaning and power by making the word a marketing tool. Icons are humble paintings of humble saints worshipped humbly in imitation of their self-effacement. For marketing purposes icons get their radiance from hubris and fame. They are touchstones of the general self-regard and narcissism.
2. Computer symbol.
3. Any well-known footballer or cricketer, the Big Pineapple, Steve Irwin, Terri Irwin, Bindi Irwin, the Irwin family, Uluru, Sydney Opera House, Dame Edna Everage, Cilla Black, the Dog on the Tucker Box, Gough Whitlam, Malcolm Fraser, Heath Ledger, Amy Winehouse, Breaker Morant, Nicole Kidman, Weary Dunlop, Dawn Fraser, Ron Barassi, Cate Blanchett, FJ Holden, the gum tree, the wattle, the cypress, the galah, the crocodile, the kangaroo, the koala, magpie, crow, *Anzac*, ANZUS, etc. Any well-known person or thing. There are business *icons* ('Business *icon* shares her story'), brand *icons* (Nike, Armani), sporting *icons* (numberless), cultural *icons* (Les Murray, Roy and HG), food *icons* (vegemite, chump chops, etc.), environmental *icons*, feminist *icons*, political *icons*. Anything that's been around for a while. Anything dinkum (e.g. 'Lee Kernaghan, Country Music *Icon*').
4. Anything or anyone you say. (Make your own list.)

> 'Katie Hopkins continues desperate attempts to become a gay *icon* by judging Porn Idol at G-A-Y.'
>
> *Mirror*, 14 March 2015

'Accounts Payable Clerk for Australian *Icon*. Our client is an Australian *icon* and market leader. They are currently looking for an accounts payable clerk.'

Job advert

'New Minister Welcomed by Wine Industry *Icon*.'

Ballandean Estate Wines press release

'When we show an Aussie *icon*, we have done so in a way that has never been seen before.'

Consultancy to Australian Tourism Commission

'Upton has the kind of glossy, glamorous social life you'd expect of a modern icon. She is friends with Cameron Diaz . . .'

www.dailytelegraph.com.au

iconic

1. Having the status of an *icon*.
2. Not contemporary (unless a contemporary *icon*).

Something old and important.

'First, their logos represent symbols of reliability, trust and quality. Second, their *consumers* associate these *brands* as contributors to their *lifestyles*. They are *iconic*. In fact, these logos are so powerful, they don't even have to include the *brand* names they were born with. Finally, these *brands* stand for something that is greater than themselves, beyond their *core* business, that symbolizes their relentless *dedication* for the advancement of society and the *consumers* they serve.'

Glenn Lopis, *Forbes*, 9 December 2012 – on McDonald's, Nike, Southwest Airlines and other *iconic brands*

'Phase 2 work includes a revitalised name, look and brand to help this community asset become an iconic Rail Trail experience.'

Mansfield Shire

'Southcorp is *committed* to being a dedicated and leading premium winemaker with a portfolio of brands and wines that range from the contemporary to the *iconic* . . .'

Southcorp media release, 2004

ideate

To conceive or form an idea. Think of something, figure out, solve, apprehend, comprehend, realise, grasp, twig, imagine, get a handle on. To have the penny drop. To be a little pretentious. As, 'I ideate, therefore I am' (Descartes).

'It really combines the real estate knowledge of the problem set that they're trying to solve, and you pair that with *product* and technology expertise that's able to take that knowledge of the problem and *ideate* how to fix it, in interesting and new ways.'

www.prnewswire.com

'Collaboration within the business sphere – or what could be called the "We" space as opposed to the "Me" space – means taking the opportunity to engage and *ideate* with big thinkers, mentors, sponsors and leaders who can assist your journey upward.'

www.smh.com.au, April 2015

The *Ideator* by Rodin.

'When you *ideate* upon a star.'

identity and culture transformation

Help in fighting fires.

> '*Cultural* Improvement *Implementation Project* (CIIP)
>
> The intent of the CIIP is to remodel and address the barriers and *enablers* that have been identified, demonstrating a clear *commitment* to cultural *reform* and compliance with continued, concentrated effort to *achieve* enduring *cultural* change, recognised as an organisation that *embraces diversity* . . . Undertake the related areas of work within:
>
> • QFES *Identity and Culture Transformation. Transforming culture* through l*eadership*
>
> • Develop QFES *cultural reform strategy*. *Implement* and measure *cultural reform*
>
> • *Capability* and workforce *framework*.'
>
> Queensland Fire and Emergency Services, Commissioner's Update, 13 March 2015

illegal maritime arrivals / illegals / illegal immigrants

1. People seeking asylum in Australia who arrive on leaky boats.
2. Queue jumpers, dodgy people, illegals.

> 'This statement provides an update on Operation Sovereign Borders (OSB) activities related to the *off-water* reception and processing of *illegal maritime arrivals*. The reporting period is from 9 am Friday 17 January 2014 to 9 am Friday 24 January 2014. During this reporting period there were no *illegal maritime arrivals* transferred to Australian Immigration authorities. Fifty-five *illegal maritime arrivals* were transferred to

offshore processing centres – 19 to Manus Island and 36 to Nauru. Five *illegal maritime arrival* detainees were voluntarily removed – one to Sri Lanka and four to Iran.'

'Let's remember that everyone in these centres is there because he or she has come *illegally* by boat. They have done something that they must have known was wrong.'

Tony Abbott

'Immigration Minister Scott Morrison has defended the use of the term "*illegal arrivals*" to describe asylum seekers, saying he is "calling a spade a spade".

"It's not calling a spade a spade," the Canon of St Paul's Cathedral in Melbourne, Stephen Ames, told PM. "It is misrepresenting the state of people who are fleeing for their lives, and to call them illegal and to perpetuate that and other dehumanising kind of labels, just doesn't acknowledge their situation."'

Age, 22 October 2013

'Illegals Aren't Immigrants They're Criminals.'

Australians Against Illegal Immigrants and Refugees
Facebook page

impact

(n) 1. collision, forcible contact, striking together.
2. An effect, consequence, upshot, result, etc.
(v) 1. To hit, dash, strike against – as an asteroid on the earth's surface or a fist on the nose. In dentistry, an *impacted* tooth is an embedded one. Bowels also get *impacted*.
2. To effect, influence, bear upon, sway, persuade, win over, inspire, engage, convince, brainwash, earbash, control, change, stimulate, make them understand, make them repent,

penetrate their minds, blow their minds, sell, make them listen, convert, bend, mindfuck, exhilarate, impress, affect, move, excite, rouse, stir, transport, move, inflame, ravish, seduce, overwhelm, fire, shock, arouse, impassion, anger, depress, soothe, stir, infect, lay them in the aisles, bore them stiff, etc. Whatever or whomever has been affected in any way (e.g. demolished, ignited, made itchy or irritable, etc.) has been *impacted*. As, 'The next *challenge* facing HR practitioners are the multiple *stakeholder* groups that all need to be *managed* . . . These may include the *impacted* individuals . . .' (HC Online)

> 'We work closely with clients to convert insights into *strategies*, whose *implementation* will have a substantial positive *impact* on performance. Consistently *delivering impact* earns the trust that is the foundation of lasting relationships. These relationships serve as a *platform* for still deeper insights and more significant *impact*.'
>
> Boston Consulting Mission Statement

> '. . . *empowering* people to lead and *impact* in every sphere of life.'
>
> Hillsong Church Mission Statement

> 'Within five hours the fire could *impact* on Whittlesea. There is a country music festival at Whittlesea. 300KV New South Wales inter connect transmission lines could be *impacted* later today. The community of Hidden Valley may be directly *impacted* upon by the fire.'
>
> Black Saturday Royal Commission

> 'These (hot weather) *events* are really *impacting* on them.'
>
> Bat Conservation and Rescue Queensland president, *Courier Mail*

'We will support our *impacted* employees throughout the process.'

GlaxoSmithKline media release, 22 May 2013

'Man behind our food revolution Barry McDonald has *impacted* what Sydneysiders eat.'

Sydney Morning Herald, 22 October 2010

'*Impact Framework*: The *Impact* Framework section discusses how DEET will *implement* the *strategy*. This includes how DEET will monitor the progress of the activity, the *impact* of that activity on the desired *outcomes* and continuous evaluation to determine whether effort is directed in the *areas* that will have the greatest *impact*.'

DEET

'Theirs not to make reply,
Theirs not to reason why,
Theirs but to make an *impact*.'

The Impact of the Light Brigade

impactful / impactfully

Full of impact. Having an impact. As, 'Impact your world' (CNN). Meaningful, influential, powerful, effective.

'I am *impactful*: What I do makes a difference in the lives of others.'

Steven R. Covey, *The 7 Habits of Highly Effective People*

'Two years in, Forest Grove's Dairy Creek Community Food Web matures *impactfully*.'

www.oregonlive.com

'Not only that, but Hayes made the transition to the NFL from track and field more successfully and *impactfully* than any before or since.'

everything-pr.com

'With the Finacle suite of solutions on Azure, we will support financial institutions in opening doors to a new era of *agility* and *innovation* in a security-*enhanced* environment, while *impactfully* shrinking their IT infrastructure costs.'

Karen Cone, Microsoft, www.firstpost.com

'More *impactful* than a locomotive. Able to leap tall buildings in a single bound.'

Superman

'Yours *impactfully*,' etc.

implement / implementation

To put into effect, action, practice, operation, service. Do. Carry out. Get it up and going. Get it running, moving. Bring about. Apply. Start, kick start. Initiate. Activate. Maintain. Institute. Proceed with.

A process for doing or not doing something while talking about it. What one does with a plan, strategy, design, initiative, process, procedures, machinery of government, etc. As, 'A clear *strategy* for *communication* of the policies will form an integral part of the *implementation* process' (University of New England).

'The Department actively monitors its performance in *implementing initiatives* announced each Budget, using the following criteria:

• *Implemented* – the *initiative* was *achieved* by the planned *implementation* date;

• On Track – the initiative is "on track" to meet the planned *implementation* date; and

• Slipping – the initiative is experiencing unavoidable delays and will not meet the planned *implementation* date.'

www.health.gov.au

'The Prime Minister has announced the government will work towards the *implementation* of the agreement by working with the Tasmanian Government to jointly appoint an independent *facilitator* to build an *implementation plan* for the principles in consultation with the signatories to the agreement.'

Email from a Federal MP

'The result appears to be a fragmented and uncoordinated approach that would efficiently be *implemented* by the heterodyning of these areas' *outputs* through a *strategic planning* document.'

From a classified document

'Thy kingdom come; thy will be *implemented*.'

implementable / unimplementable

Can be done. Can't be done.

'There are a lot of *implement*, immediately *implementable* things that can be done . . .'

Bob Mansfield, ABC radio, May 2004

> 'Last time he [Bill Shorten] tried this the Treasury said it was *unimplementable* in various ways.'
>
> Joe Hockey, *Sydney Morning Herald*, 23 April 2015

> '. . . we have been getting rid of the ones that are simply *unimplementable*.'
>
> Joe Hockey, *Bendigo Advertiser*, 22 April 2015

> 'Call me *implementable*.'

inappropriate

1. Not appropriate, proper, apt or fitting.
2. Bad, wicked, iniquitous, nefarious, egregious, criminal, vicious, depraved, etc. As, 'A Glenmont man is facing charges after police say he had *inappropriate* sexual contact with an underage girl . . . He's charged with rape, criminal sexual acts and endangering the welfare of a child' (WYNT.com).

> 'Identify *Inappropriate* Content. *Inappropriate* content includes but is not limited to:
>
> • Words or images that personally attack, humiliate or defame an individual.
>
> • Content that threatens, discriminates, harasses, menaces or causes offence including stalking.
>
> • A fake profile of an individual or school.
>
> • Depictions of nudity, pornography or child abuse.
>
> • Depictions of excessive violence.
>
> • Content that is illegal, gives instructions for illegal activity or advocates terrorist activities.'

'When I'm good I'm very, very good, but when I'm *inappropriate* I'm better.'

Mae West

inappropriate behaviour

Riots, self-mutilation, attempted suicide, hunger strikes, etc. by refugees held in Australian detention centres.

'I think the principal explanation is that there are some people who do not accept the umpire's decision, and believe that *inappropriate behaviour* will influence people like you and me, who have certain *values*, who have certain views about human rights, who do believe in the sanctity of life, and are concerned when people say, "If you don't give me what I want, I'm going to cut my wrists" . . . in many parts of the world, people believe that they get *outcomes* by behaving in that way.'

Philip Ruddock, Minister for Immigration, ABC, 2001

'Today's inquiry also heard claims of physical and sexual abuse against children by staff on Nauru. Kirsty Diallo, who worked for Save the Children in Nauru in 2013, told the inquiry of *inappropriate behaviour* by guards who stroked girls' hair, and made them sit on their laps.'

ABC, 31 July 2014

incentivise / incentivate

Encourage, motivate, inspire, inspirit, embolden, etc. Also, 'Incentivation' (John Howard election slogan, 1987).

'Using sex to *incentivise* men to do housework is a major turn-off.'

Age, 22 June 2015

'To best *incentivise* others you need an incentive solution that provides tangible results and *incentivises* the kind of *behaviours* that increase your business performance.'

www.pointsshop.com.au

'What would make the biggest difference in *driving behaviour change* amongst *consumers*? Two answers were jointly selected in response to this question – the first was about talking the *consumer's* language and ditching jargon, the second about *incentivising* the *consumer* to *change behaviour* . . .'

'. . . many *stakeholders* are concerned about Labor's plans to *incentivise* the wine industry.'

Sen. Peter Whish-Wilson, *Advocate*, 12 December 2012

initiative

1. First step in a process; the initial step, an originating act. An attempt to resolve or confront a situation or problem. Gumption, spirit, get up and go, etc. Something one seizes. A plan of action. Self-reliant enterprise.
2. Any step. Anything done or proposed. The organisation established to do it (e.g. Proliferation Security *Initiative*, Depression *Initiative*, Urban Stormwater *Initiative*, Hugo Mutation Databox *Initiative*, Western Australian Herbicide Resistance *Initiative* – WAHRI). Many *initiatives* are *strategic*. Many are exciting. Some may be identified.

'We want our staff to put the *values* into practice. The *values team* has identified a range of additional *initiatives* to support and instil our *values* throughout the organisation . . .'

Department of Treasury and Finance, Tasmania

'The Industry Growth Centres *Initiative* (the *Initiative*) is the centrepiece of the Government's new industry *policy* direction and part of the Industry *Innovation* and *Competitiveness Agenda*.'

www.business.gov.au

innovate / innovation / innovative

1. (v) To come up with something new or a new way of doing things. '[T]he thrilling power to create' (Amazon employee). 'Inventing the future' (Jeff Bezos, Amazon).
2. (n) An item of managerial stuffing, esp. in *mission and vision* statements, professional curriculum vitae, as in '*driving innovation*', 'adding *stakeholder value* through *innovation*', having *innovation* in one's DNA, etc.
3. (n) A bit of trickery. As in: 'Unfortunately, Berri Truly has not met our *performance benchmarks* and Lion has advised customers and growers that we have deleted the product. However, we will continue to *innovate* in the juice category to deliver more choice for consumers and benefits for other stakeholders.' (Berri having previously *innovated* in the juice category by selling Mexican juice under a famous Australian label – although, as the press release says, it was the product's failure, not the company's.)

'Welcome to the Public Sector *Innovation Toolkit*. The Toolkit has been developed to assist individual public servants, public sector teams and agencies who want to increase the extent and effectiveness of their *innovation* efforts.'

innovation.govspace.gov.au

'O brave *innovative* world, that has such people in't.'

Shakespeare, *The Tempest*

input

1. (n) Contribution, help, advice, offering, suggestion, something put in. (v) Put in. As, 'In March 2003, a second round of staff workshops will be held for staff to *input* to and confirm the QSA Strategic Plan 2004–2006' (Change Management consultancy).
2. An idea, remark, song, joke; a design for a new fighter aircraft or hairclip, or an actual fighter aircraft or hairclip; everything that goes in is an *input*, including: 'Acceleration techniques for stakeholder *input* and sign off & Empowering the business'.

> 'She is a bright cheery cook but one cannot but wonder why her producer has not suggested a speech coach coupled with some input of expanding her adjectives.'
>
> Letter to the editor, *Sydney Morning Herald*

> 'To define the purpose it is sometimes useful to consider *input* factors, throughput or process factors and *output* and *outcome* factors.'
>
> Queensland Health

> 'Also I had lunch with Jenny and she is feeling loved and *engaged* and is now back *in the loop*. She is going to *input* into the channel manuals.' (The listener explains 'This person is, of course, *hot-desking* from out of town . . .')

> 'I am the Alpha and the Omega, the *input* and the *outcome*, inputteth the Lord.'

inspire

Animate, enliven, exalt; give inspiration to; awaken a creative or spiritual impulse, as one might expect from a political leader or team leader or any other kind of leader. As, 'Come, Holy Ghost, our souls *inspire*.' 'Ronald McDonald never sells to children. He informs and *inspires* to magic and fun' (Shelley Rosen, McDonald's Representative, *Fed Up* movie).

> 'Shifting workplace behaviour to *inspire learning*: A journey to building a *learning culture*.'
>
> www98.griffith.edu.au

> 'How *Vibrant* Workplaces *Inspire* Employees to *Achieve*.'
>
> COMCARE National Conference, Melbourne, 9 September 2014

> '10 office styling tips that will *inspire* your employees.'
>
> www.businessinsider.com.au

interconnectedness

1. 'Everything connects.'
2. Sort of like, you know, it's amazing, weird.

> '"Spirit of Learning" encourages the integration of all dimensions of ourselves whilst understanding our essential *interconnectedness* with each other and our environment.'
>
> ReaLearning *Innovative Consultancy*

interface

(n) Relationship, relations, point of contact, where organisations meet, etc.
(v) To deal with, communicate with; talk to, dialogue with, write to, fax, ring up, email, tweet, have a drink with, meet (with), etc.

> 'Reporting to the director, the role *facilitates* the work of the *HR* functions, *continuously improves strategies* and procedures, whilst *interfacing* the internal and external environments.'
>
> Manager – administration, Monash University

> 'Results-oriented, *customer-centric* professional seeking to *leverage* experience with multiple *implementations* to help organisations exploit the benefits of Siebel and CRM. Adept at *facilitating* user sessions, defining new *processes*, documenting business requirements, evaluating *change* requests, *capturing* and *prioritising* bugs . . . Easily *interfaces* with users, executives, development *team*, and partners.'
>
> Resume

> 'You interfacin' to me?'
>
> *Taxi Driver*

in terms of

1. For.
2. About.
3. Nothing.

> 'I've been briefed, obviously, this morning on the latest developments that occurred yesterday and last night . . . and then in turn what's likely to happen today as well *in*

terms of weather events. Obviously the *event* that occurred yesterday, that moved across the state, that storm band that moved across the state was very, very intense; anybody who was in Melbourne last night, who experienced that, would understand the intensity of it . . . *In terms of* the SES response, there's been a very significant SES response . . . *In terms of* the affected areas, again, the SES will go through this, but there were 3800 calls as I've said . . . *In terms of* damage to government assets, there've been some damage to government assets across the state . . . *In terms of* insurance, the insurance industry has activated 24/7 service lines . . . Finally if I can, just a few other points: *in terms of* today, there are a number of public *events* that are on today.'

Victorian Premier John Brumby, 7 March 2010

'. . . Mr Baillieu promised to restore language programs in Victorian schools, lamenting what he said had been a "language decline" over the past decade. "I'd say we have dropped the ball *in terms of* opportunities in front of us," Mr Baillieu said.'

Age, 26 September 2011

'They're moving things around the different baskets, but it will be the end game *in terms of* putting numbers in square brackets *in terms of* tariff reductions, if there's significant requests on time frames *in terms of* phase-in.'

Mark Vaile, Deputy Prime Minister, *Canberra Times*, 6 December 2003

'For *in terms of lifestyle* we've got the germs of a ripper concept to think *in terms of*.'

Sir Les Patterson, *In Terms of My Natural Life*

'Much Ado *in terms of* Nothing.'

internal alignment

Aligned within (as one would like to be).

> 'Clarifying the unique *vision* and *value* of the organization and giving staff relevant and tangible *tools* for their *communication* purposes will assure *internal alignment* for Pact's *strategic* priorities.'
>
> www.pactworld.org

internal clients

Staff, students, patients, inmates, residents, etc.

> 'To influence and support our *internal clients* to *communicate* effectively . . .'
>
> City of Port Phillip, job description

> 'The benefits of Cleaner Production and Eco-efficiency will be promoted to *internal clients* (college staff and students) and to the wider *community*, including contractors that provide services to and for the College.'
>
> Action Plan for WA Central TAFE

> 'We will *delight* all our customers, both *internal* and external.'
>
> BAE Systems

internal resources

Staff, employees, *hires*, human capital, workers, people, men and women, folk, *internal clients*, etc.

> 'At *Go-Live*, the final transfer of knowledge and ownership will occur between the *consultants* and the *internal resources*.'
>
> SAP consultants

involuntary separations

Dismissals, sackings, layoffs, people let go, etc. As, 'These dismissals or "*involuntary separations*", as Defence calls them, were not necessarily related to abuse, a Defence spokesman said' (www.abc.net.au).

> 'Initial Jobless Claims (Wed) . . . "Initial claims have been below the 300k threshold for 11 consecutive weeks, a sign that *involuntary separations* have reached their nadir," Nomura economists said.'
>
> www.businessinsider.com.au

> 'Smithers, pack up your desk, you're *involuntarily separated*.'

irrefutable

1. Beyond doubt or dispute; watertight; incontrovertible; only the mischievous, treacherous or unreasoning could deny it.
2. Not necessarily so. As, '[It is] hard to imagine how anyone could doubt Iraq possesses weapons of mass destruction' (*Washington Post* in an editorial, headline '*Irrefutable*').

> 'The things that you're li'ble to read in the Bible aren't necessarily irrefutable.'

issue

1. The matter to be resolved. As, 'While it is hot, I'll put it to the *issue*' (Shakespeare).
2. Any argument, difficulty, injury, bone to pick, sore spot, difference of opinion (faith-based or rational),

complaint or *problem* existing between one party and another, or in one single entity. Whatever is going on between people or organisations, or within them; ditto machinery – as, 'We are currently experiencing an *issue*' (Foxtel message when screen went blank). 'We have an issue with one of the engines' (Qantas). One can have an *issue* with anyone or anything, including life itself. As, 'To be or not to be, that is the *issue*.' 'Lance's knee has been causing *issues* . . .' (A football coach. The *issues* have caused Lance to retire).

> 'It's a very important *issue*. I know how important an *issue* it is. It's not the only important *issue* and I've got to say as far as an incoming Coalition government is concerned, the priority will be on things like reducing cost-of-living pressure and increasing job security.'
>
> Tony Abbott on the same sex marriage *issue*

> 'Let me not to the marriage of true minds admit *issues*.'
>
> Shakespeare

iteration

1. What is said or performed again. What repeats.
2. Mathematics – an algorithmic technique. In computer science, to do again with a different value, often in sequence. Hence the 'ability to *iterate* on an idea' is a required skill among software engineers.
3. Business (especially closed loop *marketing*) – several can create a *time crunch*. As, 'If several *iterations* were required, the cycle could create a time crunch' (DM Review).

> '*Iteration* drives emergence.'
>
> Sigma Consulting Group

'Partnering for Profit: Creating *Value* from *Internal Business Alignment*

Recently, organizations have *focused* more intently on locking the next *iteration* of procurement *value*, beyond the "*low-hanging" fruit*.'

Good Procurement Guide: Launch & Creating Value from Internal Business Alignment Workshop, Government Reform Commission

'So rather than coming up with a product idea and launching one big thing, it's about testing – it's very *iterative* . . .'

Australian Financial Review, 9 April 2014

'Repeat. Again and again. Reiterate. Practice makes perfect. If you want to be a better writer but, like me, you know you're not actually great at it, I suggest you try *iterating* a short piece of work, over and over. How many *iterations*?'

C. G. Gray, blog

'The *iteration* that hath been, it is the *iteration* that shall be.'

Ecclesiastes, King James *iteration*

J

job seeker

1. An unemployed person. A person who has experienced an involuntary career *event*. A *churned* person. A *client* of the Department of Human Services. A person on the dole. One who has 'entered into a Job Plan', has met his or her mutual obligation requirements and not 'incurred a failure' in this regard.
2. A *client* earning $260 per week.

> 'Job seeker surge pushes jobless rate up.'
>
> news.com.au

joint priority effect list (JPEL)

A 'kill or capture' target list in Afghanistan.

> 'We also can see the behavior of Task force 373, a Special Forces "kill or capture" squad, who pursue the *Joint Priority Effect List (JPEL)*, an euphemism for the U.S. assassination list in Afghanistan. There are many events associated with them, one resulted in the death of seven children and others resulted in the deaths of a number of other innocents. You can also see how people get on the *JPEL* list; they seemed "nominated" by regional governors in Afghanistan, or by intelligence authorities, often with, it appears, little evidence, and of course no additional judicial review.'
>
> Julian Assange, WikiLeaks Press, 25 July 2011

journey

1. Expedition, trip, trek, tour, outing, A–B, etc.
2. Life.
3. A customer's experience.

'In the continuation of this *journey*, the Conference aim is to *address* the need to identify what has been the *impact* of getting research right?'

'Optimising *Impact*' Health Conference 2006

'Knowing the *customer journey* across the sales cycle is a living map on how to use optimized content for awareness, interest, consideration, purchase, retention and advocacy.'

Lee Odden, Top Rank Online Marketing

'As John Maxwell states in his wonderful book, *The Success Journey*, life is a *journey*, not a series of meaningless destinations. My *journey* is dedicated to helping others build *authentic* relationships that stand the tests of time and change.'

Byrd Baggett, author, motivator, etc.

'The *journey* of a thousand miles must begin with a single step in the *Customer Life Cycle*.'

Lao Tzu

K

key

1. (n) Something to open a lock; a means of access or control; pitch or tonality, etc.
2. (adj) Initiatives, decisions, inputs, outputs, outcomes, focus, issues, players, priorities, stakeholders, measures, assumptions, indicators, etc. are *key* whenever they are not *core*. (As in, 'There are two *key issues going forwards*.') Crucial, critical, vital, decisive, necessary, indispensable, influential, dominant, all-pervading, principal, main, essential, splendid, primary, most important, substantial, significant, crucial, *colourful*, educative, noteworthy, effective, productive, popular, etc. Chief, foremost, paramount, pre-eminent, etc. Of consequence, etc. *Core*.

> 'The hard working women and men of Australian small business were delivered surety to make the most of the Government's Jobs and Small Business package today with *key* measures passing through the Parliament.'
>
> Joe Hockey, 15 June 2015

> 'To stay informed of the views and expectations of *key stakeholders* and interested *communities*, the department has formed *key partnerships* with interested communities and *accountabilities*.'
>
> New South Wales Department for Women

> 'Moving from 29 *indicators*, the new SMAF has one *strategic* and one desired *outcome* and 12 *key indicators*.'
>
> Public service commission, Canada

key deliverable

The sort of *deliverable* on which much depends.

> 'Examining new *performance management*/measurement models that will be emerging to change the *key deliverables* of the finance professional in a new technology world.'
>
> Conference brochure

> 'Another *key deliverable* in the establishment of the Smart Water Fund was to provide a *platform* for specific research and *development* into the *key challenges* facing the Victorian water industry.'
>
> The Smart Water Fund

> 'So Moses went down unto the people,
> and spoke unto them *key deliverables*.'

key doors

Doors of some kind, probably metaphorical.

> 'In the wholesale *channel*, Burberry *exited doors* not *aligned* with *brand* status and invested in presentation through both *enhanced* assortments and *dedicated*, *customised* real estate in *key doors*.'
>
> Lucy Kellaway quoting Burberry CEO, *Irish Times*, 9 July 2014

key enabler

1. Locksmith or burglar.
2. One who is able in a *key* way. A useful person or thing. A very useful person. As in, 'Having X being able to focus on these matters in particular is a bonus for the School and he will be a *key enabler* of our IT *strategy implementation* in addition to providing strong support for the IT Manager . . .' (from a Melbourne school).

Also a *strategy*, viz.: 'Gatekeeper is the Australian Government's *strategy* for the use of Public *Key* Infrastructure (PKI) as a *key enabler* for the *delivery* of online government services' (www.finance.gov.au/policy-guides).

Or anything else that helps, as in: 'However, there may be a way for government CIOs to *leverage* a crisis to reposition IT as a *key enabler* rather than just a drain on the budget' (www.cio.com.au).

> 'The position will be a *key enabler* in realising the "Culture & Capability" *change* pillar of our *Customer-Centric Transformation*.'

> 'Come, follow me, and I will make you *key enablers* of men.'
>
> *Matthew* 4:19

key indicators

Signs, markers, measures – *key* ones.

> 'Toby's Individual Student Profile shows that he is *achieving* all the *key indicators* of Phase B on the Writing Developmental Continuum. He is also mapped as *achieving* Writing *key indicators* C1, C2, C3, C4 and C5. Although Toby is not yet operating in Phase C, he will not need to undertake the Writing validation task because he is already achieving both C2 and C5, which are part of the validation sub-set of *indicators* for Writing.' (i.e. Toby does not write well, but he is improving.)
>
> Sample student report, Queensland Studies Authority

key performance indicator (KPI)

Quantifiable measures of an organisation's success, e.g., a business might agree that turnover is a *KPI*; a school that the number of students graduating is the measure; a poultry farm, the number of birds killed and dressed; a hospital, the number of patients sent home in better health than they were enjoying when admitted. As, 'The total discharge compliance score is based on the number of medical records for which all four *key performance indicators* are complied with. For some patients, e.g. same day patients, they will only be able to comply with a maximum of 2 PI's. Where an *indicator* is determined to be "not applicable" then, for the purposes of the audit, it will be deemed to having [sic] *achieved* compliance. In all cases, if compliance were *achieved* to all relevant *indicators*, then that would mean that the Total Discharge Compliance Score is *achieved*' (i.e. You can go home tomorrow) (Victorian Department of Human Services).

> 'At Microsoft's CEO summit in May, the software giant's own CEO, Steve Ballmer, spoke passionately about the importance of having "digital dashboards": real-time desktop displays of *key performance indicators (KPIs)* that show critical business ratios such as profit per sales employee per week, customer satisfaction in dispute resolution and the status of outstanding issues with major suppliers.'
>
> www.cio.com.au

key stakeholders

Shareholders, staff, *customers*. *Key* people holding stakes. Hierarchies within these groups. People responsible for *key stakeholders* come from *stakeholder relations*.

> 'Reporting directly to the Head of Learning Australia you will present true consulting expertise across specific *internal client* groups. Working closely with these *key stakeholders*, you will provide solution *leadership* management to

ensure the *achievement* of agreed *strategic* and business objectives between Learning and the business. Building effective and constructive relationships you will *pro-actively engage* and advise the business to *achieve quality learning outcomes*.'

Job advertisement, www.seek.com

knowledge management (KM)

1. Managing an organisation's intellectual capital; rounding up (*harvesting*), *capturing* and sharing the skills and experience of its employees to increase productivity and innovation.
2. A common species of *consultant* – *knowledge* managers.
3. Virus.

'The Discovery and Re-Discovery of Knowledge. *Knowledge Management* is making a resurgence in all areas. Organisations are realising that they must retain the knowledge not just from retiring baby boomers, but also from Gen Y and Millennials, who tend to move organisations with more frequency than past generations. These factors brings [sic] a reinvention of *Knowledge Management* as new *processes* and *strategies* for *collaboration* and learning are *developed* using *enhanced* and adapted *KM* practices – giving organisations the opportunity to reap real benefits.'

kmaustralia

'Here's how we like to pretend *knowledge management* got started: Analysts, *consultants* and managers noticed that there was this really important type of information that was going unmanaged. So we called it "*knowledge*" and set about managing it.'

Dr Dave Weinberger, Harvard University

knowledge officer (chief)

1. Officer chiefly of knowledge.
2. Officer of chief knowledge.
3. Official knowledge chief.

> '*Chief Knowledge Officer*. The Australian Tax Office (ATO) employs around 20,000 people across the country, and manages in excess of 11 million *customers* through its nationwide network of offices and *call centres* . . . In essence, this represents an outstanding opportunity to create and build a *holistic knowledge management* function in one of Australia's significant, *customer focused* organisations.'
>
> Job advertisement, ATO

> 'CKOs have the responsibility for an organization's most valuable asset – its knowledge. And leveraging that intellectual capital is no easy task. To be successful in this type of role, a CKO needs to have a strategic mindset, leadership qualities [and] be able to advocate KM and motivate employees.'
>
> Helbling & Associates Inc.

knowledge sharing

Sharing knowledge – what else would it be? Essential to human survival, therefore essential to your business. As, 'Sharing knowledge has helped mankind survive and evolve into the intelligent and productive species he is today. In the animal kingdom and indeed in business, *knowledge sharing* can make the difference between survival and extinction' (Soccerwidow).

Something you do on a sort of *cultural journey* collaboration *workshop* thing. As: 'As an example of the type of support we provide, scheduled the third week of May is a *knowledge sharing* and collaboration *workshop* with 45 senior, like minded, executives from across the organisation coming together to explore and set the direction for the *cultural journey* the organisation will go through to support the *knowledge sharing agenda*' (Efficiency Quality Service newsletter, May 2011).

L

ladders off

> 'Citi's audio brand was composed especially for Citi and *ladders off* our purpose of "Driving Success".'
>
> Citibank

language

A headlock. 'Management language is about two things: making yourself look powerful, and making yourself look efficient. It's a weapon in the fight all UMs have to fight, every hour of every day. The *language* you use is the headlock by which you subdue your staff' (neurotaylor.com). C.f. Caliban:

> 'You taught me *language*, and my profit on't/Is I know how to curse./The red plague rid you
> For learning me your *language*!'
>
> *The Tempest*

leadership behaviours

Behaviours that get people to follow – e.g., force of argument or personality, charisma, empathy, personal example, strength of idea, terror, etc; desperate plight or weak-mindedness of followers. Whatever made Moses, Genghis Khan, Napoleon, Lenin, Gandhi, L. Ron Hubbard, etc., great leaders. Whatever gets your employees to work harder and more productively. As, 'Top Nine *Leadership Behaviours* That *Drive* Employee *Commitment*', e.g. 'Walk the talk', 'strategic perspective', 'driving for results', etc. (Zenger Folkman – 'Extraordinary Performance. Delivered').

leadership initiative

Doing something.

> 'Creating McDonald's Animal Welfare Council – the industry's first independent board of academic and animal protection experts. The Council has led to additional *leadership initiatives* for the well-being of cattle, poultry and hogs.'
>
> McDonald's Corporate Social Responsibility

> 'About the Advancing Leadership Initiative Program
> The Advancing Leadership initiative is a stream of ACELG's Governance and Strategic Leadership program area aimed at broadening leadership capacity and development opportunity for "aspiring" professionals working within Australian Local Government.'
>
> Australian Centre of Excellence for Local Government

> 'Come now therefore, and I will send thee unto Pharaoh, that thou mayest take additional *leadership initiatives.*'

leading edge

Cutting edge. The technology frontier. Nothing quite like it in the history of the world.

> 'We are expert coaches, trainers and *facilitators*, who *achieve* results for our *clients* by the *consistent* application of universal and timeless principles, combined with the use of *leading edge* learning technologies.'
>
> Wilfred Jarvis Institute

Lean

1. The kind derived from the Toyota Production System that, following none of the management handbooks, manages sustained growth by '*aligning customer* satisfaction with employee satisfaction, and offering *innovative products* or services profitably whilst minimizing unnecessary over-costs to *customers*, suppliers and the environment' (Wikipedia).
2. The kind that is the opposite of (1), but rather a form of Taylorism sometimes known as 'corporate *lean*'.
3. Another goldmine for *consultants*. *Six Sigma* is a descendant of *Lean*.

> 'Having an army of *Lean* "black-belts" descend on our hospitals might make for good news for senior managers who are under pressure. It might also improve some patient *outcomes*, and lead to local cost savings. However, it is doubtful that championing *Lean* will save the NHS £2 billion a year. The savings, if they do materialise, are likely to be modest. And they will likely be burdened by costs such as additional *change* fatigue, conflicts between admin and clinical staff – and of course the bill to pay for all the *Lean* gurus and their Kaizen blitz.'
>
> Andre Spicer, The Conversation, 11 November 2014

learning

1. Present participle of learn.
2. Lesson. What has been learned (sort of). As, 'We are sharing the *learnings* from the Deepwater Horizon accident to help *enhance* the capabilities needed to help prevent this type of accident from happening again' (BP Spokesman).

'We would be foolish not to pick up the *learnings* of this and take it to the next generation of how we deal with these.'

Victorian Fire Services Commissioner, 11 March 2014

Some *learnings* are *key*. As, 'The Postgraduate Certificate delivers *key learning* via a carefully selected suite of three *core* units, providing the foundation *learning* required to succeed in today's *challenging business environment*' (Macquarie Graduate School of Management). C.f. 'I shall the effect of this *key learning* keep/As watchman to my heart.' *Hamlet*

'I have learned my *learning*, Dad, and I won't do it again.'

learning event

1. A day in school; piano lesson; trip to the museum; clip over the ear; etc.
2. The following: '. . . a *learning event* is defined as: A learning, training or development activity that has been completed via attendance at a workshop, course or conference or via e-learning, a coaching or mentoring session or a team "away day" or half day etc. (of at least 2 hours duration). In the case of e-learning this may be a cumulative total.' (Note: . . . staff are entitled and expected to undertake a minimum of 3 *learning events* per annum.)

'The degree to which UCL staff meet its target for training take up is a *Key Performance Indicator* (KPI) and the percentage of managers undertaking *management development* activity each year is reported as a *KPI* to UCL's *Human Resources* Policy Committee (HRPC) and to UCL Council.

The learning/training records of staff are *captured* via UCL's *Learning Event Recording System*.'

www.ucl.ac.uk

'Business and Arts meet in the middle at creative *learning event.*'

UNSW Business School

learning program

Program that needs clarifying. As:

'Element 1: Define parameters of the *learning program*

Performance Criteria for Element 1:

1.1. Clarify purpose and type of *learning program* with *key stakeholders*

1.2. Access and confirm the competency standards and other training specifications on which to base the *learning program* . . .'

From the Certificate IV in Training and Assessment

less than lethal

Undeadly.

'Tasers provide one in a range of *less-than-lethal* options.'

NSW Minister for Police

level playing field

C.f. 'Bigfoot Spotted In Yellowstone Park.'

leverage

Advantage, bargaining chip, whatever gives power over others. A company might *leverage* its *brand*, reputation, assets (including human capital) – anything. To succeed in business one might *leverage* intelligence, experience, scandalous rumours, sexual allure, sense of humour, ability at karaoke, golf, etc.

'I *implemented* the development and *enhancement* to the functionality of the existing geographic information and mapping systems by *leveraging* off opportunities within interagency initiatives.'

Job application

'Based on the derivative side of its books, Long Term Capital had an astoundingly high debt-to-capital ratio. "The off-balance sheet *leverage* was 100 to 1 or 200 to 1 – I don't know how to calculate it," Peter Fisher, a senior Fed official, told Greenspan and other Fed governors at a Sept. 29, 1998, meeting.'

Washington Post, 15 October 2008

'In the language we were all then coming to learn: Nadya had *leveraged* her disability payments into six babies, collateralized them (as a state liability likely to pay revenues for years to come), and then quite brilliantly *leveraged* those six babies into eight more.'

Mark Greif on Nadya Suleman, the Octomom,
n+1 Spring 2010

'Australia is really good at *leveraging* all its ethnic communities to create an Australian way of life. I think there is a fantastic can-do spirit and a very healthy level of the entrepreneurial.'

Tyler Brule, *Belle*, July–August 2004

'For what is a man profited, if he shall gain the whole world by *leveraging* his own soul.'

lifestyle

1. A *marketing* term for Life. As, 'In the midst of *lifestyle* we are in death' – hence *Lifestyle* Funerals, Geelong, Victoria. ('He had a short *lifestyle* but a happy one.') Something to be segmented and targeted. Aspirational life.
2. Anything that occurs on a patio.
3. Something to which one has a *commitment*, even a passionate commitment. Enhanced *lifestyle*, etc.
4. 'Mode of living as identified by a person's activities, interests and opinions (AIO)' (Marketing textbook definition). 'Personality and self-concept are reflected in lifestyle' (Marketing textbook).

> 'We will stand up for the Australian families in all conscience we cannot, we cannot support this unfair Budget and its attack on the wallets and *lifestyles* of Australian families.'
>
> Bill Shorten, 12 June 2014

> 'The love for beautiful things, the knowledge of the functional and technical aspects of the product, the belief that domestic life is an individual space to conquer so that freedom of choice can truly nourish, in short, the determination to empower an authentic *life style*, unconditioned and untainted by consumerism, is the mission and goal of Legnoart.'
>
> On a box containing a set of cheese knives

> 'Creating a *framework* that respects the rights and needs of people who seek to become Australians, to enjoy the *lifestyle* we largely take for granted, while preserving that *lifestyle* competitively for our own citizens, is perhaps one of the most perplexing *issues* we face as a nation.'
>
> Katter's Australian Party

'Greater love hath no man than this; that he lay down his *lifestyle* for his friends.'

'. . . The Resurrection of the body. And the *lifestyle* everlasting.
Amen.'

lifestyle choice

1. Selection of one brand over another.
2. Selection of Australia over tyranny, persecution, death, famine, etc.

'What we can't do is endlessly subsidise *lifestyle choices* if those *lifestyle choices* are not conducive to the kind of full participation in Australian society that everyone should have'.

Tony Abbott, 10 March 2015

'In the main, people who have sought to come to Australia and make asylum claims do not come from a situation of persecution; they come from a situation of safety and security . . . They may not be able to go back to their country of origin but they are making a *lifestyle choice*.'

Philip Ruddock, January 2002

lifestyle outcome

'Two In One For A Successful *Lifestyle Outcome*.'

Real estate advert

'Decisions and Implementation

In preparation for our third meeting we will . . . Prepare your *Lifestyle Outcome* Report.'

www.abetterlife.net.au

'The index that measures change in the quality *lifestyle outcome* (pictured below) shows the composite average of the individual indicators.'

www.gpiwellingtonregion.govt.nz

' "It's the whole idea of shopping as an experience, catering to the customer and creating a *lifestyle outcome*," Imperiale said, adding, "margins right now in the women's shoe department are better than they've ever been in history." '

www.jsonline.com

lifters and leaners

Lifters. People of enterprise and energy who 'lift' themselves and take the country with them, e.g. Joe Hockey. As, 'We are a nation of *lifters, not leaners*' (May 2014). The government must 'reward the *lifters* and discourage the *leaners*'. People with successful *lifestyle outcomes*.

Leaners. Bludgers, sluggards, parasites, 'the caterpillars of the commonwealth, which I have sworn to weed and pluck away' (Shakespeare). People who want something for nothing, e.g. Oliver Twist – 'Please sir, I want some more.' People with unsuccessful *lifestyle outcomes*.

'Joe Hockey had a Mitt Romney moment in Australian politics where he says that half of the Australians who are receiving payments from the Government, support from the Government, he very clearly accused them of being the *leaners*, not the *lifters*.'

Bill Shorten, 12 June 2014

light up the strategy

> 'Microsoft's *strategy* is *focused* on *productivity* and our desire to help *people* "do more". As the Microsoft Devices Group, our role is to *light up this strategy* for *people* . . . We expect these *changes* to have an impact to our *team* structure . . . We plan to *right-size* our manufacturing operations to align to the new *strategy* and take advantage of integration *opportunities* . . . We plan that this would result in an estimated reduction of 12,500 factory direct and professional employees over the next year.'
>
> Stephen Elop's email to employees, 17 July 2014

live (the brand/culture, etc.)

A way of life.

> 'In today's marketplace, cultural intelligence exists when a company trusts itself enough to *live the promise of its culture* in how its *brands communicate* with its audience and consistently *delivers* on that promise in the recruitment, retention and *development* of its employees.'
>
> Glenn Lopis, *Forbes*, 9 December 2011

long pole in the tent

The difficult part of the project.

> 'We're really talking about the hardening, about the miniaturization sciences involved in creating the nuclear detonation. That's not the *long pole in the tent*. The *long pole in the tent* is the fissile material.'
>
> Former Director of US National Intelligence
> General Michael Hayden, 21 November 2014

'"That's going to be the *long pole in the tent*, but we always knew that," Bezos said. "The FAA has their hands full trying to figure out how to regulate drones."'

www.cbsnews.com

'BOLTON: He is saying we have been sold out. The Americans have given the Iranians everything they have wanted. They have given them more political legitimacy. They've essentially legitimized their uranium enrichment program, which whatever constraint you want to put on it is *the long pole in the tent* for a would-be nuclear proliferator.'

www.foxnews.com

low-hanging fruit

Easy pickings. Gains made without much *efforting*. Even *misaligned* companies can pick them. Mad if you don't take them, but there's a whole new world up higher. (Also any easy sexual conquest. Gonads. Other.)

'Partnering for Profit: Creating *Value* from *Internal Business Alignment*.

Recently, organizations have *focused* more intently on locking the next *iteration* of procurement value, beyond the "*low-hanging' fruit*".'

From the Good Procurement Guide: Launch & Creating *Value* from *Internal* Business *Alignment Workshop*, run by the Government Reform Commission'

'"At the same time, it would also provide State Governments with additional funds to build more and better infrastructure and provide services for communities – all without introducing a new tax – so this type of reform should be low hanging fruit that COAG could safely pick," he said.'

Hinchinbrook MP, Andrew Cripps

low key

Low pitch. Discussions and meetings which are informal, discursive, friendly and on which nothing much depends are described as *low key*. Meetings on which much depends, or at which threats are made, are not so commonly called *high key*, and *mid key* meetings are unknown.

'A series of informal *low key* meetings for regional industry leaders, government officers and industry organisation managers to exchange information, develop *strategic* alliances and discuss regional *strategic issues* in a no recourse, non-threatening environment.'

Sunraysia Mallee Economic Development Board

main game

1. The most important game, match of the day.
2. The most important element in the mix. Where it's at. What it's *about*. When you boil it down, *at the end of the day*. What the *bottom line* is. That on which all else depends, and to which all else is like unto a feather in a gale. In the 1980s the *main game* was the economy. Survival is another one. God, getting a male heir, war, starvation and disease have also been *main games*, and in some places remain so. Some would say climate change is the *main game* at present, but others say it is *absolute crap*. Getting elected is the main game in politics, not that it's a *popularity contest*.

> 'On Adelaide radio station FIVEaa, Treasurer Joe Hockey said his priority was the budget, describing the iron ore issue as "not the *main game*".'

> 'The release of the *Productivity* Commission's draft report into climate adaptation at the end of last month could have been a spark that changed the debate in Australia. That's because it implicitly suggested that adapting to climate change – regardless of whether its origin is anthropogenic, "natural", or whatever – is now the *main game*.'
>
> IPA News, May 2012

make a difference

Internal clients' key input. What every team player wants to make. Corporate injunction to managers and employees, possibly borrowed from football coaches. To *add value*. More *efforting* to earn your keep. To do enough to survive the next round of job cuts. 'I'm here to make a difference.'

'If you want to be part of an exciting new opportunity to *make a difference* and excel in an environment that rewards results, initiative and hard work and practices *meritocracy*, then we want to talk to you. Join us at Evolution Realty.'

www.evolutionrealty.com.au

'These *strategic* themes will enable Synergy to realise its *vision*: By 2009 we will *transform* Synergy into a brilliantly successful retailer. The skills, experience and *passion* of *our people* will make Synergy the *brand* of choice in a highly competitive energy market . . . We will *make a difference* in our community by *delivering* on our environmental and social *commitments*.'

Synergy

manage out

Dismiss a proportion of employees; cull, let go. Application of performance reviews or *anytime feedback tool*. 'Purposeful Darwinism' (Amazon employee).

'An Amazon spokesman previously confirmed that the company seeks to *manage out* a certain percentage of its workforce every year.'

map / mapping

Visually *mapping* a production path from 'door to door'. A *Lean strategy*. A job for a *consultant*. Or a teacher – even one in a remote school.

'The EsseNTial *Learnings* are organised into the Inner Learner, Creative Learner, Collaborative Learner, and Constructive Learner domains. Each domain has a set of culminating *outcomes* and *developmental indicators* to help *map* a learner's progress through the *Key Growth* Points and Bands.'

Northern Territory – hence EsseNTial, get it? – Curriculum Framework

'Read more about how the Kaizen Institute has helped *customers* use *Value Stream Mapping* to identify muda in their Current State and design a Future State that *focuses* on *Adding Value* for the *customer.*'

Kaizen Institute

'The Rich Task to Essential Learnings Mapper (Version 2): A computer-based tool for mapping the alignment of Rich Tasks and the draft Essential Learnings. The mapper was developed as a pragmatic response to the need for teachers to demonstrate how their enactments of the Rich Tasks, Blueprint tasks or school-developed tasks satisfy systemic requirements under the QCAR framework.'

Queensland Department of Education, Training and the Arts

marathon not a sprint

It's not easy. No quick fixes. Won't be solved overnight. *Scoping*, etc. required. Probably nothing will ever come of it. Don't blame me/us.

'As I've said before, this is a *marathon, it's not a sprint.*'

Joe Hockey, Treasurer, ABC, 16 July 2014

'. . . *it's a marathon not a sprint* and we are very *focused* on doing what is right over the medium and long term for the nation.'

Joe Hockey, Treasurer, *Sydney Morning Herald*, 17 July 2014

'Well, it was always going to be *a marathon, not a sprint*.'

Mathias Cormann, Minister for Finance, ABC, 19 August 2014

'As my good friend and colleague Mathias Cormann often says, "*It is a marathon, not a sprint*".'

Joe Hockey, Treasurer, AFR, 25 August 2014

'Senator Cormann says pursuing important economic reform is a "*marathon, not a sprint*".'

Sky News, 12 April 2015

market failure

Inefficient allocation of resources in markets in equilibrium. Where the pursuit of private interest is not in the public interest, especially if the public is subsidising the private; e.g, climate change, 'the greatest market failure in human history' (Nicholas Stern, chief economist World Bank). As, 'Greenhouse gas emissions are a classic externality, where everyone on earth subsidizes oil companies and consumers of fossil fuels. Fossil fuels are under-priced by $40 trillion, which is estimated to be about the cost future generations will pay for the damage' (Stan Sorscher, *Huffington Post*, 6 August 2015).

Inequitable distribution of wealth, private wealth/ public squalor, unemployment, industrial collapse, failure of essential services, social breakdown, etc. 'Invisible hand' not working. Tragedy of the Commons, etc.

market segmentation

Marketing's means of making certain that no one is left out; all human beings have a price, a *product*, a *need*, a *want*, a flow, a crack through which a *message* can be squeezed; ‘No man is an Island, entire of itself’, etc. As, ‘*Market segmentation* can be defined as the *process* of dividing a *market* into distinct subsets of *consumers* with common *needs* or characteristics and selecting one or more segments to *target* with a distinct *marketing* mix’ (Marketing textbook).

marketing

Indispensable, highly sophisticated drivel. Hidden persuasion. Making a silk purse from a sow’s ear; making the consumer think he’s a silk purse, not a sow’s ear. Manipulation of the baser instincts, greed among them but far from the only one: viz. Samuel Butler 1890, ‘All progress is based upon a universal innate desire on the part of every organism to live beyond its income.’

> 'Marketing is fundamentally about driving need for products and services.'
>
> Oracle's 'Customer Experience Reference Architecture'

> '[A]nybody who's occupied this office has to remember that success is determined by an intersection in policy and politics and that you can't be neglecting of *marketing* and P.R. and public opinion.'
>
> Barack Obama

massage the figures

To loosen them up, make them *flexible*, improve tone and appearance, get them working as they should, make them look and feel like new.

> 'Police *massaging of figures* on rape involved a practice whereby officers classed allegations as crime-related incidents rather than crimes, meaning the cases were not investigated properly.'
>
> *Guardian* UK, 20 November 2013

> 'Mr Tilbury accused police of trying to *massage the figures* in a bid to put a positive and unrealistic spin on the new Frontline 2020 policing model.'

Also, 'moving the goalposts': As, ' "I believe it is clear that WA Police have tried to covertly *move the goalposts* so that the statistics show the new operating model is working," Mr Tilbury said.' Moving the *KPIs* too: As, 'The dispatch and response times highlight that fact and the new *KPIs* (*Key Performance Indicators*) have conveniently made it look a lot better than it really is' (*Perth Now*, 31 May 2015).

mate, mateship

A men's cult in Australia.

> 'Socialism is just being *mates*.'
>
> William Lane, Australian utopian and mate

> 'They tramp in *mateship* side by side – The Protestant and Roman/They call no biped lord or sir/And touch their hat to no man!'
>
> Henry Lawson, etc.

> 'We value excellence as well as fairness, independence as dearly as *mateship*.'
>
> John Howard, Draft Preamble to the Australian Constitution

matrix management structure

Structure for a university.

> 'ITS last year introduced the *matrix management structure* and the service owner *model* (i.e. portfolio-based) to provide clear management *accountabilities*, an agile response to *change* and *greater focus* on *delivering* superior service and *value* to the University. The decision taken will facilitate this by giving service owners *greater* ability to influence required *business outcomes*, noting that service owners are ultimately *accountable* for *ensuring delivery* of service *changes* to their respective *client* groups. This decision, along with many other *changes* we are going through in ITS, is vitally important if we are to keep pace with our changing business environment and *evolving customer* needs.'
>
> In an email from the Executive Director IT and Chief Information Officer at a Melbourne University, April 2012

mentoring moment

One of these: 'A *mentoring moment* is an intersubjective coming to know in *dialogue* that *engages* unitary humans in a *transformative process*, confirming beliefs and *values* in creatively imagining and launching projects . . . The human-to-human *engagement* in a *mentoring moment* is unpredictable and everchanging as *value* priorities shift with different experiences and new understandings' (Nursing Science Quarterly).

meritocracy

A social and organisational arrangement based on the idea that merit, rather than inheritance, nepotism, brute force or rat cunning should determine status, power and wealth. It is very much in favour among the relative few who have status, power and wealth, warmed as they must be by the sense that their status and influence (and every dollar of their handsome incomes) have been well-earned. The powerless must live with the sense that they too have earned their status, a stigma that feudalism did not confer on the poor. Just why the meritocratic (and inevitably smug) elites would not 'harden into a new social class' (in the words of the inventor of the term) and consolidate their power through nepotism, cunning and various forms of inherited privilege is not very well explained.

> 'With the coming of the meritocracy, the now leaderless masses were partially disfranchised; as time has gone by, more and more of them have been disengaged, and disaffected to the extent of not even bothering to vote. They no longer have their own people to represent them.'
>
> Michael Young, author of *The Rise of the Meritocracy* (1958), *Guardian*, 29 June 2001

> 'It must be what Blair thinks. How else can he believe we can create a genuine *meritocracy* without nobbling private education – one of the main mechanisms by which the upper-middle classes retain their stranglehold on wealth and power? Blair's view must be that the current system is already not far off being *meritocratic* and that, generally speaking, the top positions are already populated by the most talented. The fact that these people invariably turn out to be privately educated upper-middle class folk is down to the fact that the lower orders are, generally speaking, congenitally less able.'
>
> Stephen Law blog, 20 May 2008

'The American system works because we believe in merit. This isn't an aristocracy, it's a *meritocracy*. By and large, talent and hard work are rewarded, whatever one's background happens to be.'

Yash Gupta, Johns Hopkins Carey Business School

'We must find ways to mobilize employees around the firm's *vision*, to then *achieve alignment* with, and *commitment* to those central *values*. We must develop a leadership mind-set that embraces *meritocracy* as a vital force in how we improve our firms, and lives.'

Omni Consulting Group

'[Amazon] Employees say that the Bezos ideal, a *meritocracy* in which people and ideas compete and the best win, where co-workers challenge one another "even when doing so is uncomfortable or exhausting", as the leadership principles note, has turned into a world of frequent combat.'

New York Times, 17 August 2015

'The Vanderbilts have asked us up for tea.
We'd go but they're not *meritocracy*.
No siree.'

message

1. *Communication*, note, memorandum. The meaning; the point. The sign within.
2. In marketing, including political marketing; the *story*, *takeout*, grab, line, *dog whistle*, underlying idea or theme, slogan, catchphrase, what they take away with them, that with which voters must be beaten senseless. *Messages* are verbal and non-verbal. They must be delivered in ways that *ensure* they

impact and *engage* listeners. Politicians in particular must be always '*on message*', even if the effect is tedious, offensive and annoying. As with this mantra, '"stop the boats", "scrap the carbon tax", "get the budget back under control" and "build the roads of the 21st century"' (Tony Abbott).

> 'The successor to politics will be propaganda. Propaganda, not in the sense of a *message* or ideology, but as the *impact* of the whole technology of the times.'
>
> Marshall McLuhan

> 'The *team* began by "documenting some objectives and measures of success. We were there to *communicate messages*, to magnify the reach, to quickly correct misinformation, and to minimise reputational damage. There were *KPIs* that were set." This, said Whitelaw, was about "giving the team really clear reasons about why we are coming in here to do stuff, rather than just being able to coordinate in our activity".'
>
> Darren Whitelaw, Assistant Director, Strategic *Communication* and Protocol Branch, Department of Premier and Cabinet, www.themandarin.com.au

> 'Plain English *focuses* on the *message*. It uses only as many words as necessary and avoids jargon, unnecessary technical expressions and complex language. In other words, plain English is the opposite of gobbledegook and long-winded, confusing *communication* . . . Organisations need to use plain English for all their *communications* with *stakeholders*.'
>
> Department of Education, Employment and Workplace Relations: authors of 'Australia's Prosperity and Well Being – National Capability – Learning, Skills, Knowledge and 7 Goals and 24 Strategies'

'Modern audiences are sophisticated, educated, and saturated with *messages* so to *impact* them requires new speaking skills.'

Business Seminars Australia

'To be or not to be, but what is the *message*?'

metrics

1. Used to assess a *process*.
2. Used to track trading trends, efficiency, productivity, etc. As, '. . . an overarching confidence in the power of *metrics*, buoyed by his experience in the early 1990s at D. E. Shaw, a financial firm that overturned Wall Street convention by using algorithms to get the most out of every trade' (*New York Times*, 17 August 2015, on Jeff Bezos, Amazon CEO).
3. Used to measure business performance: As, 'the *metrics* indicate that performance improved by . . .'

'The SCOR (Supply Chain Operations Reference) model provides a set of *performance metrics* and supply chain practices where the supply chain performance is contingent on the maturity of supply chain practices.'

Professor Umit S. Bititci, University of Strathclyde

'Previous research and leading practices . . . provide *key* metrics that can improve workforce *productivity* and *performance*, they also enable their *HR* personnel to translate human capital data into *executable strategy*.'

Unlocking the DNA of the Adaptable Workforce: The Global Human Capital Study

'The CSIRO Strategic Plan for 2003–2007 outlines our organisation's goals, strategic objectives, targets and performance *metrics* for the next four year period. Focussing on delivery and execution, it is the second in a series of strategic plans that are guiding our vision for the future . . . Our goals will be achieved by our unremitting excellence in research, focussing on key national challenges and embracing global opportunities. We will deliver outcomes of true value and impact, unleashing our creative abilities. We are building a research enterprise with truly global connections and stature.'

CSIRO

Metric for Metric

Shakespeare

migrate

1. Move people
2. Move *issues*.
3. Move.

'To this end, the Project *team* have undertaken a detailed testing *strategy* that unfortunately resulted in some unexpected results on *key* components of the *HR* module, as such we determined that it was more *appropriate* to defer the project by two weeks and resolve some of the open *issues* in a development environment rather than *migrate* them into a production system and try to resolve them through a support period.'

SAP Upgrade and Improvements Project

'*Best-in-class* organizations are *migrating* towards a more *strategic mindset* by emphasizing deep *partnerships* with *internal customers* and suppliers.'

Good Procurement Guide, Government Reform Commission

'*Migrate*, baby, *migrate*.'

J. O'Keefe

millennials

People born c.1980–2000. Generation Y. Young people. Youngs. A marketing category. Prefer brands that are *authentic* and *artisanal*.

> 'But to put out products that do well with *millennials*, it helps to actually have a lot of them on staff.'
>
> Lucia Moses, *Digiday*

> 'We wanted to make sure there was a platform for *millennials* within Time Inc. to communicate across brands, across franchises, across age groups," said Rahn . . . We specifically wanted to streamline *communication* between *millennials* and *leadership* . . . They are regularly asked for their feedback on new products and services that are aimed at *millennial customers* or the company as a whole. *Millennial input* helped lead to new benefits options that let employees lower their healthcare costs by taking spin classes and wearing Fitbits, for example. In addition to traditional mentoring programs, the company is looking into *reverse mentoring*, where young employees mentor older ones.'
>
> Lucia Moses, *Digiday*

> '*Millennials* are the first digital natives; the first people to have their lives instantly, and constantly, chronicled online. And even if they grew up during a great recession, they have been inundated with information.'
>
> Tanya Dua, *Digiday*

See *early-onset nostalgia*, *authenticate*, *artisanal*.

millennials (entrepreneurial)

'Future value creators' whose value needs to be *unlocked*. People to be encouraged, propelled up the *talent pipeline*.

> 'Dow Chemical found that aggressively hiring *entrepreneurial millennials* was the fastest way to create more "short-cycle innovation" alongside the company's long-cycle R&D processes.'
>
> R. Charan, D. Barton and D. Carey, 'People Before Strategy', *Harvard Business Review*, July–August 2015

mindset

A set of assumptions from which escape is difficult. Mental inertia. Mental gridlock. The square outside of which one cannot, or is not allowed, to think. Belief, faith, ideology, mania. To be of a *mindset* is to be of a mind – to think or believe. There are right *mindsets* and wrong ones that need changing: As, '. . . changing *mindsets* and empowering people to lead and *impact* in every sphere of life' (Hillsong Church Mission Statement).

> '. . . ethical challenges come about because of a culture of indifference or a set of behaviours that model a "if only we had the time" managerial *mindset*.'
>
> Dr Attracta Lagan, National Director of Ethics and Sustainability Services, KPMG

> 'Sappi believes that a *strong leadership culture drives* collective *mind-sets* which is crucial for *executing* effectively our *strategic* priorities.'
>
> Sappi Europe

'The new Windies head coach . . . is advocating for a change in the *mindset* of the players which he said should be informed by the state of the game.'

www.jamaicaobserver.com

'*Mindset* Workshops take this thinking one step further. Designed to make change from the inside out, our workshops capture mindsets first to embed change in the long-term.'

mindset.com.au

'Changing *mindsets* is so very hard to do.'

Hal David and Burt Bacharach

mission

1. An errand or *goal*; that for which one goes or is sent forth, or which one imagines it is one's purpose to pursue. As in: 'She thinks catching butterflies is her *mission* in life.'
2. An organisation's statement of common purpose – a *mission statement*. That which, when enacted, *drives* the vision. As in: 'Thus the prerequisite for the success of a national *vision* is an active citizenry that identifies with and owns the *vision* and *mission*, and which sees itself as a central agent in the success of national *goals* – a nation that is *driven* by its *vision* and which in turn *drives* that vision through enacting the *mission*' (David Ntshabele, Director of Communications, Office of the President, South Africa). Note: while they are often conducted in the course of them, *missions* are not wars. As, 'I think strictly speaking it's best described as a *mission* rather than as a war' (Tony Abbott PM, 3AW, 16 September 2014, announcing 600 military personnel were being sent to the Middle East).

mission creep

Going further than the *mission* decrees, esp. in war or 'very *significant* counter-terrorist operation' (US Secretary of State, John Kerry); from a couple of dozen advisers and spies, to a couple of million military personnel, etc.

> 'Prime Minister Tony Abbott insists Australia's expanded *commitment* to Iraq does not represent "*mission creep*". "It's not *mission creep*," he said. "It's the successful execution of the original *mission*."'
>
> *Australian Financial Review*, 3 March 2015

mission statement

Vision statement. Statement of principles, *core values* and *key goals*. Company creed. Usually seen in the reception area, but becoming less common.

> 'Every business needs a purpose that says what it is and a *vision* that describes what it wants to be. This purpose and vision come together in the *mission statement*.'
>
> e-Business Plan tutorial

> 'Therefore, policies, *strategic initiatives* and operational plans will be put in place to ensure that a *quality* service, relevant to this *vision* and *mission statement*, are maintained.'
>
> James Cook University, chaplaincy

> '"If you're going to launch a space satellite or if you're going to revitalize downtown, you've got to have a plan," said Councilor Walt Skowron. "I don't really see a *mission statement*. I'm looking for a *mission statement*."'
>
> www.reporterherald.com

model

1. (n) Archetype; plan in miniature; exact copy, etc.
2. Substitute for something concrete or an effort to say what you mean. As, 'David Murray's financial system inquiry recommended against an up-front, or ex-ante, levy, saying there should be an ex-post *model* in which a levy would be imposed on the banks if the scheme were triggered by a failure and there were insufficient funds recovered through a bank's liquidation to recoup the government's costs' (*Australian Financial Review*, 12 April 2015).

> 'The QSA Grammar *Scope* and Sequence that accompanies the English Essentials and Standards is underpinned by a functional *model* of language, but foregrounds traditional grammar terminology.'
>
> Queensland Department of Education, Training and the Arts

> 'Offering communities enhanced outcomes in add*ressing sustainability issues* is an emergent collaborative *model* integrating *knowledge*, competencies and resources from *diverse* organisations – *multi-stakeholder partnerships* (*MSP*).'
>
> Commentary: *Sustainability and Innovation*, CSIRO

(v) 'We will be *modeling* various sensitivities [to?]determine the best *strategies* to *optimize* our *strong* originations forecast and *manage asset growth* and capital. In addition, we will *prioritize* the launch of new *growth initiatives*, as well as the timing of these investments in comparison to the revenue projections' (in a corporate memo from a US-owned Canadian company).

modernise

Make up to date, in keeping with progress and the general trend, including the trend toward somewhat higher prices. Harmonise your business with the modern world, including the terrible cost of things these days. Ease the pain felt by customers as they *transition* to modernity, including the cost of living there.

> 'The main themes were fairness and simplicity – we have these themes in our key objectives in *modernising* our price structures . . . A further move towards simplicity and fairness is our decision to *harmonise* the prices changed in the Northern and Central pricing zones . . . To ease price *transition* for our Northern *customers*, we propose to *harmonise* these charges over nine years . . .'
>
> Draft Water Plan, 2013–18, Coliban Water

monetise

Turn into money – for old rope, etc.

> 'Spotify wants to *monetize* your mood with ads based on your favorite playlists.'
>
> venturebeat.com

> '*Monetising* the Queensland arts and creative industry sectors. *Monetisation* is the driving force behind business start-up communities. *Monetisation* – regardless of the venture operating on a niche artistic or cultural business model – is a reasonable requirement of any "concept" that attracts government, angel or venture capital investment.'
>
> www.arts.qld.gov.au

move / moving forward

Not stationary, torpid or inert. Not just milling about. Going forward. Migrating forward. Transitioning forward. Forward ho! Forward! Onwards! Mush!

> 'Today I seek a mandate for the Australian people to *move Australia forward.*'
>
> Julia Gillard, PM, upon calling an election on 17 July 2010. She said 'moving forward' 36 times in a 31-minute press conference – possibly a record. ABC

> 'The *brand strategy moving forward* is about *mapping* a new approach to *design*, facilities and *communications* that reflect BAC's *goal* to *deliver* an airport that, among other things, has a distinct sense of place.'
>
> Brisbane Airport Corporation spokeswoman, *Courier-Mail*, 27 April 2013

> 'We would *move forward* in conformity with what was happening in the past.'
>
> Rick Santorum, US Republican politician

move on

Also move *forward*, *going forwards* – whatever suggests progress, especially away from something unpleasant or likely to cause feelings of guilt or embarrassment, or for which one may be held to account. Hence favoured by cads, con-men, carpetbaggers, politicians, priests and others on whom responsibility falls. As, Barack Obama decided not to pursue the torturers or the previous administration that sanctioned them, preferring to 'look to the future not the past'. Let's not dwell on the past, honey; let's not wallow in the fens of history; let's not waste public money setting up inquiries; let's not waste time arguing the toss about who said what and whether they meant it. You and I might want to have this debate, Alan, but I don't think the Australian people want to have it, Alan. I think they want to *move on*. In fact I know they do.

> 'I think the public wants to *move on*.'
>
> John Howard, PM, moving on from the 'children overboard affair' in the 2004 election, ABC

> 'JOURNALIST: Why did you use Comcars on your book tour?
>
> TONY ABBOTT: I think I've fully dealt with it. Time to move on . . . Let's move on. Let's move on.'
>
> *Sunshine Coast Daily*, 10 July 2013

> 'We are going to upgrade you with immediate effect. We are going to allow you to move on in order that you can you use your talents and skills more effectively and thus upgrade your career and opportunities.'
>
> www.ftd.de

> 'I'm through with you/ too bad you're blue
> I'm *movin' on*/ I'm *movin' on*.'
>
> Hank Snow/Ray Charles

move / push the needle

Improving. As, 'How Do You Push the Needle Forward on Transformational Mobility?'

> 'Our *focus* is on *moving the needle* for organizations *in terms of* business *outcomes* through our customised, tailored, open and coaching programs.'
>
> Mount Eliza Executive Education

> 'This *workshop* will introduce participants to the concept of complexity and complex adaptive systems as well as some emerging principles and practices of adaptive leadership and management aimed to improve the probabilities – but never guarantee – that people and organizations can *move the needle* on complex issues. Collective Impact 3.0 is about scaling collective impact and building the practice internationally.'
>
> www.csi.edu.au

> 'Applying Collective Impact to *Move the Needle*.'
>
> sacoss.org.au

moving target

1. Prey – tiger, deer, wallaby, etc.
2. Enemy soldier or agent, or enemy weapons – tanks, aircraft etc. Targets to be 'taken out'.
3. *Clients* or *customers*, including *valued* ones. As in, 'Since *Millennials* are *moving targets*, I wouldn't assume that what the experts have to say represents the last word when it comes to mounting an effective marketing campaign for *Millennials*' (Enterra Insights Blog).

multiculturalist

1. Advocate of cultural diversity and pluralism. Expanding 'the family of the nation' (Al Grassby).
2. Reverse racist, member of minority group, cultural or *moral relativist*, persecutor of the majority, the mainstream, the ordinary people. A politically correct person. Not on *Team Australia* (see *caffè latte*). As, '. . . Aborigines, *multiculturalists* and a host of other minority groups' (Pauline Hanson, 1996).

'The naïve . . proclaim *multiculturalism* as a triumph of tolerance when in fact it undermines the cultural values and cohesiveness that brings a nation together.'

Senator Cory Bernardi

'The Republican Party of Bush, Hastert, Frist, Rove, et al., is a *multiculturalist*, diversity-mongering, pro-immigration enemy of the interests of *ordinary Americans*.'

View from the Right Web Forum, September 2003

'I've shifted from being a critic to a supporter of *multiculturalism*, because it eventually dawned on me that migrants were coming to Australia not to change us but to join us.'

Tony Abbott, PM, September 2014

multi-stakeholder platform

More than one stakeholder on (or in) a platform.

'What we need is a *multi-stakeholder platform*.'

World Economic Forum chairman Klaus Schwab.
Jonathan Lynn, 'Jargon Hunting at Davos'

N

narrativity

1. The 'narrativeness' of a narrative or a piece of music or some other work.
2. An *empowering driver* in marketing.

> 'Through narrative practice we can enrich and explore the interpretative horizon of our situation and we can develop a more *authentic managerial language* that *empowers* us to face complexity and dilemmas as drivers of welfare *innovation*.'
>
> *Narrativity* in Organizations, Klaus Majgaard, 2012

> '*Narrativity* Corporate Story Consultancy'

needs

1. Whatever is required.
2. Whatever is desired.

> '*Marketing* is fundamentally about *driving need* for products and services.'
>
> From Oracle's 'Customer Experience Reference Architecture'

> 'What are the expressed information *needs*/wants of farmers as perceived by Intermediaries?'
>
> The Regional Institute Ltd, Key Evaluation Question

> 'Leave in for 1–5 minutes, according to your hair *needs*.'
>
> Hair conditioner instructions

> 'From each according to his needs, to each according to his desires.'
>
> Karl Marx

negative impact

Effect on public of sleeping people who are not members of it.

> 'Chief Inspector John Fish told the press that "the public rely on police to reduce the *negative impact* of rough sleepers".'
>
> Ally Fogg, *Guardian* UK, 30 May 2013

negative patient outcomes

Golden staph, erroneous amputation, bedsores, death, etc.

> 'This article concludes that nursing injury rates are linked to the nursing shortage and less nursing time at the bedside, both of which have been scientifically linked to *negative patient outcomes*.'
>
> www.ncbi.nlm.nih.gov

> 'One *negative patient outcome*, we wake eternally,
> And death shall be no more; Death, thou shalt die.'
>
> John Donne

negative stakeholders

An unwanted kind.

> 'Does the candidate have proficiency in managing *negative stakeholders impacting* her own workplace situation?'
>
> Ernst & Young

negative uplift

1. Stationary? As you were? Down, downwards, falling? Up – not?
2. Funding cut. As in: 'Savings in the secondary care sector are being driven for the most part by two levers – pay restraint imposed nationally and a reduction in the PBR tariff (achieved partly by redesign and partly by *negative uplift*)' (www.publications.parliament.uk).

networking

To exchange business cards, information, glances etc. Hobnobbing, socialising, fraternising, consorting. Seeking advantage and influence. Have a drink, take tea, dine with. Do what's necessary. (More if it's agreeable.)

> '2.50 pm. Coffee and *Networking*.'
>
> Governance seminar brochure

> 'I *networked* my arse off.'
>
> Participant in governance seminar

neuro linguistic programming (NLP)

1. Variety of *knowledge management* derived from Large Group Awareness Training (est, Landmark *Forum*, etc.).
2. A 'methodology' taught by *consultants* (in 21 days) to other *consultants* who teach it to business.
3. Brainwashing, mind games, thought control, etc. Hogwash, etc.

'*NLP*ers ask the question, "If another person can have fun playing with their pet spider, what can we learn about them that we could teach the phobic person so they can play with spiders, too?"'

www.nlpinfo.com

'A methodology which allows you to track how people are thinking, what they *value*, and how they make their decisions, and how this helps or hinders their *processes*.'

The Consultant's Consultant

nimble

1. Agile, deft, quick, balletic, like a mountain goat, etc.
2. Public servant.

'A *nimble* Commonwealth public sector can carefully manage its own costs, respond rapidly and *realign* its *resources* to *address* changing realities and priorities, to continually serve the Australian people better.'

www.finance.gov.au

non-continuing

Dejobbed senior executives. Senior executives handsomely compensated for not continuing.

'*Non-continuing* senior executives.'

Annual report

'Bob's partner is Ailsa, Jeff's *non-continuing* wife.'

non-core

1. The truth, heart, essence, innermost part – not. A non-binding vow.
2. Non-*key*.

> 'The fleet business was *non-core* to our plant hire division and reflects *management's* intention to *exit* our *non-core* operations.'
>
> CEO of Austrim Nylex

> '*Core* promises and *non-core* promises.'
>
> John Howard, PM

> 'You made a vow that you would ever be true,
> But somehow that vow was *non-core* to you.'
>
> Pat Boone

non-invitation

Banned, excluded, sent to Coventry, etc.

> 'A decision has been made that, at *this point in time*, periods of *non-invitation* will not be imposed by the Metropolitan West School Sport Board in relation to the use of compulsory swimwear.'
>
> Letter informing a schoolgirl that a ban on her taking part in inter-school competition had been overturned. *Courier-Mail*, 9 June 2011

O

objective setting

A *process.*

> 'The role of the Liaison Librarians *project team* is to: *Facilitate* the *objective-setting process*, work with those in similar roles to reach consensus on role-specific objectives and *KPIs*, obtain *buy-in* from *stakeholders* during the *planning process* by seeking *feedback*, reporting back to *stakeholders*, keep in mind the overall aim of the *objective-setting process*.'
>
> Internal memo, University of Sydney Library

offerings

What is offered: stocks and shares, slaughtered beasts, frankincense and myrrh, a T-Box. As, 'Telstra's decision to ditch its T-Box *offering* in favour of a new streaming device to rival Apple TV has led to warnings it could erode its part-owned pay-TV service Foxtel's customer base.'

> 'We have established a specialised unit called La Trobe Sport that will *drive* our vision to be the University of first choice for the study of, participation in, and partnering in sport in Australia . . . Our Sport Unit will work closely with all areas of the University to *enhance* the sport *offerings* and research *outcomes* that already exist, as well as build new courses to suit the changing sporting market.'
>
> La Trobe University

office

Delivery vehicle.

'*OFFICE* OF LEADERSHIP AND ORGANISATIONAL CULTURE

The *Office delivers* the University's *strategic* organisational and *leadership development* requirements. The Office will take *forward program* areas of *leadership*, management *development*, succession planning and equity *strategies* that will play a *significant* role in *delivering* the *strategic vision* of "*growth* and *sustainability*" for the University.'

Charles Darwin University

off-line

Discuss an *issue* outside the meeting. As, 'I think we should take that *issue off-line*, Jenny.'

offshored / offshorable

Sent *offshore*. Able to be sent *offshore*. Jobs done for lower wages and in worse conditions abroad. Cheap labour; child labour; slave labour – whatever labour *grows* the company, is good for the *bottom line*, leads to continuous improvement, etc.

'A similar analysis of any company's corporate centre would show that about a quarter of those positions are *offshorable* as well. So the savings can be enormous even if some operations are kept onshore for redundancy.'

American Banker, 3 July 2003

'Suncorp has made an accelerated multi-locational contemporary *offshoring strategy* capable of adding serious long-term *value* to its actual businesses, *customers* and share-holders *in terms of* cost, revenue and capital efficiency *outcomes*.'

Outsourcing adviser Sri Annaswamy, *Australian Financial Review*, 23 July 2013

omnibus variation

An anthology or collection of variations.

> 'The individual variations are being coordinated in an *omnibus variation* to streamline the Territory Plan Variation process.'
>
> Letter to residents about an information session from Manager, Community Engagement, Chief Minister, Treasury and Economic Development Directorate, ACT

onboarding

Preparing employees for their jobs.

> 'Expressions of Interest are now open for the positions of Employee Relations Officer and Recruitment and *Onboarding* Specialist.'
>
> From a University staff online newsletter, 22 May 2013

> 'If you are a new employee click here to access your introduction package and *onboarding* documentation.'
>
> www.bne.catholic.edu.au/bce-employment/new-employee-and-staff-benefits/Pages/New-Employee-Onboarding.aspx

ongoing

1. Going on. That of which we're in the midst. Time present. Time. Time continuing. Continuing *in terms of* the present moment. As in, 'You are asking me a question in the context of an *ongoing* investigation' (George W. Bush, 11 July 2005) – as opposed to a question in the context of something that has ended or not yet begun. Continuing, and

therefore beyond investigation, analysis, opinion or comment. Unresolved. It's not for me to say. These things are not for us to know.

2. A *time period* of indeterminate length. A lengthy *point in time*. Not an *appropriate* time. Proceeding through the immeasurable vastness of time. As long as a piece of string. A spin-doctor's special. As, 'There are *ongoing* security *challenges* that we face and Prime Minister Allawi is determined to address those *ongoing* security threats' (Scott McLellan).

> 'A: I appreciate the question. This is an *ongoing* investigation at this point. The president directed the White House to cooperate fully with the investigation, and as part of cooperating fully with the investigation, that means we're not going to be commenting on it while it is *ongoing*.
>
> Q: But Rove has apparently commented, through his lawyer, that he was definitely *involved*.
>
> A: You're asking me to comment on an *ongoing* investigation.
>
> Q: I'm saying, why did you stand there and say he was not involved?
>
> A: Again, while there is an *ongoing* investigation, I'm not going to be commenting on it . . .'
>
> Scott McLellan, 11 July 2005

> '. . . The difficulty for me in relation to these matters is I can't talk about *ongoing* activities in which our security agencies are *involved*.'
>
> Philip Ruddock, ABC, 8 June 2005

'*Ongoing* parallel qualitative work indicates that explicit consideration of personal values attached to potential *outcomes* challenges women's perceptions of the optimal decision and this may influence their resolve to achieve a vaginal birth.'

University of Bristol

'All will be revealed in the fullness of the *ongoing*.'

'The *ongoing* is on my side.'

'. . . Creeps in this petty pace from day to day to the last syllable of the *ongoing*.'

on message

In election campaigns you must stay *on message*, or people will not know what you stand for. You stand for what the people stand for, or at least what your *focus* groups stand for, so don't start talking about Plato's *Dialogues* or reciting Emily Dickinson. Don't mention anything that you can't tie to the 'ladder of opportunity', or '*leadership*' or 'security', whatever is judged to be the *key message*. And jobs. Jobs, fairness, and opportunity. Mention these until they're sick, until you can see their knees buckling or your own are giving way. And when that happens mention them again. Recite them one by one. And don't forget to say 'Australian'. And 'all Australians'. And 'access and equity'. And mention '*mateship*', mate. And jobs. And *growth*. But keep it simple. And don't get personal. Of course he's a 'lying rodent'. We know that, but the mob don't like us saying it. And it only confuses them. It's noise. It's off *message*.

on-pass

Passed on.

> 'The papers were often *on-passed* to students.'
>
> *Age*, 14 October 2011

on-sell

Selling on; selling – real estate, intellectual property, pork bellies, potatoes, underpants, hostages, etc.

> 'So criminal gangs according to security sources are taking people and then *on-selling* them to insurgents and terrorists.'
>
> ABC

> 'Death of an On-salesman' by Arthur Miller.

on track

Implemented by the due date; aligned with the schedule. No need to get it done before then.

> 'One year after presenting its *Vision* 2020, Siemens is *on track* with the *implementation* of its concept for the company's *strategic realignment*.'
>
> Siemens AG press release, May 2015

> 'Are we helping to *grow* the Australian economy, *build* prosperity, create jobs? We're *on track* to do that.'
>
> Joe Hockey, Hobart *Mercury*, 13 May 2015

> 'Federal Treasurer Joe Hockey has confirmed the government is *on track* to deliver a budget surplus by 2019–20, as forecast in the mid-year economic fiscal outlook.'
>
> Student News Network

See *implemented.*

on-water

On the sea or even a big lake. Comment will not be made about matters that occur in such places. C.f. *operational matters.*

> 'Q: What's become of that boat of asylum seekers?
>
> LT. GEN. ANGUS CAMPBELL: I will not comment further in relation to *on-water matters.*
>
> REPORTER: This business is of great public interest.
>
> CAMPBELL: I will not comment further in relation to *on-water matters.*
>
> REPORTER: Have they been . . .
>
> CAMPBELL: I will not comment further in relation to *on-water matters.*'
>
> ABC, 8 November 2013

> 'Q: Were the Australians the first to arrive on the scene?
>
> SCOTT MORRISON: Well, again, I'm not going to go into *on-water* operations of what other potential partners have been engaged with.
>
> Q: This is an issue of great public interest, and where the boat goes the plight of these people is part of that. Why can't you be more forthcoming?

SCOTT MORRISON: Because that would go to our conduct of *on-water* operations.'

Scott Morrison, Minister for Immigration

'Thank you, Madam Speaker. Commenting on *on-water operational matters* at sea would be to telegraph tactics employed by the government as to how these measures were handled.'

Scott Morrison, Minister for Immigration

open cut event

Something that happens in an open cut, specifically a fire in a brown coal open cut; but a dance party in an open cut, we must presume, would be also an *open cut event*.

'I've no doubt that this will be a catastrophic *event* that changes the way in which we deal with brown coal *open cut events*, and in particular those that are very close to communities . . .'

Victorian Fire Services Commissioner, 11 March 2014

operational matters

Matters not for discussion. Secret matters. 'On water' matters, for example, are operational matters. As, 'I'm just not going to comment on operational matters' (Tony Abbott, PM). Not sport for journalists (or voters). As, 'The public expects us to solve the problem, not to engage in sport for commentators' (Tony Abbott, PM).

'Q: What sort of assistance did you give them?

SCOTT MORRISON: Well, again, we're not going to go into the micro detail of these *operational matters*.'

'Look, in relation to any of the *operational matters*, I don't have any comment.'

Peter Dutton

'LEIGH SALES: So just to be clear, who is the leader and what is the focus on his capture?

KEVIN ANDREWS: I'm not going to go into *operational matters* obviously.

LEIGH SALES: Can you name the leader of IS?

KEVIN ANDREWS: I'm not going to go into *operational matters*.

LEIGH SALES: I don't think it's operational, I think it's a matter of public record . . . The specific person to whom I have been referring is Abu Bakr al-Baghdadi.'

ABC, 15 April 2015

See *on-water*.

optimising

1. Maximising. Making the most of.
2. Augmenting and *enhancing outcomes* for companies and individuals. Remedy for people with the wrong impression of themselves.

'"Lifewise International Pty Ltd. *Optimising* Personal Performance." Including "Practical *tools* for changing faulty self-perceptions, *achieving* life goals and improving general presence and image, *communication* and presentations."'

Lifewise International Pty Ltd

optionality

Degree to which an option is optional?

> 'So it just increases the options and the *optionality*.'
>
> Chief Financial Officer for Qantas, ABC, 28 August 2014

options (navigating)

1. A choice, the exercise of choice, that which is offered for choice.
2. The appearance of choice.
3. Balderdash.

> 'Nurofen pain-specific products provide easier navigation of pain relief *options* in the grocery environment for *consumers* who are experiencing a type of pain.'
>
> The makers of Nurofen, on the ACCC's report that at least four Nurofen products sold as formulations for specific ailments all contain the same active ingredient

> 'To not be, or not to be?'
>
> Hamlet

> 'The money, or the money?' 'The box, or the box?'
>
> Bob Dyer

ordinary Australians (concerns of)

1. Australians whose opinions are the *benchmark* of relevance and worth, including moral worth. If ordinary people are not concerned by injustice, or famine, or fire-blight in New Zealand apples, the media should not be concerned,

and people who are concerned are not *ordinary Australians* but likely members of an *elite*.
2. A rather patronising expression to describe not many Australians.

> 'I don't usually use the expression "*ordinary*" very often myself. I try and avoid using it, it sounds rather a patronising expression.'
>
> John Howard, March 1999

> 'PRIME MINISTER: And I think Australians, I don't like using the expression *ordinary* . . . I mean we are Australians.
>
> Q: How many *ordinary Australians* do we know – not many.
>
> PRIME MINISTER: No, that's right. We're Australians.'
>
> John Howard, radio interview, October 2000

> 'I mean, that is the sort of arrogant dismissal of the views of *ordinary Australians*, that many of them find disconcerting.'
>
> John Howard, November 1999

> '. . . to try and generate a momentum of hostility and concern about the *impact* of it on the lives of *ordinary Australians*.'
>
> John Howard, June 2000

> '. . . you suggest we are indifferent to the position of the *ordinary* worker.'
>
> John Howard, debate, 2001

> 'Coalition Government that has put more money, more disposal [sic] income, into the pockets of *ordinary Australian* workers.'
>
> John Howard, June 2001

'No *ordinary Australian* family wants a situation of enormous medical bills for a major illness for one of its members.'

John Howard, December 2003

'I've always believed that good economic management is about giving *ordinary Australians* the freedom and opportunity to live their lives as they wish.'

John Howard, July 2004

'And, I mean, I said to him, in all honesty – I forget what his name was – I said: I don't have an immediate answer to that, but I said: I feel for you and I understand it. And he said: look, I am just an *ordinary Australian* . . .'

John Howard, Press Club Address, October 1998

outcome

1. 'Natural result; consequence' (*American Heritage* Dictionary).
2. Result achieved after *targeting* and agreement.

A consequence of *inputs* and *outputs* and dependent on alignment. Elements of a *scenario*. Companies, government departments, education curricula and schoolrooms are *outcomes-based*.

'. . . ultimately we've got to get the right policy *outcome*, and the best place to start is with the best policy *outcome*.'

Joe Hockey, 30 March 2015

'In the recent evaluation by the Australian Council for Educational Research, school and community members reported that Direct Instruction was having a positive impact on student *outcomes*, but the researchers were not yet able to say whether or not the initiative has had an impact on student learning.'

The Conversation

'A *focus* on *outcome targets* without an emphasis on improved employment practices will not *deliver* support from men and will not result in *sustainable* changes in organisations to improve gender equity *outcomes*.'

www.eowa.gov.au

'In order to achieve the *Mission Statement*, procurement must be central to the Council's business and operational decisions from the point at which the public service *outcomes* the Council wishes to deliver are identified, through the lifecycle of the requirement and the review of the delivery of those outcomes following implementation.'

Highland Council Procurement Strategy

'I encourage our minds to shift to one word, *outcomes*. *Outcomes*, *outcomes*, *outcomes*. Long-term *outcomes*, state and federal *outcomes*, Labor and Liberal *outcomes*, for-profit and not-for-profit *outcomes*. Whatever does your biscuit, the key from here is *outcomes*.'

Rob Oakeshott

'You don't have to have a lot of *outcome* from it the next day, but one that ends up in a hospital and an ambulance you would expect to have an *outcome*.'

Dr Peter Larkins, AAP, 10 September 2015

'A Commissioning for *Outcomes* Statement is a written "story" of the *outcomes* the program is trying to achieve for *clients* and the broader community, and it sets out how that will be monitored to improve *outcomes* for clients.'

www.atdc.org.au

> 'We are such stuff/As dreams are made on; and our little life/Is rounded with an *outcome*.'
>
> Shakespeare, *The Tempest Event*

outcome – unanticipated adverse

1. 'Definition of *unanticipated adverse outcome* – Death, temporary and/or permanent disability requiring intervention' (Kaiser Permanente, 'Communicating *Unanticipated Adverse Outcomes*').
2. Being found liable.

> 'A Cautionary Note About Words
>
> While *unanticipated adverse outcomes* of care must be explained to the patient, there is no requirement to admit liability, assuming that there is any. Nonetheless, a patient may be inclined to suspect that an *outcome* that differs significantly from the anticipated *outcome* is the result of negligence and may attempt to probe the practitioner about fault.'

out of touch

1. To not understand the desires or concerns of *ordinary Australians*; or some powerful constituency such as farmers or people wanting to buy a house for the first time. To understand but not care. To neither understand nor care.
2. To imagine that a principle or your own judgement should prevail over popular prejudice. Unpopular. Often 'arrogant and *out of touch*'.

> 'An exclusive 7News ReachTEL poll has found more than half of all Australians believe Treasurer Joe Hockey is "*out of touch*".'
>
> 22 August 2014

'Treasurer Joe Hockey says he's not fazed by claims he is *out of touch* for telling young Australians to "get a good job that pays good money" if they want to buy their first home.'

Advocate, 19 August 2015

output

What comes out. All *inputs* have been *outputs* at some stage. A system of accounting. 'Government's desired or intended *impacts*/effects on the *community* resulting from a set of *outputs* and other factors including *community* action' (Victorian Department of Treasury and Finance).

'This process involves the following steps: *strategic alignment* with the *vision* on where to take the company, competitive differentiation, first scan attractiveness of the idea, feasibility organisational capabilities to execute cross-department inclusion, consistency of process, buy-in to *output*.'

Report provided by consultants Booz Allan Hamilton

'Project *outcomes* are *achieved* from the *utilisation* of the *outputs delivered* by a project. Not to be confused with Agency Budget *Outcomes* and treasury arrangements.'

Tasmanian Government

'In sorrow thou shalt bring forth *outputs*.'

outsource

(v) 1. To sub-contract. To out-task. To *offshore*. To *downsize*. To contract with other companies to provide goods and services and perform business *processes* formerly done in-house. To lower costs by doing this, especially by *outsourcing* to India and China where labour is cheaper.

To keep your workforce *flexible* by this means. To *downsize* or *release capacity*. To multiply the number of *consultants* in the world. To strip jobs from the in-source and create them in the *outsource*. To *globalise*. To put us in touch with the people of Bangalore. An unstoppable trend, whatever you think of it.

> 'With the Government's emphases on improved efficiency, reduced staffing *levels* and *core* business activities in public sector agencies, training services are among those *non-core* activities which should be considered for *outsourcing*, either as an entire function or specific courses.'
>
> Department of Transport, Victoria

2. Delegating any task to another entity, for example war to robots: As, '[Stephen] Hawking cautioned governments against a future where militaries *outsource* dangerous combat to "autonomous robots" that will likely – and here's the scary bit – be "beyond meaningful human control".'

> 'When you Google "what's causing the ache in my right knee", what you're really doing is *outsourcing* the cognitive load of finding that information to one of the finest, most complex pieces of mass artificial intelligence the world has ever seen.'
>
> Laura Demasi, *Brisbane Times*, 30 July 2015

over-firm denial

1. No
2. Yes.

> 'Conservative Party chairman Grant Shapps admitted he had "*over firmly*" *denied* continuing his work as a web marketing

expert under the name Michael Green, after being elected in 2005.'

BBC

'Those in favour say, "Aye" or "No". The contrary, "No" or "Aye". The question is resolved in the affirmative or negative.'

oversight

1. (n) Unintentional omission.
2. (n) Supervision or care.
3. (v) To oversee, watch over, look over, supervise, run, keep an eye on, superintend, handle, guide, *monitor*.

'This includes *oversight* of activity *management* and close consultation with *key* officers within the MAFF.'

'There's a somebody I'm longing to see,
I hope that he turns out to be,
Someone who'll *oversight* me.'

Duke Ellington

ownership (taking)

1. The state of owning – a house, a copyright, an idea, etc.
2. Military: 'You break it, you own it', where 'it' is a country. Also shopkeeping, where 'it' is a vase or tea cup.
3. Business: Making an idea one's own – or an *issue*, problem, solution, process, plan, strategy, scenario, principle, values, mission, vision, *input*, outcome, etc.

'You know you're gonna be *owning* this place.'

Colin Powell to President George W. Bush, 2002

'Because of their involvement and *ownership* of the *issue* many *stakeholders* will have *knowledge*, *networks* and resources which can add significant *value* to your project.'

NSW Environment Protection Authority

'Local *ownership* is more than "pressing of hands into concrete". It is about treating people with respect by openly sharing information and decision-making to allow understanding whilst not apologising for the "constraints".'

Vital Places, specialist consulting service

HELP!
COMMUNICATION
ANALYSIS
LANGUAGE
IN
AUTO-CHURN
NOUNS
SPIN
END USER EXPERIENCE
MEDIA
KEY DELIVERABLE
PLAUSIBLE
DENIABILITY
REALITY CHECK
SALE
MONETISED
SYNERGISTICS
UPTICK
ON WATER
SEAMLESS
CLIENT BASE
EARLY ONSET NOSTALGIA
THE PAST
THE CLOUD
LIFE
HELP!
PLANET CRISIS
Petty

P

package

Suite of elements comprising an *initiative*, *plan*, *strategy*, policy, pork barrel, bribe, campaign, offer, etc. (E.g. 'Great Barrier Reef Marine Park Structural Adjustment *Package*'; 'Forest Industry Structural Adjustment *Package*', etc.) *Packages* are delivered. They contain *deliverables* and, sometimes, Ethics. Broader than a code.

> 'This Code of Ethics is an integral part of the broader Ethics *Package*. The Ethics *Package* has now been revised to more closely reflect our changing work and our *values*. The complete Ethics *Package* is available on the EPA website. The Ethics *Package* will be a dynamic document and will be constantly amended as new *needs* and *issues* arise. All staff are encouraged to provide *input* into this process to *ensure* the Ethics *Package* remains a *relevant* and significant guide to assist our work.'
>
> EPA, New South Wales

> '. . . What we're doing today is expanding the reach of the *package* . . . to anyone who is *impacted* negatively by the *historic* rezoning of the reef.'
>
> Minister for the Environment, 27 August 2004

package (the complete)

1. A kind of footballer – as in: 'Michael Voss is the complete package'.
2. The real deal, the whole caboodle, the full kit. Also sometimes racehorses, greyhounds, entertainers.

> 'This is the most complete swimming *package* I have ever seen.'
>
> Murray Rose on Ian Thorpe

paradigm (shift)

1. *Model*, exemplar or archetype. Movement from one *model* to another is a *paradigm shift*.
2. Change in the way you organise the office. What *consultants* claim to bring, and management after paying them, feels constrained to agree. As a revolution is heralded by a new language, the idea that a *paradigm shift* has occurred might serve as justification for new and constantly repeated terms.
Companies are attracted to the idea by the famous negative examples of IBM, which was so locked into an old *paradigm* of the computer business that it could not make the shift to the PC; and the Swiss, who invented quartz watches but, being caught in an older watch *paradigm*, left the Japanese to manufacture them.

An old millenium term. As, 'The reaction described in the preceding paragraph could be viewed as a *paradigm shift* to borrow a term from old millennium management terminology' (Bottom Up Management).

> 'You've also got to measure in order to begin to affect *change* that's just more – when there's more than talk, there's just actual – a *paradigm shift*.'
>
> George W. Bush, July 2003

partner / partnerships / partnering

Teams. *Synergistic* combinations. Teaming up. Joining forces. What you do with someone you trust or, if you don't trust him, with someone in whom you see the prospect of advantage: As in, 'There are *ongoing* security *challenges* that we face and Prime Minister Allawi is determined to *address* those *ongoing* security threats. And we're there to *partner* with him in those efforts' (Scott McLellan, 20 September 2004).

> 'I'm asking you today to consider *partnering* once more with your University to achieve *ongoing transformations*.'
>
> Letter from the University of Melbourne's 'Advancement Office'

> 'We will provide *human capital solutions* with intelligent workflow making your people more *productive*, *innovative* & *strategic*. By *partnering* with us your organisation will become more *competitive*, profitable & valuable.'
>
> EmployeeConnect

> 'The Plan provides a set of over-arching *areas* of *focus* designed to link with established and new *partnerships* and *initiatives* that address current and emerging wellbeing and safety *issues* in the community.'
>
> 'Community Safety and Crime Prevention Partnership Plan for Macedon Ranges Shire', 2011

passionate

1. Susceptible of passion, the passions – fear, hate, love, joy, etc. Given to rage, vehemence, ardent desire, lust, wild enthusiasm, deep sadness, etc. Fervent. Moved by passion rather than reason.
2. Keen on something, such as cooking or ice cream or *value creation*. What one needs to be about one's job, one's everything.

> 'Byrd Baggett CSP, Developing authentic leaders and *passionately* engaged teams since 1990.'

'A *passionate* family residence.'

House for sale, Mt Macedon, Victoria

'Arnie Fertig, MPA, is *passionate* about helping his Jobhunter-coach *clients* advance their careers . . .'

Yahoo Finance, 12 August 2015

pathways

1. Tracks, paths, usually leading somewhere.
2. *Pathways* to success, *pathways* to good living, to wellness, to inspirational success, to happiness, to a flat stomach. Tracks *going forwards* – and sideways and underground. Tracks that make you sleepy just following them on the page.

'Your *pathway* from *strategy* to *process* to repeatable *value creation*.'

Jim Collins

'The purpose is to equip us better to achieve the "ambition inspired by *achievement*" which underpins our new *strategic plan* . . . It is now imperative that we define the *pathways*, the priorities and the *performance indicators* that will make a reality . . . This position is intended to *optimise* the *feedback* loop in which energy and *initiative* at the "*cutting edge*" is encouraged and also shapes and is influenced by corporate *strategies*.'

The University of Sydney's new organisational structure

penetration

1. To break into, pierce, force entry. To get through – a wall, a thick skull, etc. To gain insight.

2. To break into or pierce jobs; or break into or pierce with jobs . . . (?) Break into or pierce *clients*; pierce with telephone, etc.

> 'In terms of *key* metrics you'll see us *grow customer* numbers, reduce *churn*, you'll see us *grow customer penetration* in digital *products*, you'll see us *grow* total digital sales and the total *value* of packages we sell.'
>
> CEO Sensis, *Australian*, 29 March 2011

> 'You'll need proven ability to develop and cultivate new relationships, as well as increasing *penetration* within existing *clients*, combined with urgency, *passion* and a *commitment* to win.'
>
> Hudson, job advertisement

> 'In areas with low telephone *penetration*, researchers have resorted to house-to-house in-person recruiting to overcome this problem. As telephone *penetration* increases, so does the randomness of telephone recruitment.'
>
> Research company

people (our)

Staff, employees, workforce, workers, *hires*, etc. Managers, leaders, team leaders, teams, brand ambassadors, drones, others. A component of 'all our *stakeholders*', even *key stakeholders*. As, '*Our people* are our *key stakeholders*' (Sappi Europe). *Human* capital, human resources, resources. *Internal clients* and *customers*, etc. Loved, valued and important part of an organisation. As, 'Without *our people*, we would not have a sustainable business.' Furthermore, 'Our Sappi Europe *People Strategy* is very closely *aligned* to both the European Business and Global *People Strategies*' (Sappi Europe).

> 'The priority we place on our *people* is what drives our *quality performance* and profitable growth, and in 2004 we made considerable investments in our *people initiatives*. Central to this was an *Accelerated Collaborative Event* (ACE) which enabled a broad cross-section of our *people* to have *input* into our *people* approach, and has resulted in six project *teams* working to *embed* the *key initiatives* across our firm.'
>
> Ernst & Young, Message from the CEOs

perceptions (managed)

What you perceive when someone has re-arranged things for you.

> 'We will ultimately need a cup redesign but the short term *action* is *manage perceptions*.'
>
> DePuy's director of hip marketing, April 2008, speaking about a faulty prosthetic hip that failed thousands implanted with it, and poisoned others with cobalt and chromium

> 'Primarily associated with corporate America, *branding* is all the things people can do to *manage perception* of a product or place, both rational and emotional, said Jack Stanton, group director of *brand planning* at Carmichael Lynch.'
>
> www.startribune.com

performance appraisal

1. Essential measure of an employee's worth. 2. Dopey idea. Not enjoyable, possibly counter-productive. Neuroscience

'clarified why forced rankings were undermining the desired *culture* of trust, collaboration and risk taking'. As, 'When people realise they are being compared with others, a "threat response" in their brains sends cortisol levels skyrocketing and makes it hard for them to take in other information' (J. Boudreau and S. Rice in *Harvard Business Review*, July–August 2015).

> 'PWC and Juniper Networks have already abandoned traditional *performance appraisals* – perhaps the most reviled standard practice in all of management – and moved toward a model of ongoing *conversation* designed to improve skills and results.'
>
> Peter Capelli, 'Why We Love to Hate HR . . .' *Harvard Business Review*, July–August 2015

> 'As of September, one of the largest companies in the world [Accenture] will do all of its employees and managers an enormous favour: It will get rid of the annual *performance review* . . . CEB found that 95 per cent of managers are dissatisfied with the way their companies conduct *performance reviews*, and nearly 90 per cent of HR leaders say the process doesn't even yield accurate information.'
>
> *Sydney Morning Herald*, 22 July 2015

performance-driven

Driven, and not by a concern for happiness, goodwill, loyalty, tradition, Christian or any other kind of fellowship, love, loathing, fear, envy, spontaneity, the pleasure principle, the principle of a fair day's work for a fair day's pay, an attachment to the ideas of Erasmus, J.S. Mill, George Orwell or John Curtin, etc., but by *performance*.

'From an *end-user* perspective, initially, there should be little change in the service. *Moving Forward*, Facilities and Services will be *developing* a more user-*focussed* and *performance-driven* cleaning regime across the campus.'

A message from the Deputy Vice-Chancellor,
Monash University

performance management (PM)

Almost universal organisational method beyond the imagination of Soviet planners. *Performance* is measured by the difference between actual and desired results. Wherever the desired exceeds the actual there is a performance *issue* which must be resolved by *performance* appraisal, *performance* improvement: i.e. by *performance management*. Justified by competitive *challenges*, especially global competition, which makes it imperative for every organisation to '*ensure strategies* are *implemented* effectively' to *deliver optimum outcomes*. As, '. . . the effective use of inter-related *strategies* and activities to improve the *performance* of individuals, *teams* and organisations . . . integrate and *align* organisational, business and individual planning and *performance* . . . a means to recognise and reward good performance and to manage underperformance of staff' (Australian Public Service Commission).

'Prepare for the performance conversation: Self-reflection – Academic Staff Development Need/s.

What skill/s, knowledge, experience/s or resources do you require as identified by:

- past performance
- proposed future *key outcomes*

• identified career *aspiration*/s

These may be either technical or behavioural development needs.'

University of South Australia

'You'll *drill down* into how to set up and roll out a performance *improvement framework* in your organization . . . You'll *benchmark* how to integrate your disparate systems into one streamlined *performance management framework* and how to inject greater *customer centricity* into your service *delivery initiatives*.'

Performance Improvement Frameworks for Government Service Delivery Conference

'The purpose of this paper is to provide the project manager with a statistical perspective to the development of the Performance Measurement Baseline (PMB) and ultimately to the statistical assessment of schedule variance. Understanding the statistical properties of the PMB adds another arrow to the project manager's information quiver. Two vantage points have been taken: Time-centric and Task-centric.'

www.pmi.org/learning/performance-measurement-baseline-statistical-view-2055

See *metrics*, *Amazonians*.

personality

1. A cult.

'By learning more about my own *Personality*, and about other *Personality* Types, I can come to a better understanding of my strengths and weaknesses. I can improve my interpersonal relationships, *realign* my expectations towards others, and gain a better self-knowledge that will help me define and *achieve goals*.'

Web page

'The DaVinci Method details how you can leverage your *personality* type the same way all great entrepreneurs have, leading to health, wealth and happiness.'

The Da Vinci Method

'For the head of the ANZ to describe me as Hugo Chavez is the introduction of *personality* into the debate.'

Joe Hockey, *Sky*, 7 November 2010

2. A marketing *challenge*.

'Each *consumer* has a unique *personality*.'

Marketing textbook

'The *brand personality* is a key tool for differentiating Victoria University. It has been defined as:

• can do, expressive, cheeky, brave

• open minded, surprising

• straight talking, individual; and

• worldly, friendly.'

'Developing "street smart" creative', outlining Victoria University's new approach to marketing

personal life

1. The side of life which is not work but for *optimal outcomes* should be *aligned* with it. As, 'Effective Time Management: Using Microsoft Outlook to Organize Your Work and *Personal Life*.' Cooking, Pilates, selfies, Sudoku,

getting fit, getting wasted, getting tatts, getting laid, etc. *Lifestyle*. Life beyond the organisation, the brand, the team, the process; yet can be made the concern of others through Facebook, texting and sexting. Life spent in front of a screen that is not the one you use at work.

> 'Inspiritive (Teaching lasting life skills) will help you to discover how *NLP* can *enhance* your *personal* and your professional *life*, and the relationships with the people you have in both.'
>
> Neuro Linguistic Programming advertisement

2. The life in which one is a *marketing target*, in which one's wants are turned into needs, in which one's *customer profile* is built.
3. The lives of others. As, 'The prevailing media narrative surrounding Taylor Swift's *personal life* paints her as a voracious man-eater or lovelorn tragic. Neither is correct, nor completely untrue' (*West Australian*, 10 May 2013). 'Nicole Kidman admits her career highlights seem to have coincided with her *personal life* "falling apart" '. Etc. What sells newspapers, advertising, etc.

pillar

Column or post, potentially *impactful*.

> 'Each objective under each *pillar* has been assessed on the basis of whether or not it would *impact* the other *pillars* as described in the *Action Plan*.'
>
> DurhamRegion.com, 26 January 2012

platform

1. Raised structure for speaking or other performance (inc. a metaphorical form of this), for boarding or alighting from trains, launching spacecraft and political campaigns.
2. Underlying computer system on which applications can be run. As, 'At our core, Microsoft is the *productivity* and *platform* company for the mobile-first and cloud-first world' (Microsoft CEO).
3. A business model arising from the internet (itself a *platform*): As, 'There are two broad business models: pipes and *platforms*. You could be running your *startup* the wrong way if you're building a *platform* but using pipe *strategies*.' Pipes (e.g. TV channels, Encyclopaedia Britannica) 'just create and push stuff out'; *platforms* (e.g. YouTube, Wikipedia) 'allow users to create and *consume value*' (Platform Thinking).
4. Required for anything that an organisation does or feels it should do. As, 'What we need is a multi-stakeholder *platform*' (World Economic Forum chairman Klaus Schwab).

> 'For about five years we've actually been providing a training *platform* for the emerging doctors . . .'
>
> Northern Star

> '*Consumer engagement levels* with the *platform* are high with downloads up to 19 per cent . . .'
>
> Radio Today

plausible deniability

1. The ability to credibly deny all knowledge of matters for which one might be presumed to bear responsibility. Pass the buck. Remain ignorant and out of harm's way. As, 'I made a deliberate decision not to ask the President,

so that I could insulate him from the decision and provide some future *deniability* for the President if it ever leaked out' (John Poindexter, referring to President Reagan in Iran Contra affair).
2. The inability to deny convincingly. As, 'I did not have sexual relations with that woman' (Bill Clinton). 'I am not a crook' (Richard Nixon). 'We are determined to find the person or persons responsible for this enormity and you may be assured that the full force of the law will be applied' (generic).
An old concept employed and given a name by the CIA, and applied to politics, crime, espionage and other infidelities. As, 'Be innocent of the knowledge, dearest chuck, Till thou applaud the deed' (*Macbeth*). Deliberately loose chains of command enable people in high office to deny giving any instructions that have gone wrong. The doctrine failed in the case of Watergate because the President was not plausible. It also fails when those given the instructions take the apparent unwillingness of the President, CEO, Mafia boss, Kremlin heavy, or other powerful person to know anything about the consequences as a blessing on proceedings and a licence to do what they like.

> 'The testimony that we did obtain from former CIA officials was often less than candid. A central axiom of clandestine activities, such as the MKULTRA Program, is that CIA must maintain "*plausible deniablity*".'
>
> www.turnerhome.com

> 'Although hard to prove one way or the other, direct orders and precise knowledge aren't the way Murdoch works, which is by string-pulling, winks and nods behind the scenes, and always some degree of *plausible deniability*.'
>
> Geoffrey Wheatcroft, *New York Review of Books*, 8 January 2015

pockets of resistance

Groups, often small, of insurgents, fanatics or *dead enders*. In 1942, Hitler acknowledged that the German army was encountering 'small *pockets of resistance*' in Stalingrad. The US army ran into small *pockets* in Vietnam and again in Iraq, where they attempted to empty them with 'mopping up activities'.

> 'Small *pockets of resistance* remain, said the spokesman, who acknowledged reports of looting in Basra.'
>
> CNN, April 2003

> 'Some 7000 enemy, well-equipped, crack NVA regulars blasted their way into the imperial city of Hue, overpowering all but a few *pockets of resistance* held by ARVN troops and the US Marines.'
>
> History 1st Battalion, 5 Cavalry Regiment

point of contact

Someone to talk to; with whom to *touch base*, *dialogue*, *network*, exchange notes, etc. As in: 'Cleo, you're the point of contact, right?'

> 'In an effort to spread the corporate *learnings* and stay *accountable* to the six-month timeline, conference calls were held every other week with the corporate *team lead* . . . First, each hospital administration designates an eMAR coordinator to serve as a single *point of contact* to *facilitate* improved multidisciplinary *communication* for shared *learnings* across the corporation.'
>
> www.psqh.com

> 'And the *brand* essence, promise and *personality* must be consistently and compellingly manifested at each *point of contact* the *brand* makes with the *customer*. Finally, the *brand's* position can be reinforced through any of the senses.'
>
> The Blake Project

political correctness, politically correct (PC)

1. Of, relating to, or supporting broad social, political, and educational *change*, especially to redress injustices in matters such as race, class, gender, and sexual orientation.
2. Too much concerned with these matters. An obsession with them manifested in tiresome and stifling conversation, oppressive social policy and ineffectual government.
3. Not believing in *moral clarity*, faith-based *initiatives*, the active presence of a partisan God, absolute good and *evil*, and the doctrine of *common sense*. Not the voice of the people: As, 'the voice of the people [was] never heard' in the governments of Hawke and Keating (Alan Jones).
4. Thought police, intellectual *elites*, *chattering classes*, *caffè latte* set, femi-nazis, academic snobs, ideologues, do-gooders, who would have people who 'talk about certain things . . . living in fear of being branded a bigot or a racist' (John Howard, 1996).
5. Demand that everyone join Team Australia; that the ABC be balanced in all things; that people in the media don't treat Anzac as contestable history.

> 'We're more concerned about *political correctness* than we are about victory, than we are about winning. We are not going to be *politically correct* any more, we are going to get things done.'
>
> Donald Trump, 15 August 2015

popularity contest

> 'I grieve for the rise of the new *political correctness* – the hypocritical demand of the conservative establishment in this country for civility in political debate.'
>
> Mark Latham, 2002

popularity contest

What politics is not. It only looks like it – what with democracy and the popular vote and the polling and advertising and fund raising and rictus smiles and all the humiliating efforts to please the punters and meet *community expectations*. But it's not. As, 'Government is not a *popularity contest*, it's a competence contest' (Tony Abbott, PM).

portal

Window, door, gate, opening, entrance, gateway, ingress, entrance etc., usually of imposing dimensions. Internet site, providing access to other sites. As, 'So if you are having trouble logging into the *portal* to get your timetable done, here are some backdoor links that skips the main login page of the *portal*' (Unimelb Adventures).

A public library is a '*Portal* of knowledge'. As, 'Creating relevance for one of Australia's great *portals* of discovery. The State Library of New South Wales.' 'Our *strategy* has helped the library to be a more engaging and experience-led destination, reinforcing its role in an increasingly competitive cultural landscape' (Frost Collective). *Portals* are common in *knowledge management*. As, 'The preliminary analysis of instructors' *utilization* of corporate *portal* in an academic institution shows that providing tools through corporate *portals* to support knowledge conversion *enhances* the effectiveness and efficiency of business *processes* and employees' learning . . .' (Kamla Ali Al-Busaidi, '*Leveraging*

Organizational Knowledge Management through Corporate *Portal*', Springer Link).

> 'Human-oriented workflow is the next frontier for *portal frameworks*. The year 2004 will be "the *year of* the *process portal*" for *portal* frameworks, whereas 2001 was the year of the content *portal*, 2002 application access, and 2003 collaboration – with each year adding to the *capabilities* of those before it. This pattern of feature creep will end with composite applications in 2007, after which *portal* and composite application *frameworks* will merge and become indistinguishable.'
>
> International Association for Human Resource Information Management

> 'But, soft! What light through yonder *portal* breaks.'

potential

1. Potential
2. That which remains to be fulfilled.

> 'He is learning to stay *focused* and *engaged* on his tasks so he can fulfill his *potential* and complete them within the set *time frame*.'
>
> Paul Chai, *Daily Life*, 3 June 2014

> 'What did you do at school today, son?'
>
> 'I learned to stay *focused* and *engaged* on my tasks so I can fulfil my *potential* and complete them (my tasks) within the set *time frame*, Dad.'
>
> 'You mean you're still a bit slow, son.'
>
> 'Pretty much.'

PowerPoint

Microsoft's presentation software; 1 billion sold since 1987.

Bedding Down the Dead

1. Overview
   - Man that is born of woman
   - Short time to live
   - Full of misery
2. *Agenda* (Almighty's)
   - Pleased to take the soul of dear exited brother
3. *Agenda* (Ours)
   - Put his body in ground (*core commitment*)
4. Implementation
   - Ashes to ashes
   - Dust to dust
5. Summary (actualised core value)
   - Certain of resurrection and eternal life

'*PowerPoint* allows speakers to pretend that they are giving a real talk and audiences to pretend that they are listening. This prankish conspiracy against substance and thought should always provoke the question, Why are we having this meeting?'

Edward R. Tufte, *The Cognitive Style of PowerPoint*, 2003

'*PowerPoint* makes us stupid.'

General James Mattis

- Be
- Not be
- Answer?

price signal – see *value signal*

1. A message to customers: as, for example, an increase in their gas bill tells them to use less gas.

> 'The [Medicare] co-payment is a *price signal*, but at $5 it signals nothing to a rich politician on $200,000 a year, even with 50 visits for the family over the year. For a low-income-earning family on $50,000, paying off a mortgage, it is a kick in the guts.'
>
> Tim Woodruff, *The Drum*, 12 December 2014

2. A message to business: a high price is a signal to produce more. Note: price *gouging* is a misreading of the signal, at best. At worst this behaviour fails to understand the principle of *consumer* sovereignty and that in a competitive economy the price of goods and services closely reflects the cost of producing them.

> 'We think it is important for people to have a *price signal* for people that can pay.'
>
> Joe Hockey, Network Ten, 20 January 2015

Price signals are sent only in market economies; in command economies they are unknown.

prioritise

1. To make something a priority – e.g. *goals*, *challenges*, *agreed outcomes*, *implementation* of *strategies*, *alignment* of *strategy* and *outcomes*, buying paper clips, having a haircut.
2. To concentrate on, *focus*, make *front of mind*, give one's all to, do first, do in the morning or by the end of the month, or within whatever is a reasonable time frame, and of course

taking account of the overall envelope. As, 'So what we've got to do is *prioritise* the expenditure in those areas but overall the envelope have committed expenditure in those areas will continue' (Joe Hockey, ABC, 22 October 2013).

> 'So, how does one *prioritise*? First, write down all the *goals* you can think of, everything you want to have and *achieve*. Next, put them into categories based on how important they are to you. Decide what is the most important, and what is the most urgent. Try to realistically evaluate which and how many *goals* you can actively pursue at once.'
>
> Single-step.com

> 'If it were done when 'tis done, then 'twere well
> It were *prioritised*.'

privatise

Sell, unload, flog, cash in, realise, hock; by share issue, sale to the highest bidder or other means, transfer ownership of a government business, agency, service or property to the private sector. People's capitalism, popular capitalism: As, 'Popular capitalism is nothing less than a crusade to enfranchise the many in the economic life of the nation' (Margaret Thatcher).

> 'Just as nationalisation was at the heart of the collectivist programme by which Labour governments sought to remodel British society, so *privatisation* is at the centre of any programme of reclaiming territory for freedom.'
>
> Margaret Thatcher

'In South Australia following *privatisation* families pay the highest electricity bills in Australia – while the billionaire owner of the network makes $420 in profit from every household in that state every year.'

Luke Foley, NSW ALP Leader, campaign speech 2015

proactive

Like 'active', but in a way that enables you to create your own 'perspective expanding experiences', etc. As, 'But if you're *proactive*, you don't have to wait for circumstances or other people to create perspective expanding experiences. You can consciously create your own' (Steven R. Covey, *The 7 Habits of Highly Effective People*).

'We take our quality-assurance *processes* seriously and have *proactively* undertaken *process* improvements to *ensure* that they are as *robust* as possible.'

Mark C. Rodgers, Citigroup, 'Citigroup Whistle-Blower Says Bank's "Brute Force" Hid Bad Loans From U.S.', Bloomberg, 16 February 2012

'Their onballers have to get *proactive*.'

Football commentator

'It would enhance our lifestyle going forwards, Muriel, if you would more *proactively* oversight my porridge.'

probletunity

A *problem* and an opportunity in one? As, 'Use "*Quality Tools*" to establish the procedures following the "*Probletunity* Story Board".'

'A *Problem* Statement is a *tool* used to document a *Probletunity*.'

New South Wales Education Department document, after Langford International Tool Time Education Handbook

'There is a *probletunity* in the affairs of men which taken at the flood . . .' etc.

process

1. Procedure, operation. Way of doing something. Organised action or undertaking.
2. Method of turning *inputs* into *outputs*. A sequence of interdependent procedures of which each stage consumes one or more resources (e.g. time, energy, money) to convert *inputs* (e.g. data, effort) to *outputs* (products) that offer more value to the *customer* (after *Business Dictionary*). Or, 'keep the cost of fulfilment to the minimum while we continue to increase the speed at which we deliver our *customers*' orders' (Amazon).
3. That to which all hopes are consigned.
4. That which *progresses*. Or sometimes stalls. Or goes nowhere. Quietus.

'It's all about the *process*. The politicians, their advisers and their spin doctors have alighted on the importance of *process*. The substantive policies and politics of a complex public issue are now subservient to *process*.'

Noel Pearson, 'Process of Recognition', *Monthly*, August 2015

'Mr Morrison said his department secretary was in PNG as part of an "ongoing *process* of collaboration". "There's [sic] been extensive levels of support and training and mentoring being provided to Papua New Guinea and Nauru to manage

> those *processes*," he said. "I haven't seen anything to suggest that there are *issues* associated with that."'
>
> *Age*, 22 October 2013

> 'While we obviously hold boys to high standards, occasionally boys can make errors in judgment and when that happens, we have to institute an education *process* to advise boys that they've behaved *inappropriately*.'
>
> Principal of elite Brisbane school

> 'We want to reassure *customers* that they have a voice in how the over-recovery of funds is managed *going forward* through our draft Water Plan consultation *process*.'
>
> In a statement from Melbourne Water after admitting they had been charging households $306 million for a desalination plant that is not yet operating. *Age*, 14 June 2012

> 'The reaction? Nothing. The inexorable caravan of *process* moved on as though nothing had happened.'
>
> Pearson, ibid.

process improvement (PI) manager

One who manages the improvement of *processes*. (But who manages the *process improvement manager*'s improvement?) As, 'Interpret *metrics* and participate in the *development* of appropriate *actionable plans* for the definition of a new and/or improvement of an existing *process*. This will include detailed tactical steps to *drive* the *changes* desired with clearly defined success criteria' (Bemis).

> 'Senior *Process Improvement Manager* – Luxembourg
>
> Our overall *mission* is simple: we want Amazon to be the place where our *customers* can find, discover and buy anything

online. Whatever our *customers* want, we will find the means to *deliver* it. With your help, Amazon will continue to enable people to discover new worlds and *implement innovation*. This is your chance to make history.'

Amazon job advert

process (objective setting)

A *process* likely recommended by a *process* manager. As, 'The role of the Liaison Librarians project *team* is to: Facilitate the *objective-setting process*, work with those in similar roles to reach *consensus* on role-specific objectives and *KPIs*, obtain *buy-in* from *stakeholders* during the planning *process* by seeking *feedback*, reporting back to *stakeholders*, keep in mind the overall aim of the *objective-setting process*' (Internal memo, University of Sydney Library).

processing centre

1. Place where raw or unrefined materials (e.g. pigs, ores, grains) are processed into a refined state (e.g. ham and bacon, foil, corn flakes).
2. A camp, detention centre or gaol in which refugees (see *queue jumper*, *illegal*, etc.) are *processed*.

product

Arising from production, manufacturing, *innovation*, etc. Goods, chattels, ideas, inventions, intelligence, concoctions, information, misinformation, art, novels, poetry, plays, football, pornography, apples, mental health services, correctional services, all services. Anything.

'"Jeffrey" has been working very well recently on the small group collaborative project which required students to *develop* their own *key* questions, research information and *develop* a variety of *products* to present their information.'

Year 7 History report

'. . . our processing infrastructure and *development* of *innovative* transactional banking *product*.'

Australian bank

'An opportunity has arisen for a Product Manager who will be responsible for *product* planning, pricing and execution of *product* initiatives throughout the *product* lifecycle. *Key* requirements of this role include; gathering and *prioritising product* and *customer* requirements, defining *product vision*, and working closely with internal and external *stakeholders* to *implement product changes*.'

Job advert for position in Mental Health Services
Marketing and Product, Seek.com

'Raindrops on roses and whiskers on kittens,
Bright copper kettles and warm woollen mittens,
Brown paper packages tied up with string,
These are a few of my favourite *products*.'

productivity

Effectiveness of industrial effort, measured by rate of *output* per unit of *input*. Just about the only thing that matters. As, '*Productivity* isn't everything, but in the long run it is almost everything' (Paul Krugman).

In its name much once held to be valuable must go (e.g., towns, suburbs, communities, employment) or be subverted (e.g., education). As, 'Investment in education is crucial to *driving productivity* growth and to *driving* a modern and prosperous economy for the future' (Kevin Rudd, PM, first line of Education Revolution statement. See Dennis Glover, *An Economy Is Not a Society*, Melbourne, 2015).

> 'The Department of Education and Training requires the services of a firm with expertise in *Business Intelligence* (BI) to develop a 5 year *strategic road map/plan*. The *road map/plan* will be used to *implement* a BI *capability framework* to meet the *vision* "To *drive* learning *productivity*".'
>
> Queensland Department of Education

product offering

Product for sale. Offered product.

> 'World Bank *Significantly* Expands Disaster *Risk Management Product Offerings* for *Clients*.'

> 'SIAL is a broad-based exhibition with a fully exhaustive food *product offering*.'

> 'When it comes to your *product offering*, you need to *focus* on the end first.'
>
> Startup Daily

> 'There are more *product offerings* in heaven and earth, Horatio, than are dreamt of in your philosophy.'

progress, progressed, progressing

(n) Growth, improvement, movement towards an objective, etc.

(v) 1. Go, *go forward*, advance, make progress, proceed, improve, kick it along, make it work, get it off the ground, up and running, etc. As, 'Have you *progressed* the *implementation* of the change platform *going forwards*, Beverley?'
2. Very little change since last time I spoke to you. Stalled, bogged, inert. May as well be dead. What happens with processes sometimes. As, 'This *process* is *progressing*, and I look forward to reporting a favourable *outcome* in due course' (Annual report).

> 'QSA should *progress* the assessment regime.'
>
> Queensland Studies Authority

> 'The network has *progressed* towards *achieving* its aim with *stakeholders* to *develop strategic partnerships* to keep young people *engaged* in education, training or employment.'
>
> Outer Eastern Local Learning Employment Network

> '*Progress*, *progress* with hope in your heart
> And you'll never *progress* alone.'

> 'I will arise and *progress* now, and *progress* to Innisfree . . .'
>
> Yeats

public interface zone

Bicycle path?

> 'Create strong identity and branding for Port of Melbourne Corporation along *public interface zones*.'
>
> Webb Dock Redevelopment

pub test

Test of what or who is credible, decent, ethical or sensible: people who are a little rat-legged (including bon viveurs, depressives, inebriates, etc.) having better judgement in these fields than the parliament, the courts, the academies and other institutions that pass themselves off as expert. As, 'Bill Shorten is failing the *pub test*' (*Australian*, 11 March 2014). Test conducted by people who phone Alan Jones' show; people who decide the fate of prime ministers: As, 'To win an election – and you're not worth two bob in opposition – to win an election, you've got to pass the *pub test*. I can tell you that the board here this morning is in meltdown' (Alan Jones to Tony Abbott, PM, 17 November 2014).

> 'It's for the Speaker to justify that this is part of her official duties, but it appears not to pass the *pub test*.'
>
> *Sydney Morning Herald*, 15 July 2015

pull the oars

No room for the unwilling.

> 'Maybe someday we'll be a big company again. But, only by responsibly delivering top notch products and services and with everyone *pulling the oars* together to make happy customers.'
>
> Alpine

> 'You are all in the boat together, and you need all to *pull the oars*, everyone doing her part. To do your very best work, you need everyone's efforts to be *aligned* and synchronized.'
>
> Anthony Iannarino, blog

'You can be the greatest leader in the world, but if the team does not *pull the oars* with you, it will not be different. That is about cultural change.'

www.parl.gc.ca

purchase cycle

The one everyone rides.

'If you're like me then you have made many purchases in your lifetime, and because of that you may not realize the *purchase cycle* we follow (from realizing the problem to the evaluating how we feel after the purchase is made). It's so ingrained in us that we barely notice our repetition. *Marketers* are obsessed with this *purchase cycle* and have analyzed it thoroughly to better understand *consumers* and to increase your shopping experiences. Allow me to show you behind the velvet curtain!'

BrandingBeat

Q

quality

Excellent, or alleged to be. As, 'He's a quality performer' 'Q. racehorse, greyhound, footballer, etc.' 'Q. product, service, experience, etc.' 'She's all quality.'

> 'Coordinator of the playgroup program, Mrs X, says "being able to spend an extended period of time coaching the playgroup teams has meant that the leaders are confident in planning good *quality* play experiences . . ."'

> 'The *Framework* is part of the Council of Australian Governments' *reform agenda* for early childhood education and care. It is a *key* component of the Australian Government's National *Quality Framework* for early childhood education and care.'
>
> education.gov.au/early-years-learning-framework

queue jumper, queue jumpers

1. A refugee who jumps an orderly line of 50 million other refugees and arrives in Australia in a wilful, dangerous and unauthorised fashion. A rude and impatient foreigner; 'not the sort of person we want here', etc.
2. Persons fleeing Iraq, Afghanistan, Sri Lanka, Syria and other happy lands, and unwilling to wait their turn, and 'come through the proper channels', etc.
3. Persons so foreign to the *Australian lifestyle* that they would risk their own lives and those of their children for freedom, democracy, etc.
4. Persons who would pay money to 'people smugglers' to save their families.
5. Persons who, in 'the familiar terms of doing good and fighting *evil*' (Philip Ruddock, July 2001), need to be fought.

'"*Queue-jumping*" emerged as a fundamental irritant to respondents, according to the paper published this week in *Journal of Refugee Studies* . . . "If they feel they've somehow *jumped the queue* or tried to sneak in then there's quite a different reaction to them, but people are generally in support of Australia taking refugees," she said.'

The Conversation, 26 October 2011

'Thou shalt not covet thy neighbour's wife, nor his manservant, nor his maidservant, nor his ox, nor his ass, nor his place in the *queue*.'

quick fix, quick fixes

There are no *quick fixes*.

quite frankly

1. To be honest with you; to spare you nothing in the way of truth, however unpleasant; what follows is my opinion unadorned.
2. I need you to believe this. Put this bit at the top of the news. Here comes the grab.

'*Quite frankly*, I think his comments were out of order.'

Joe Hockey, ABC, 17 May 2015

'And *quite frankly*, I would rather have a fair system where everyone pays the same amount of tax for the same sort of good . . .'

Joe Hockey, ABC, 20 August 2015

'No I don't, no I don't and *quite frankly*, I would say to everyone: please do the job you have . . . Polls are volatile and *quite frankly*, nothing illustrates that better than what just happened in Queensland.'

Joe Hockey, ABC, 5 February 2015

'And unto Adam he said, *Quite frankly*, because thou hast hearkened unto the voice of thy wife, and hast eaten of the tree, of which I commanded thee, saying, Thou shalt not eat of it: cursed is the ground for thy sake; in sorrow shalt thou eat of it, *quite frankly*, all the days of thy life.'

R

range of strategies (in school reports)

> 'His concrete understanding of number and place value allows him to effectively *implement* a *range of strategies* to solve addition and subtraction problems.' [School report]
>
> When I take away the bullshit from this, I guess he can add and subtract. [Parent]'
>
> Paul Chai, 'I don't understand my children's school reports', www.dailylife.com.au

rapid disassembly

Explosion of airbag. As Takata Corporation, after several people were killed, many others were injured and 14 million cars had to be recalled: 'an inflator that exploded with excessive force was said to have gone "high order", while an inflator that ruptured and sprayed metal shards "*rapidly disassembled*"' (Reuters, 3 December 2014).

rationalise/rationalisation

1. Invent plausible reasons for behaviour that has less rational (or creditable) causes.
2. Subject an organisation, an industry or a national economy to something similar: namely, that they are more efficient – and 'conformable to reason' – when fewer people are employed in them and fewer services provided.

> '. . . it has been the reduction in operating costs that has been the more important factor in sustaining high rates of return. This reduction has been achieved through a variety of means including the *rationalisation* of branch networks, the migration of transactions out of branches to low-cost

electronic delivery systems and the automation of back-office processing . . . Overall, the number of bank branches fell by almost a quarter over the decade, while the number of full-time equivalent employees in banks fell by around 20 per cent.'

Marianne Gizycki and Philip Lowe,
'The Australian Financial System in the 1990s'

'Every living thing is linked by bonds of communication and some degree of shared nature. These bonds create a duty – a duty that is easy to follow, so long as we listen to our nature and tune out the voices of fanaticism and *rationalisation* (which all too often work together).'

Sarah Bakewell on Montaigne, *Guardian*, 7 June 2010

reach out

Howdy, etc.

'How do I *reach out* to my manager on the first day?
My first day at work is coming up soon and I would like to know how to *reach out* to my manager and tell him that I would be on campus on the said date and would love to have 1:1 with him . . .'

workplace.stackexchange.com

'Emphasizing that the prevalence of public *data* has *transformed* the ability of small internal *teams* to *reach out* and rapidly build something entirely new, DiGiammarino points to the OI ecosystems created by growth companies like Netflix, OpenTable, and Kiva (as well as – of course – Amazon).'

Innovation Excellence blog

real world

World lived in by *real people*; not chattering classes, *caffè latte* set, greenies, ABC, *Guardian* and Fairfax reading leftie luvvies, femi-nazis, etc. Not '*7.30 Report* Land'. As, 'Now it might be easy for you to sit there in *7.30 Report* Land and say that was easy to do; let me tell you, mate, it wasn't' (Kevin Rudd, 12 May 2010). Where the ducks are. World not lived in by Joe Hockey or Bronwyn Bishop. World without politicians and bureaucrats. But with a royal family, Harry Potter and other real world celebrities and scientologists. Lovely place, full of good people and common sense.

> 'Perhaps the most worrying issue is that the report glosses over the long-term problems of the *real world*.'
>
> John Daley, The Conversation, 5 March 2015

> 'Joe Hockey needs to get back in touch with the *real world* for a while.'
>
> *Sunshine Coast Daily*, 10 June 2015

reality check

1. Check to see if we are dreaming or in the *real world*. As, 'How do we know if we are sleeping, and all our thoughts are a dream; or if we are *boiling the ocean* in a waking state?' (after Plato).
2. A condescending put-down beloved of people without imagination. As, 'Time for a reality check, Toots.'

> 'Their insights on cloud solutions and cloud platforms are included in a white paper and an infographic titled "Cloud *Reality Check* 2015."

This white paper provides a perspective on why businesses are *migrating enterprise* applications to a cloud computing environment and pinpoints the specific *challenges* where *enterprises* are still struggling.'

NTT Communications

'What is required in this latest period is a *reality check* that accepts a unitary Iraqi state has effectively ceased to exist between its Shiite, Sunni and Kurdish enclaves.'

Tony Walker, *Australian Financial Review*, 5 June 2015

re-brand

To deceive, dissemble, bullshit, bear false witness. To give something a new name when the existing one is passé – or not. As, 'King's London sounds more like an aftershave than a credible university', after King's College was *rebranded* without a noun to say what it was and at a cost of 300,000 pounds (*Times Higher Education*, 16 December 2014). Popular among university administrators and manufacturers of shampoo, motor vehicles and pre-mixed drinks. Also politicians: As, 'Good government starts today' (Tony Abbott). Also military campaigns: e.g. '*War on Terror*' was (unsuccessfully) *re-branded* as the 'struggle against violent extremism' (SAVE) in 2005. 'As the struggle evolves some of the language evolves' (US official).

'What's in a name? If you're the newly created Australian Border Force, the answer is about $10 million – splashed on military-style uniforms and thousands of signs at airports and detention centres to create a fresh, hardline image. Australia's newly named paramilitary border force began operating in July, triggering the 10th *rebranding* of the immigration bureaucracy since World War II.'

Age, 26 August 2015

'The APIC 2008 conference was amazing with incredible presentations addressing all of the hot topics for infection prevention. Yes, you read correctly – in Denver APIC took the bold step of re-branding our profession. This rebranding included a new title for our work. From Denver onwards we will be known as INFECTION PREVENTIONISTS. It's a mouthful but promises to elevate the profession in public, professional and governmental arenas all around the world.'

A Day In The Life Of An APIC Board Member blog

'In 2008, Mercy Health & Aged Care underwent a *rebranding*. As a consequence of this process, the following facility names have changed . . .'

www.mercy.com.au

rectification time target

Time it takes to fix something (ideally).

'. . . the extent of our geographical area can often challenge our ability to meet our *rectification time target*. In order to keep prices as low as possible, we are proposing several slight reductions in service levels.'

Draft Water Plan 2013–18, Coliban Water

redacted

Censored.

red ocean

Opposite of *blue ocean*.

'So why the dramatic imbalance in favor of *red oceans*? Part of the explanation is that corporate *strategy* is heavily influenced by its roots in military *strategy*. The very language of *strategy* is deeply imbued with military references – chief executive "officers" in "headquarters", "troops" on the "front lines". Described this way, *strategy* is all about *red ocean* competition. It is about confronting an opponent and driving him off a battlefield of limited territory. *Blue ocean* strategy, by contrast, is about doing business where there is no competitor. It is about creating new land, not dividing up existing land. Focusing on the *red ocean* therefore means accepting the key constraining factors of war – limited terrain and the need to beat an enemy to succeed. And it means denying the distinctive strength of the business world – the capacity to create new market space that is uncontested.'

Harvard Business Review

redundancy

The condition of being sacked, *downsized*, *decruited*, *churned*, laid off, let go, etc. That which leads one to the profession of *job seeker*. Unemployed, lacking paid employment, unwanted, etc. Efficiency-gain *output*. An *involuntary career event*. Implementation cost. An *unlocked* cost saving. An excess resource, now *rationalised*. The condition preceding that of being a *job seeker*.

'It's easy to spend your *redundancy* payout but it pays to be cautious. Unless you are retiring, your *redundancy* payout will have to last you until you get another job, and this may take longer than you think.'

ASIC Money Smart

re-engineering

Rebuilding, redoing, remaking, reorganising etc., a company or corporation, a political party or any other organisation (aka business *process re-engineering*). More than a lick of paint. Usually costs jobs. Also applied to *mindsets*, especially strategic ones (c.f. re-education).

> '*Reengineering* itself got a flood of new practitioners, who discovered that even if they didn't know what they were doing they could always just *drive* a bunch of layoffs and (courtesy of the same information flows that made our *reengineering* efforts) the organization would survive somehow while the *consultant* basked in the glory of the cost-savings.'
>
> pikasoft, 15 May 2015

> 'Employers will be challenged to *re-engineer* the workplace, rethink jobs and reshape the way to attract, engage and manage people if they are to *drive* business performance amidst a growing global economy in 2015, according to a recent research report.'
>
> www.insidehr.com.au

> 'The *reengineering* of *strategic* mindsets is arguably our *core challenge*.'
>
> Kevin Rudd

reframing

Changing, varying, altering, but in a special way.

> 'The *reframing* of the descriptors of the Australian Curriculum achievement standards is a reminder to view and discuss a child as a capable and changing learner who is connected to

> their [sic] prior experience and at the start of their [sic] first phase of schooling.'
>
> Qld Education 'Reporting student achievement and progress in Prep to Year 10 . . .'

> 'You've *reframed*,
> That sparkle in your eyes has gone . . .'
>
> Billie Holiday

relationship

1. Connection or association, often very powerful: as, 'When a love-*relationship* is at its height there is no room left for any interest in the environment . . .'; but also complex: as, 'It is always possible to bind together a considerable number of people in love, so long as there are other people left over to receive manifestations of their aggressiveness' (Freud). For these reasons, probably, fodder for literature, art, media, Facebook, Instagram, LinkedIn, Pinterest, Twitter, texting, telephone, etc.
2. Commercial connection or association: between one organisation and another; an organisation and its *customers/clients*, including internal *clients*: an organisation and the *community*, etc. *Relationships* are valued, even 'enjoyed'. *Customer-focused relationships* are common. *Relationships* are grown and managed. Some consultants are *relationship* managers. *High value* or *key relationships* are those which return the most commercial benefit to the *relationship-focused* organisation.

> 'By now, you have a *robust* profile on LinkedIn, you tweet several times a day with hashtags, you have a Facebook page, several videos on YouTube, and you've even created several clever boards on Pinterest. You attend a handful of *networking*

events every month, and you venture out to interesting *events* like SXSW a couple of times every year. But after all that, how do you build your social circle and influential contacts in *key* centers of influence? How do you maintain, nurture, and ideally, bridge the gap between *relationship* creation and *relationship* capitalization? How do you turn friends and followers into active, interested social currency?'

David Nour, Mashable

'David Nour is the *thought leader* on *relationship* economics, the quantifiable value of business *relationships*. The Nour Group, Inc. helps organizations *drive growth* through unique return on their *strategic relationships*.'

Mashable

'As part of our *commitment* to our *clients* we are *realigning* your *client management team* to further service your current and evolving *needs* and to strengthen your *relationship* with us.'

Bank letter

relationship builder

How does one know?

'Are you a *relationship builder* and have a high desire to succeed in life?'

Job advertisement

relocate

Move.

'The bottling functions will be *relocated* to a venue in close proximity to the location of which the water is sourced.'

Bottled water company

'If Mohammed won't *relocate* to a venue in close proximity to the location of the mountain, the mountain must *relocate* to a venue in close proximity to the location of Mohammed.'

reposition / repositioning

1. (v) To move. (As in: deck chairs on *Titanic.*) To hide, cover up, camouflage, etc.
2. (n) A make-over. *Rebranding*. As, 'The purpose of a very modest *repositioning* is to deal with these concerns sensitively and constructively' (Vice Chancellor, King's College after rebranding to King's London). Surface *change*. The *repositioning* is intended to take place in the *consumer*'s head. 'A temporary, yet quirky, transit campaign to cover up former M Tram, Swanston Trams and The Met logos on trams has been launched alongside a major *repositioning* campaign for the entire Melbourne tram network, now run exclusively by Yarra Trams' (Yarra Trams). Note: trams will not be *re-positioned.*

> 'Fresh can assist you to analyse and define your *brand goals*, create and *develop* your new *brand* and corporate identity, or *reposition*, redesign and revitalise your existing *brand* to meet your corporate *strategic goals*.'
>
> Fresh

required no longer

Goodbye; farewell; au revoir, old son; all over red rover. Regrettably fired.

> 'Since the acquisition was completed, we have reviewed the future direction of the business to maximise its *potential* and

ensure its *on-going growth* in line with that of the wider Merlin business. Regrettably this has meant that some positions at Melbourne Aquarium are *no longer required* and we have *consulted* with those employees affected.'

Crikey, 21 May 2012

requirements traceability matrix

An RTM. Note: for the mystified version follow instructions on box.

'The *Requirements Traceability Matrix* (RTM) is a mechanism for *managing* the *life cycle* of a requirement throughout the project. It tracks what happens to each individual requirement from baseline (after initial approval) to final "*go live*" or *implementation*. The *Requirements Traceability Matrix* records what happens to each and every requirement by way of status *changes* and phase artifacts. This matrix is also referred to as a Coverage Matrix by the BABOK Guide.'

www.business-analysis-excellence.com/
requirements-traceability-matrix-demystified

'Duties extended to the design of a *scope* management system using a *Requirements Traceability Matrix* (RTM) for managing *change*. The benefits of this system deployment and associated *governance processes* exceed US $9 million. Responsible for the *development* of *risk management plans* for the *initiative* including all supporting *risk management* documentation extending to mitigation and contingency *plan* formats.'

www.sevenconsulting.com

reset

Repositioned, rebranded, rectified, re-engineered, required.

> '. . . chief executive Rhys Holleran said in a statement he was confident the Kyle and Jackie O Show "has been positively *reset* for 2012" and would provide an "advertiser-friendly environment".'
>
> *Age*, 20 January 2012

resources

1. human resources, human capital, humans, etc. Assets, commodities. As, 'Labour is a commodity like every other, and rises or falls according to the demand' (Edmund Burke). Employees, staff: thus under-resourced – under-staffed. 'The only reason for these words seems to be dehumanisation. "Shedding excess *resources*" sounds less upsetting than "sacking people" ' (Human Resources trainee). 'The labor of a human being is not a commodity or article of commerce' (Woodrow Wilson). But it is, being what the human being sells and commerce buys, or dispenses with.

> 'An *executable strategy* for *leveraging* transferable skills and exploring cross *team synergies* will result in higher *competency* and *resource utilisation* in an organisation.'
>
> '*Leveraging* cross *team synergies*', Sunder Ramachandran and Madan Ramachandran, www.ascent.com

> '. . . In local government, the theory of *asset management* is often *challenged* by a number of factors including Council decisions, staff stress due to workload, and *resource issues*. Ngaire will explain her *strategies* for making progress in this environment . . .'
>
> 2009 National Local Government Asset Management and Public Works Engineering Conference Australia

responsibility assignment matrix

A structure.

> '*Responsibility Assignment Matrix* (RAM)
>
> A structure which relates the project organisation structure to the work breakdown structure (WBS) to help ensure that each element of the project's *scope* of work is assigned to a responsible individual.'
>
> www.tmr.qld.gov.au

results driven

Driven by results. Very like outcomes driven. Or just driven. A useful ability. A *mindset* not needing re-engineering.

> 'Going through university, I had always thought *marketing* was a *brand-focused* activity, rather than what it is now, which is a very *targeted* and *results-driven* numbers game.'
>
> 'Mint Wireless' Justus Hammer talks data and *results-driven marketing*', CMO

> '*Key* Selection Criteria:
>
> Demonstrated ability to think laterally, question assumptions, problem solve and be *results driven*.'
>
> City of Port Phillip, job description

> 'Let me say it again: we have *architected* our business for a high speed broadband world . . . This is not old Telstra any more, it is the new Telstra, highly competitive, highly *focussed* and very *results-driven* in terms of what we do . . .'
>
> Sol Trujillo, Telstra Investor Day, 6 November 2008

> *Results Driven* Cleaning, Gordon Park, QLD.

reverse engineer

1. To take apart some man-made thing – computer, car, toaster – in order to better understand the way it works, and to reproduce and improve upon it.
2. The quickest *lever* in the circumstances.

> 'There has to be a greater *synergy* between, let's call it our policy *leadership* in this, which has been *focused* so much, legitimately, on targets and global *architecture*, almost *reverse-engineered* back to the means by which you can quickly *deliver outcomes*, and on the demand side in our economy we're looking at potential advances in terms of 20 to 25% range if you do this *across the board*. It all takes cost, but let me tell you it's probably the quickest *lever* you can pull given the *challenges* we face.'
>
> Kevin Rudd, PM

See *re-engineering*.

revisit

1. To go back to, return.
2. To have another look, reconsider, check, refresh the memory. As, 'I think we should *revisit* the implementation strategy.'

> 'In response to requests by service providers, the team has been supporting organizations to sit down with service users, families, boards and staff to start looking at the task ahead. For most organizations, the best place to start is to get *stakeholders* together and *revisit* the organization's *mission* and *core values* and *realign* on purpose and direction.'
>
> ACROD, National Industry Association for Disability Services

'Colleagues: As you are aware NSI is reviewing its Business Lines to improve the *performance* and *sustainability* of the Institute by strengthening the *value adding* connection between and across the *customer service points*. During the course of this project, roles and responsibilities of Business Lines will be clarified and the dimensions of Business Lines will be *revisited*.'

Northern Sydney Institute of TAFE

'Like dogs *revisiting* their vomit . . .'

revitalise

1. Make lively and vital again.
2. Sack people and abandon standards of grammar, spelling, accuracy, etc. Substitute *lifestyle* and celebrity clickbait for depth, international news and investigative reporting. Dumb down.

'Fairfax Media has announced plans to *revitalise* its newsrooms in regional Victoria with a significant investment in new systems, training and equipment for journalists and sales staff . . . If the proposal goes ahead the company expects voluntary *redundancies* of around 80 full-time equivalent positions across Victoria.'

Bendigo Advertiser, 11 March 2015

right-size

Staff-balancing change.

'Ford in Australia will "*right-size* our business" by "staff-balancing *changes*", according to chief executive Marin Burela. "We would be taking *proactive* steps *in terms of* reducing our *throughput* through our build operations . . . In line with the production *down-balance* we have also taken the opportunity to take a good look *strategically* where we are, what we're doing and how do we *move forward*."'

Age, 16 October 2008

risk management

Managing risk. Minimising risk. Taking risks (*risk-taking*). Covering your arse. Having an *exit strategy*. Having insurance. Having *common sense*. Stating the obvious. Laying off.

'The training is *focused* on performance *outcomes*, skills and knowledge required to identify risks and apply established *risk management processes* to a subset of an organisation or projects operation that are within the person's own work responsibilities and area of operation. *Key learning outcomes* of the *risk management processes* are: Identifying risk within your workplace. Analyse and evaluate risk. Treat risks. Monitor and review effectiveness of risk treatments. Face to face classroom *delivery* will be used to *facilitate* the underpinning knowledge requirements.'

Down to Earth Results

'The NSA Report is obsessed with framing the debate over surveillance around the neopositivist vocabulary of "*risk management*", but we know from history that political liberty will always suffer when a dominant regime deems a nation, its leadership or its population a "national security threat".'

Geographical Imaginations. Posts about Edward Snowden by Derek Gregory

risk-take

Take risks.

> 'They *risk-taked* all night.'
>
> AFL football commentator

> 'Hardly surprising really that a *risk-taker* like Ms Russo was a wrong fit for the risk adverse [sic] environment of the legal profession.'
>
> CareerOne Job Network

> 'The best *outcome* is that the child will "*risk-take*" within the boundaries of personal safety.'
>
> RTA NSW

road map

Something to follow.

> 'I am eager to *ensure* this *transformation* provides a clear *road map* and clarity on the objectives which underpin it, so that we can all constructively *engage* with it.'
>
> News Ltd CEO to staff

> '"Rebuilding America's Defenses" became the *road map* for foreign policy decisions made in the White House and the Pentagon; PNAC had the Vice President's office in one building, and the Defense Secretary's office in the other. Attacking Iraq was central to that *road map* from the beginning . . .'
>
> William Rivers Pitt, August 2004

robust

'We appreciate Dell showing *strong* support for the bulk of our *product offering* and the strength of our *road map*.'
Scott McLaughlin, a spokesman for California-based Intel BL

'Richard Eary: First going on to Next G, *in terms of* the *road map*, *in terms of* devices, obviously I think the launch of the dongles on megs, and early next year, can you just give a feel in terms of what the *road map* is going to be actually for physical handsets?'

Telstra Investor Day, November 2008

robust

1. Strong, vigorous, sturdy, hale and hearty, lusty, strapping, durable, etc.; e.g. An English oak is a *robust* tree, Bruce Willis a r. sort of chap.
2. A good kind of anything – r. discussion (aka 'full and frank exchange'), r. organisation, r. quality assurance, r. debate, even r. opportunity, as in: 'The *process* includes independent assessment and decision making by the Planning Assessment Commission, featuring a *robust* and comprehensive opportunity for community members to have their concerns considered by decision makers' (NSW Minerals Council).

'We've always had a *robust* party room, and I hope that will always continue.'

Tony Abbott, PM, April 2015

'World class commissioning will be *robustly performance managed*.'

Michael Sobanja, Dip HSM Dip IoD Cert HEFRSM, Chief Executive, NHS Alliance

3. Not biased or inconvenient.

> 'If someone raises a concern about the *robustness* of some research that's been done, on which other people might rely, it's quite appropriate to have the *robustness* of that tested out . . . I mean, his concern is with the *robustness* of some work . . . I am turning my mind, as is the department in consultation with me, as to how we can be sure that we can get some *robust* and reliable information.'
>
> Amanda Vanstone, ABC, 10 February 2005

rocket science (not)

Easy, simple, straightforward, comprehensible, uncomplicated, not as hard as it looks, plain as the nose on your face, etc. As, 'It's not *rocket science*, Jeremy.'

rockstar

An outstanding employee. As, 'If your employee isn't an asshole but simply a *rockstar* – a *culture* fit but a little weird, wacky, or eccentric – what do you do? The *key* is to bring out the awesome and minimize the disruptive from them' (Four Signs Your *Rockstar* is an Asshole', Techco).

rocopoly money

'[Q]uarterly bonuses for Citigroup employees paid according to the number of existing borrowers they could lure into new loans . . .' 'The more gullible the consumer appeared, the more coverages I would try to include in the loan' (former CitiFinancial employee quoted in Andrew Cockburn, *Harpers*, April 2015).

roll-out

(n) Commencement, beginning, *implementation* of the *plan* or *strategy* – e.g. military invasion, new computer program, etc. Go *live*.
(v) To put the plan into *action*, *implement*, *go live*, etc.
(As in: When's *roll-out* on the monitoring *strategy*, the *empowering vision*, breakfast? etc.)

> 'Effective at *knowledge transfer*, training, and *roll-out* support, including *development* of training materials and user documentation.'
>
> Resume

> 'You'll *drill down* into how to set up and *roll out* a *performance improvement framework* in your organization . . . You'll *benchmark* how to integrate your disparate systems into one streamlined *performance management framework* and how to inject greater *customer centricity* into your service *delivery initiatives*.'
>
> *Performance Improvement Frameworks* for Government Service *Delivery* Conference

rubber hits the road

Business as car, truck, bicycle or wheelbarrow tyre: determining traction, grip, how fast it can go. The nitty gritty, where truth will out, etc.

> 'That is where the real diplomatic *rubber hits the road*.'
>
> Michael Sainsbury, *Crikey*, 25 February 2015

> 'Kevin Rudd made a lot of promises, but not much *rubber hit the road*.'
>
> *Inside Story*, 3 February 2015

'"This is where the *rubber hits the road in terms of* the future of the world economy and I look forward to meeting with my fellow finance ministers and central bank governors over the next few days as we shape the destiny of the world economy," Mr Hockey said.'

Sydney Morning Herald, 20 February 2014

'Our *mission* and our *values* decide how the *rubber hits the road*.'

Business leader speech

'Where the *rubber hits the road in terms of strategies* and *goals*.'

Corporate document

run it up the flagpole (and see if anyone salutes)

To put forward a *plan* and see what the response is. Take soundings. Test the water. Throw something into the ring. Throw it at the wall and see if it sticks. Something to do at a *brainstorming* session, *workshop*, think tank, etc. Probably began in advertising agencies in the US where they run up flags all the time, c. 1950s.

'We'll *run it up the flagpole* and see who salutes that booger.'

Texas House Speaker Gib Lewis

rural values

The *main game* for country folk.

S

scalable

As with mountains, walls, etc., easily done. As, 'Queensland Corrective Centres are fully *scalable* to ensure prisoner numbers, which fluctuate for a range of reasons, can be accommodated at any given *point in time*' (www.dailymercury.com.au). Little *efforting* required. Low cost, handsome return. Ripper.

> 'Adopt efficient, *scalable*, security *enhanced* cloud-enabled services to help expand reach and improve citizen participation in government affairs.'
>
> www.microsoft.com

> 'In preserving the principles of sustained *impact* and *accountability*, the approach has the potential to bring *scalability* and *innovation* to shared-*value initiatives* that underpin *strategic* competitiveness.'
>
> *European Financial Review*, 14 April 2015

scope / scoping

To research, analyse, evaluate, document, study, look at, look over, peruse, read, check, scrutinise, skim.

> 'Traditionally, curriculum *frameworks* are descriptions of what is known to curriculum *developers* and which is then *scoped* and sequenced for the benefit of learners [sic].'
>
> Queensland Studies Authority

> 'The Training Working Group of the former Vertebrate Pests Committee (VPC) initiated this *scoping* study into past and present pest animal training and capacity building.'
>
> Pest Smart

screw the pooch

1. (vulgar) Avoid productivity. Waste time. As, 'Are you going to sit there and *screw the pooch* all day?' Polite version of earlier military, 'Fuck the dog': to fritter or idle away time (*Slate*, 14 January 2014).
2. (vulgar) To blunder or make a catastrophic mistake. As, in *The Right Stuff* (1979) Tom Wolfe reports it as slang used by test pilots in the 1950s. The test pilot who *screwed the pooch* was the one who died in the wreckage of his plane. In business, to stuff up a deal, a meeting, a relationship, etc.

> 'Sweet Jesus, Harry, you surely *screwed the pooch* last night, didn't you?'
>
> Charlton Heston in *True Lies* (1994)

> 'Of course, and we have royally *screwed the pooch* on that front.'
>
> Clarissa Ward, re Syria, *Face the Nation*, 16 December 2013

sea change

1. A slow but profound change; in Shakespeare's *The Tempest*, one wrought by the sea:

'Nothing of him that doth fade,
but doth suffer a *sea change*,
into something rich and strange.'

2. *Lifestyle change*. As, 'Find Real Estate & Property For Sale by *Seachange* Realty – Emu Park.' 'A loose coalition of 56 high-growth councils, called the *Sea Change* Task Force, is lobbying state and federal governments for an estimated $5 billion it argues is needed for infrastructure work in coastal regions over the next 15 years' (AIM, 1 November 2004).

3. Change in market conditions. As, 'I have been describing the *sea change* going on as a belief that the dollar has topped and oil has bottomed' (Jim Cramer, 4 May 2015).
4. Any change.

> 'The *migration* of internet usage from desktops to a plethora of new devices has ushered in a massive *sea change* in the *relationship* that *brands* have with *customers*, according to Adobe CEO Shantanu Narayen.'
>
> Which50, 28 July 2015

> '*Sea Change* Foundation is dedicated to *achieving* meaningful social *impact* through *leveraged* philanthropy that addresses the most pressing problems facing the world today.'

seamless

Without seams. As, 'Christ's seamless shroud'; 'Ace seamless gutters', etc. Invisible seams. Insignificant seams. Seamless where no seams are possible anyway: as, 'A seamless transition'; 'a quick, seamless interaction from real world to digital'.

> 'In 2008, COAG agreed to *implement* regulation and competition reforms under the National *Partnership* Agreement to Deliver a *Seamless* National Economy.'
>
> www.coag.gov.au

> 'The prototyping process will: Contribute to increasing the effectiveness of the public sector to build *seamless* government experiences.'
>
> design.gov.au

> 'The "Meet You There" tagline acts as an invitation to experience *key* brand elements through clever headlines and energetic images of people gathering in different settings. "Wi-Fi, Mai-Tai, Say Hi" shows guests coming together, *seamlessly* blending business and leisure – also known as "bleisure".'
>
> Sheraton Hotels press release, 21 June 2011

selfie

Photo of self.

> 'Essentially a glorified self-portrait, the *selfie* has become "the" method used by celebs to show they are just like the rest of us.'
>
> www.profoundry.co

senior living

Housing and other amenities for old or obsolete citizens. A category of real estate for people for whom the wheel is coming full circle, who hath borne most . . ., etc.

A *lifestyle* and *marketing* category. As, '*Senior Living* Marketing Experts Dan Gartlan and Nicole Wagner to Speak at Two Upcoming LeadingAge Conferences . . . This informal setting will allow attendees to get a hands-on insight exploring a series of proven *tactics* and *strategies* that can help *engage* new audiences and draw prospects to their facilities. "Integrated *Marketing Strategies* to Attract Prospects to Your *Brand* and *Drive* Occupancy" will focus on Gartlan's *innovative* Attraction *Marketing* program and the techniques that can strengthen current marketing programs and *enhance* results' (PRWEB 26 August 2015).

Also extremely senior living. As, 'Treasurer Joe Hockey has raised the prospect of people living until 150 to explain why Australians should accept cuts to government benefits and pay a greater share of their health costs' (*Sydney Morning Herald*, 19 January 2015).

> 'Paradise Village *Senior Living* has lovely fruit and pine trees, and a nice courtyard for each building with fountains and gorgeous landscaped grounds. We also have a beautiful clubhouse, and salon.'

> '. . . will you still need me, will you still feed me, when I'm in *senior living*?'

separated (and dis-established)

Let go.

> 'We had something like 44 *separations* as of the first of July, 2012 and we will have something of the order of 30 positions *dis-established* and we expect that that will mean . . . real losses of capacity.'
>
> Crime and Misconduct Commission (Queensland) Chairman Ross Martin (he later clarified his answer to say the 30 *dis-established* positions were included in the 44 *separations*)

service owner model

Vitally important, portfolio-based model for a university business with customers. As, 'ITS last year introduced the matrix management structure and the *service owner model* (i.e. portfolio-based) to provide clear management *accountabilities*, an *agile* response to *change* and greater *focus* on *delivering* superior service and *value* to the University. This decision, along with many other changes we are going through in ITS, is vitally important if we are to keep pace with our changing business environment and evolving *customer needs*' (email from Executive Director IT and Chief Information Officer at a Melbourne university, April 2012).

servicing the target

1. Military. Bombing the bejesus out of the target.
2. Space. 'The experimental servicing satellite ESS applies robotics to resolve the problem of *servicing* a non-cooperative *target* in or near to a geostationary orbit, a region of space still out of reach to manned spaceflight' (European Space Agency).
3. Other. *Servicing the Target* by Cherise Sinclair (The 'ascendant erotica queen', *Rolling Stone*). 'A discharged Army Ranger, Ben considers his job as a BDSM club security guard to be an excellent hobby . . . He's never been tempted to join in. But everything changes when the notorious Mistress Anne . . .'

set the agenda / agenda set

To decide what the game will be and how it will be played. Politicians try to set the *agenda* so that they can play the game on their terms. When they fail in this, they become defensive and reactive; they get 'on the back foot' and it may show up on television.

To *set the agenda* is to be *proactive*, positive, to get 'on the front foot', to show leadership, etc. This may involve *pushing the envelope* on policy. If there is no policy worth announcing, or you're losing on that front, you can always talk about threats (inc. budget crises, military crises, boat people crises, etc.) and keep repeating the words 'Team' and 'Australia'. Or you can head for the bush and get in touch with *ordinary*, *common-sense* Australians and rural *values*.

This way (contrary to 'the *Agenda Setting* Function Theory, which suggests that the media can't tell you what to think but it can tell you what to think about'), you'll be setting the media *agenda*, and that's more important than the policy *agenda* anyway. Meanwhile the people will think *they* are *setting* the policy *agenda* which adds to the beauty of the whole *initiative* and proves the soundness of the *strategy*.

> 'This has been Joe Hockey's show – hosting the dignitaries – *setting the agenda* in a shifting global climate.'
>
> *Australian Financial Review*, 21 September 2014

shareholders

Easily forgotten category of human beings. More than half of all Australian human beings. Human beings to whom companies, who are also human beings, have obligations. *Stakeholder* subset. Source of happiness and despair.

> 'Interviewer: . . . do you think that executives of the company were somewhat blind to the moral responsibility and moral *issues* in all of this?
>
> Meredith Hellicar: We are human beings. You cannot be blind to this awful, awful disease, and none of us has been blind to that . . . But – and we can't rewrite history. The fact of the matter is, we can't wish away our legal and fiduciary responsibilities and as much as we would like to in many respects, at the end of the day, we're custodians on behalf of the *shareholders*. We have obligations to our *shareholders* and you know, I think perhaps that's been forgotten in all of this.'
>
> Chair, James Hardie Industries, August 2004

> 'Applying these studies to *shareholder* empowerment, it is misguided not to respect increasing *shareholder* power as an end in itself . . . If participation is a *key* factor contributing to individual happiness, and the pursuit of happiness is the natural underlying objective of all human beings, then participation rather than passivity becomes the rational choice.'
>
> James McConvill, Online Opinion, 26 April 2006

shifting the goalposts

Changing the rules while the game's being played. A low, unprincipled act, contrary to the spirit of business or politics.

shoot the puppy

See *swallow the frog*

shortfall

1. Not enough. Less than what is needed.
2. Less than what is generous or expected or just or proper, etc. An insufficient amount. Stingy, paltry, mean, etc.

> 'We were truly, truly sorry that there was a *shortfall* in our initial funding of the foundation. We do regret the anxiety and concern that that *outcome* may have caused sufferers and their families and the community.'
>
> Chair, James Hardie Industries, August 2004, speaking about an underfunded foundation for victims of asbestosis

> 'Accredited Home Lenders Holding Co. became the latest player in mortgages to the poor and credit-blemished to admit that it was grappling with a liquidity *shortfall*.'
>
> *The Times*, 14 March 2007

shortly

(adv) Of, pertaining to or heralding a void of indeterminate dimensions, often set to music or advertising. The longest recorded *shortly* is five of Vivaldi's *The Four Seasons*. 'A customer service representative/operator will be with you *shortly*.'

> '*Shortly* the Rockies may crumble
> Gibraltar may tumble . . . etc.'

> 'Better shortly than never.'

showcase / showcasing

Exhibiting, revealing, showing, demonstrating, making known, starring, trotting out, displaying, with. As, 'Ski resort *showcasing* spectacular views.' Etc. What one does with talent and all *vibrant* things.

> 'Cr John Foss says he is looking forward to the festival, which *showcases* the *vibrant* culture and *lifestyle* of the Surf Coast Shire.'
>
> Groundswell, The Surf Coast Shire Community Newsletter

> '*Showcasing iconic* locations in both Australia and overseas, *LowRange* is hosted by John "Roothy" Rooth, Australia's best known four wheel driver, bush mechanic and camp fire cook.'
>
> Roothy's LowRange

> 'Penthouse *Showcasing* a Designer Renovation.'
>
> L. J. Hooker

'*Penthouse showcasing* erotic photography as an art form.'

Penthouse

'*Showcasing* your strategy through storytelling.'

Westpac

'Ironically, *showcasing* your newfound six-pack won't be just about the abs.'

www.muscleandfitness.com

sidebar meeting

Extra meeting. Not the main one. As, 'Not now. Let's *dialogue* it in a *sidebar meeting*.'

signage

More than one sign, including signs of a 'way-finding' kind: as, 'Follow the *signage* to Mildura.' One sign. Signs as infrastructure. For the time being, one need not speak of the *signage* of puberty, diphtheria, religious mania, etc., nor speak to the deaf in *signage* language.

'Way-finding *signage* is infrastructure that provides information to motorists, cyclists and pedestrians on how to find services and places of interest within urban and natural environments. It is important that way-finding *signage* makes visitors feel comfortable and safe when experiencing new environments.'

Webb Dock Redevelopment Development Guidance Note

'For the purpose of the Comprehensive *Signage* Policy, this category of signs does not include regulatory, warning, guidance, destination and street *signage*.'

Mornington Peninsula Shire

'. . . outward and visible *signage* of an inward and spiritual grace.'

'Oates was showing *signage* of exhaustion.'

'We will review the risk *signage* at the site . . . We consult with *stakeholders* at the end of each season.'

Parks Victoria ranger after a woman drowned at a beach, *Age*, 24 January 2012

significant

Full of meaning, import, consequence, etc. Much less than that – even to the point of insignificance.

'The vigorous, vaguely quantitative words, "*significant*" and "significantly" are used 5 times on this slide, with meanings ranging from "detectable in a perhaps irrelevant calibration case study" to an amount of damage so that everyone dies to a difference of 640-fold.'

Edward R. Tufte, on the Boeing PowerPoint slides that led NASA to ignore a hole in the Columbia space shuttle

'As you reflect upon the *cultural* promise of your organization and yourself, there is one more thing that is *embedded* in the success of these *brands*: they seek to be *significant*. Your *cultural* promise defines your *significance* factor. The more your organization dedicates itself to the promise of the *culture* you are trying to create, the more your people and *brand* look to be not only successful, but also *significant*.'

Glenn Lopis, *Forbes*, 9 December 2011

'Q: So Mr Morrison, you are not even going to confirm there is a boat, you are not going to say what is happening if people are in the water? . . .

A: What I have said is that it is our practice to report on *significant* events at sea . . . If there was a *significant* event happening then I would be reporting on it . . .

Q: So could you clarify, sir, for us – at what point does an event become a *significant* event involving a boat on the water?

A: When you see me here standing and reporting on it.

Q: And you are standing here reporting.

A: I am not. I am saying there is no such report for me to provide to you today . . .

This should come as no surprise to you . . . This is another day at the office for *Operation Sovereign Borders*.'

Sydney Morning Herald, 4 July 2014

silos

1. Storages for wheat, etc. Welcome.
2. Storages for knowledge. Unwelcome. May be human nature. As, '*Silo* Mentality in business is so common that it is assumed to be a fundamental problem of human nature, and thus viewed as yet another element managers must manage' (www.perceptiondynamics.info).

'Juniper had too many *silos* and too many priorities. It was top heavy and conflict avoidant.'

Harvard Business Review, July–August 2015

'But if you look at their [teachers'] performance, from a knowledge perspective, they may in fact represent the ultimate in hermetically sealed knowledge *silos*.'

Wayne Hewett, Setting up Communities of Practice

'Treat *customer* experience as a *competence*, not a function: *Customer service* is everyone's *priority*, not just that of the contact center. Call it "*customer experience*", "*customer* advocacy", "*customer* insight" – anything, Temkin pleaded, that avoids dumping it into a *siloed* department.'

Jessica Tsai, 'The 5 Levels of Customer Experience Maturity'

'It's also important to note that *silos* can be vertical or horizontal. Individual units can have high barriers between them or senior *leadership* can be completely isolated from lower *management* levels.'

www.forbes.com

silver bullet

No such thing. Never has been and never will be, and no-one ever thought there could be. Phantom. Rhetorical device to highlight one's own common sense. As, 'while we know there is no *silver bullet* to fix the health system, there is a growing and urgent call, especially from *key* health *stakeholders*, for *change*, through sensible *reform* measures, to put the patient back at the centre of all of our efforts' (Premier of Tasmania, 26 July 2014).

situational awareness

Awareness of a situation.

'As the Marines entered Nasiriya, their "*situational awareness* became clouded" because of deviations from the maneuver plan, the urban environment and communications problems, according to the report.'

CNN

'Actually, their work at paying attention, at developing *situational awareness* makes them more alive, more aware of their world and their life, helps them avoid ever having to use their handgun, and if they do, makes it more likely they'll survive to enjoy those additional years of inspirational awareness.'

Mike McDaniel, The Truth About Guns

skill set

Personal collection, assembly, anthology, arrangement, etc., of skills. Employees of quality organisations, including football clubs, have *skill sets.* At this point in their development, farmers, mechanics, jockeys, people engaged in home duties and many other vocations may have extensive assortments or whole rafts of skills, but they do not have them in sets.

'Explaining why they had spent more than 600 million dollars on them, DFAT said that private security contractors had "high quality and contemporary *skill-sets,* invaluable in-country knowledge, and experience in specific operating environments".'

Age, 1 March 2015

'Enhancing your *skillset* to outgrow a pure transactional role and *drive* the *paradigm* toward higher awareness and *utilisation* of *data* intelligence.'

Australian Chief Information Officer Summit, July 2013

skin in the game

A 'widely used and imperfect aphorism of uncertain origins' (Michael Corey). Having some personal involvement in the game – i.e. business, politics, gambling, war. As, 'Warren Buffet prefers shares in companies whose executives are heavily invested in their enterprise.'

> 'A NEW technology investment fund is at the heart of the *strategy* for *transforming* the CSIRO under former Silicon Valley venture capitalist Larry Marshall . . . He says the 3900 patents within the CSIRO are a "Pandora's box" of technology that should be mined for commercial opportunities. But that mining of opportunities will only work commercially if the CSIRO itself can show it has *skin in the game*.'
>
> www.queenslandcountrylife.com.au

social capital

Society. Society rediscovered, and found to be actually necessary and actually good for business. Recognition of an 'important *downside*': 'communities, groups or networks which are isolated, parochial or working at cross-purposes to society's collective interests (e.g. drug cartels, corruption rackets) can actually hinder economic and social development' (World Bank). Education, health, welfare programs, charities, training, sport, networks, the arts, people are all *social capital.* Social resources; the resources of communities.

> 'Investment in *social capital* is investment in success.'
>
> Wayne Baker

'*Social capital* refers to the institutions, relationships, and norms that shape the quality and quantity of a society's social interactions . . . Not just the sum of the institutions which underpin society . . . the glue that holds them together.'

World Bank

'Business has to *deliver*: by good *governance* on its own part, by building *social capital* on the part of communities and the nation.'

Business speech

socialise

1. Mix with people; get out and about.
2. Nationalise. Bring the means of production, distribution and exchange under public or state control.
3. To be rendered or render oneself fit for social intercourse.
4. To circulate for *feedback*. As, 'We need to *socialise* this idea with the management team.'

'A number of activities were undertaken to reinforce *Values*, including a *Values socialisation* program to more than 7000 employees and a "*Values* of the Month" program.'

Corporate Responsibility Report, Coca-Cola Amatil

Solution Architect

As follows: 'The purpose of the *Solution Architect* role is to lead *strategic* design, *scoping* activities and support the *implementation* of information *solutions* that meet organisational *plans*, *needs*, and *functions*, and assure their *alignment* to enterprise *goals* and the overall IS *architecture*. The role has primary responsibility for maintaining and deploying the *Enterprise Architecture*, with particular emphasis on Technology Infrastructure and the Security *Framework*' (New Zealand District Health Board).

solutioneer

(n) *brainstormer*. As, 'The types of *workshops* we run include: Decision Making, *Alignment* (Conflict Resolution), *Visioning*, *Planning*, *Scope Development*, *Solutioneering* (*Brainstorming*)'.
(v) brainstorm. As, 'We're *solutioneering* the data issue.'

> 'James Burke is a brilliant historian and sociologist who combines his knowledge to create relevant connections of how our world was changed and some of the problems with these changes. His statement here is an inspiration for approaching these problems. It is useful for a *Solutioneer* because it provides an approach to take and encourages us towards control of our own destiny.'
>
> www.solutioneers.net

solutions

What *lifestyle* demands and the free market provides. What the computer industry creates, along with the need for them. As, 'innovative *solutions*', staffing *solutions*, hair *solutions*, shoe storage *solutions*, military *solutions*, style *solutions*, 'QMI *solutions*: empowering business.' What you need to be part of if you don't want to be part of the problem.

> 'In my lifetime all the problems have come from mainland Europe, and all the *solutions* have come from the English-speaking nations across the world.'
>
> Margaret Thatcher

'Tern *Solutions* specialises in running *team* workshops at all levels in an organisation with group sizes of up to 40 people. We do more than just *agenda* time-keeping and *conversation* queuing.

Our *workshops* are an integral part of our *consultancy engagements* and prove to be effective in quickly *addressing issues* and *aligning teams* and *team* members.'

www.tern.com.au

space

Not outer, but inner. A region of the mind, a little like the afterlife in being so hard to describe. Some people get in the wrong *space*, some in just a different *space*.

'A new bit of jargon has recently entered the Canberra lexicon. People talk about being in this or that "*space*". Just now, Julia Gillard and Tony Abbott are both in the "*space*" of seeking ways to get Australians off welfare and into work.'

Michelle Grattan, *Sydney Morning Herald*, 1 April 2011

'I've made it perfectly clear to local government that failure in that *space* is unacceptable and if there were to be failure in that space then obviously the state government would have to take action.'

Peter Gutwein, Tasmanian Treasurer, *Examiner*, 19 May 2015

spend

(v) Outlay, e.g. money. As, '*spend* a penny'. 'Don't *spend* it all at once', etc.
(n) The money. The penny. What one spends. Expenditure, spending . . . etc.

'Traditionally, it's been the procurement guy who wants to know how much *spend* is used towards contingents.'

Forbes

'This report shows a list of cost centers ranked by *spend* with a running total of *spend* amount and the percentage of *spend* for a selected date range. You can drill down by cost center to view *spend* for the cost centers in the next level of the hierarchy structure.'

SAP

'Hey, big *spender*,
Spend a little of your *spend* with me.'

spilled

Made redundant, let go . . . etc. As, 'According to workplace union Professionals Australia, 33 GRDC workers, or about half the organisation, were told their jobs have been "*spilled*" and that they would have to apply for changed roles within a week' (*Age*, 17 June 2015).

spin

Story telling. Probably derives from 'spinning a yarn'; but it might also refer to the spin bowlers put on a cricket ball or pitchers on a baseball with the intention of deceiving. In tennis and table tennis, spin is used to control the flight and bounce of the ball and to keep it in play, and it is the same in politics. *Spin* aims to control the interpretation of events where the events themselves cannot be controlled.

Politicians instinctively put a *spin* on events, but in the interests of keeping the story consistent and leaving the pollie to practise being genuine and spontaneous, people known as Media Advisers, Media *Strategists* or *spin* doctors are employed to persuade the media to buy it. Successful *spin* creates the political equivalent of staff sign off by the media. *Spin* doctors or *spin*meisters are often journalists on leave from the press gallery.

It is true that *spin* embellishes and manipulates the truth, and that sometimes outright lies are told. But just as often *spin* is the only way to convey the truth, to defeat lies and confusion (see Aristotle), to properly counsel patience, to put words and events in context. As much as the media sneers at *spin*, they also depend on it. The relationship is interdependent if not downright incestuous. Companies, business leaders, NGOs and government departments all employ *spin* doctors.

stability and reconstruction operation

Not war. Warish.

> '"The United States is not sufficiently structured or prepared for the next SRO (*Stability and Reconstruction Operation*)," Bowen concluded, using Pentagon jargon for modern military campaigns.'
>
> www.huffingtonpost.com

staff signoff

Stage in a *strategic plan* – agreement, capitulation. Get workers' names on it. On board, in the cart, etc. Give them *ownership*, a say in things. Mug them in a *strategic* context.

> 'I plan to return to staff with an emergent QSA *Strategic Plan* for fine-tuning and *staff signoff*.'
>
> Consultancy document

stakeholder process ownership

What every hospital needs.

> 'IPHoA management philosophy seeks *continuous improvement* in the *quality* of all the *processes*, *products* and services of an organisation. It emphasises the reaction to *process* variance, *stakeholder process ownership*, the importance of measurement, the role of the *customer* and the involvement of employees at all levels in an organisation in pursuit of such improvements.'
>
> Independent Private Hospitals of Australia

stakeholders

1. Person or organisation with a stake, i.e. a share or interest.
2. People in a nursing home; people engaged in *senior living*.
As, 'At Easter the *stakeholders* all wore bonnets and those who could joined in singing "It's a long way to Tipperary".'

> 'We have consulted with our *stakeholders* in industry and across government to update the *plan* so it reflects current *challenges* and government priorities to pursue the ICT-as-a-service *agenda* and a cloud-first approach to ICT delivery.'
>
> Ian Walker, Queensland Minister for Science etc., 2014

> '*Sustainability* is determined by an organisation's ability to create and *deliver value* for all *stakeholders*.'
>
> Principles of Business Excellence, Gracedale Private Nursing Home

> 'It is standard practice for Australian government agencies to have stock of corporate gifts available for customary purposes to assist with *stakeholder* relationships.'

Statement regarding 2000 Border Force-branded plush dogs to be given to international dignitaries and visitors,
Age, 6 September 2015

All *stakeholders* are relevant but some are more relevant than others. As, 'An *implementation strategy* for the NIQTSL (National Institute for *Quality* Teaching and School *Leadership*) will consider the roles, functions, governance arrangements, operational and funding requirements, *performance indicators* and relationships with relevant *stakeholders*' (Federal Department of Education, Science & Training).

Some are more key: 'Relevant *stakeholders* (*key* and other) can be brought together through the Steering Committee to consider all relevant issues of the MPS proposal for the community, and to drive the process of development' (WA Department of Health).

> 'And Moses called unto them; and Aaron and all the other key *stakeholders* returned unto him. And Moses messaged them.'

start-up

Small business just starting. First step on the road to fortune. As, 'Launching a beverage *start-up* in a saturated market, dominated by the Red Bulls and Monster Energy drinks of the world, isn't for the faint of heart' (CNBC, 29 July 2015). Where entrepreneurs begin life. The pulse of private enterprise, often started with a government grant.

> 'Hockey says Labor's changes to the taxation of employee share schemes have put a handbrake on *start-ups* . . .'
>
> *Business Review Weekly*, 3 July 2013

state of the art

On the frontier of innovation; the *cutting edge*/leading edge of design, technology, management, ideas, fashion inc. facelifts, haircuts, etc. New in every respect except the term for it.

> 'Our wargame specialists design games to reveal operational *synergies*, accommodate a wide range of *scenarios*, and explore the role of the latest technologies. Our *state-of-the-art* wargaming and modeling facilities give senior defense and business executives the ability to test advanced concepts, conduct integrated training, and *engage* in real-time interactive *scenarios*, including distributed simulations.'
>
> Booz Allen Hamilton consultants

step up to the plate

1. (US baseball) What a batter does when it's his turn.
2. To come forward; put oneself on the line; become engaged; take one's turn; do one's duty; be accountable; accept responsibility; do what's necessary, proper, right, appropriate, manly, brave, etc.

> 'When disasters strike our shores – whether they take the form of bushfires, earthquakes or mass murder – it is often local government leaders that *step up to the plate*.'
>
> President of the Australian Local Government Association, 2002

> 'He encourages individuals to become self-motivated while challenging them to *step up to the plate* of personal responsibility.'
>
> Byrd Baggett – on Byrd Baggett

stove-piped

Failure to properly share and analyse information before passing it onto leadership, especially intelligence information, often with the intention to mislead, e.g. 'Each department has its own *horizon scanning* policy *development* machinery. If I was to identify the first risk, it is this work is *stove-piped*' (Jon Day, UK Senior Intelligence official).

> 'Some of the *stove-piping* is broken down to get departments together about the *issues* that are approaching.'
>
> Director of the UK Civil Contingency Secretary, *Telegraph*, UK, 21 April 2015

> '"Due to time constraints, TSA's technical environment evolved in a decentralized manner, leading to *stovepiped* systems with limited information sharing and technical standards," the report said.'
>
> www.nationaldefensemagazine.org

strategic delivery channel

Channel for a library's *value proposition.*

> 'The Academic Outreach team is a *strategic delivery channel* for the library's *value proposition*, in a one on one environment with primary *stakeholders* – academics, researchers and HDR students . . . *Strategic* initiatives and objectives are developed in *alignment* with University goals as part of the annual *strategic planning process* in which all Library teams participate. Library goals are met through cross team projects and team plans which are guided by the *Vision*, *Mission* and *Goals* and the Library's *performance indicator framework*.'
>
> University of Wollongong

strategic imperative

From imperative: must be done; and strategic: tactical, calculated. Something that must be done tactically, or something that must be done if the strategy is to succeed. As, 'This marginalisation of women is not in keeping with Cricket Australia's "*strategic imperative*" of attracting more women and girls to the game over the next four years' (Angela Pippos, *New Daily*, 27 November 2013).

> 'At Vistage, we see opportunities in the *challenges* and we are continuing our *commitment* to our four *strategic imperatives* . . . *Build* our *brand*. *Grow* our business organically. Expand internationally. *Leverage* technology.
>
> As I'll be talking about these imperatives more specifically during the coming weeks, I'd like to ask you to consider these three questions: 1) What are your *strategic imperatives*? 2) Do all your *people* know what they are? 3) Is your company *culturally* and structurally positioned to *achieve* your *strategic imperatives*?'
>
> blog.vistage.com

strategic issue

An *issue* that the company needs to manage. An *issues* management consultant can help.

strategic oversight

1. Something missed in the *strategy*. Something missed, e.g. position of the enemy forces; resistance of the enemy forces; failings of one's own forces. Stuff-up, cock-up, etc.
2. Not the other way of doing it. Oversight – overseeing – at the *strategic* end of the spectrum.

'We, the undersigned members of the Joint *Strategic* Planning Subgroup for Oversight of Afghanistan Reconstruction, are pleased to present the Inspectors General Fiscal Year 2013 Joint *Strategic Oversight* Plan for Afghanistan Reconstruction.'

Joint Strategic Planning Subgroup For Oversight Of Afghanistan Reconstruction

'*Strategic oversight* of resources by government.'

Victorian Department of Treasury and Finance

strategic philanthropy

An expression of *Corporate Social Responsibility* based on the Macedonian or Panhellenic model: 'I do not ask what is becoming for you to receive, but what is becoming for me to give' (Alexander the Great).

'Few phrases are as overused and poorly defined as "*strategic philanthropy*". The term is used to cover virtually any kind of charitable activity that has some definable theme, *goal*, approach, or *focus*. In the corporate context, it generally means that there is some connection, however vague or tenuous, between the charitable contribution and the company's business . . . In fact, most corporate giving programs have nothing to do with a company's *strategy*. They are primarily aimed at generating goodwill and positive publicity and boosting employee morale . . . True *strategic* giving, by contrast, addresses important social and economic *goals* simultaneously, *targeting* areas of competitive context where the company and society both benefit because the firm brings unique *assets* and expertise.'

Harvard Business Review, December 2002

'. . . corporations remain wary about *engaging* in social programmes that *enhance human capital*, especially if these programmes do not contain an immediate, direct, and measurable benefit to the *core* business . . . Building on recent advances in social-*impact* (SI) investment, we develop a *partnership* approach that *outsources* the *risk* that corporate investors and *shareholders* see in *strategic philanthropy* and that compensates corporations for incremental societal benefits inherent in *strategic philanthropy*.'

European Financial Review, 14 April 2015

strategic plan

Planned strategy. Contains *core visions* and *outcomes* – and *strategies*. *Drives* things. Linked to *actions* of delivery *programs*. *Strategic planning* – planning with a plan in mind.

'Organisational Strategic Direction

Holroyd City Council has established a set of plans that outline the *long-term vision* for the future of our city, which has been created in *partnership* with our *community*. The Living Holroyd *Community Strategic Plan* provides the *core vision* for Holroyd's future and the *key community outcomes* that form the basis of Council's *planning*. The *Delivery* Program (incorporating Council's Annual Operational *Plan*) establishes a rolling program of *actions* and *priorities* outlining how Council will work toward *delivering* the *strategies* contained within the *Community Strategic Plan*. It is these *plans* that drive our organisation and all staff have a responsibility in understanding that each program, each service and each decision identified in the Operational *Plan* is linked to the *actions* of the *Delivery* Program which in turn respond to the *outcomes* and *strategies* of the Living Holroyd *community Strategic Plan*.'

Holroyd, NSW, advertisement for a landscape architect

strategic staircase

Growing the company in a *strategic* direction (upwards) one step at a time. 'The staircase approach of continuously compounding skills and options . . .' (McKinsey).

> '5.3: Officers are currently *aligning* the budget setting and business *planning process* and a revised approach to Star Chamber and service planning is being introduced and is covered elsewhere on the *agenda*. This will include a corporate balance *scorecard* and *strategic staircase* at corporate and *strategic* levels.'
>
> Slough Borough Council

> '*High Performance Culture Process*
>
> The *process* starts with a reality scan to assess the organisational climate and *culture*. From the reality scan you can now define your current reality and design your case for change on a *strategic staircase*, which will assist you to *achieve* the future intent.'
>
> www.ihpconsulting.net

strategic window

Similar window to *window of opportunity*.

> 'For every *strategy* there's a "*strategic window*". A period of time during which that *strategy* will work. But if you slip your schedule too far – if you miss that *strategic window* – your *strategy* simply won't work. Please be aware of your *strategic window*.'
>
> Bill Birnbaum, Monitoring Implementation of your *Strategic Plan*

'There is a tide in the affairs of men, which gathered at the *strategic window* . . .'

strategies (implement a range of)

1. Something quite complicated.
2. Add and subtract.

'His concrete understanding of number and place *value* allows him to effectively *implement a range of strategies* to solve addition and subtraction problems.'

School report

strategise

(v) Think of, come up with, devise a *strategy*; or do something according to a *strategy*. As, 'One of the first *actions* of the Taskforce is *strategising* ways to increase producers' awareness of management options to prevent the introduction and spread of Bovine Johne's disease' (www.animalhealthaustralia.com.au).

'*Strategise* your shopping.'

www.weightwatchers.com.au

'UC students *strategise* for science.'

www.canberra.edu.au

strategy

Without one, life is all but impossible. A science or art of military command; means of securing the objects of war. So with business or politics: essential, so long as it is the right *strategy*; so long as it is not dogma, an idée fixe, a redoubt for ideologues, egomaniacs or the entirely self-interested, an obstacle to more creative and intelligent thought. As, 'However beautiful the *strategy*, you should occasionally look at the results' (W. Churchill).

> 'The *key* advantage in CONSORTIA's approach to business and *strategic planning* is the capability of our *consultants* to *facilitate* deep levels of discussion and practical *outcomes* in *delivering* on the *strategic agenda* through *strategies* that effectively maximize *human resources*, *optimize communication strategies* and have strong underpinning *metrics* to *enable* both *accountability* and clear *delivery* of results.'
>
> CONSORTIA. *Leadership*, *Strategy* and *Performance*

> 'We must earn the prosperity we seek and this budget lays down the right *strategy*.'
>
> Joe Hockey, Federal Treasurer, *Australian Financial Review*, 25 August 2014

> 'Today, one hardly talks about *strategy* without using the language of competition. The term that best symbolizes this is "*competitive advantage*". In the *competitive-advantage* worldview, companies are often *driven* to outperform rivals and capture greater shares of existing market space.'
>
> *Harvard Business Review*

strong / stronger

Not weak, insipid, feeble, weedy, wishy-washy, namby-pamby, pathetic, etc. Like an oak tree. Like Achilles, the Terminator, etc. As, 'You know, in the old days . . . bing bong [acts firing rifle]. When we were *strong*, we were *strong*' (Donald Trump, 15 August 2015).

'"We have a *strong plan* . . . one other point I make today is the opposition leader can talk about jobs until the cows come home, and she has been doing a lot of that, but I make the point, you cannot create jobs unless you have a *strong* economy and you only have a *strong* economy if you have a proper *strong* economic *plan* and you have a *strong* stable government to deliver that *plan*," he told reporters on the Sunshine Coast . . .'

Campbell Newman, from a doorstop interview in which he used the word 'strong' 23 times

'That is what the LNP is offering. We have an economic *plan*. We have a *strong* team.'

'Our (*strong*) plan – Real *Solutions* for all Australians: The direction, *values* and policy priorities of the next Coalition Government (16 page summary/pamphlet).

p. 3: . . . we have developed our *plan* to offer Hope, Reward and Opportunity for all Australians. Our *plan* is to build a *stronger* Australia by building a *stronger* economy, a cleaner environment, *stronger* borders and more modern infrastructure. The Coalition's priority is to build a *stronger*, more productive and *diverse* economy . . .

p. 4: Our aim is to *deliver* a *stronger* Australia; a *strong* and prosperous economy . . .

p. 5: The need to build a *stronger* economy . . . It is imperative that Australia adopts a *strong* economic plan . . .

p. 6: We have an economic plan for Australia – a plan to *deliver* a *strong*, prosperous economy . . . We believe a *strong*, productive and prosperous economy . . .

p. 8: We will develop *stronger* people-to-people relationships . . . We will create a *stronger* economy and *deliver* higher productivity growth . . .

p. 9: We have an economic *plan* for Australia – a *plan* to help small businesses grow and create *stronger* jobs growth . . . we will build a *stronger*, more diverse 5-Pillar economy by building on our strengths as a nation and building *stronger* industries to produce *stronger* jobs growth . . .

p. 10: Our economic *plan* will *deliver stronger* jobs growth right across Australia . . .

p. 11: We believe that *strong* families are the bedrock of a healthy society . . . We will ensure older Australians and seniors enjoy a secure retirement by *delivering* a *stronger* economy . . .

p. 12: A *strong*, growing and prosperous economy is central to everything . . . Our aim is to build a *stronger* Australia with a *stronger* economy . . .

p. 14: We will *deliver stronger* borders . . .

p. 15: The Coalition's *strong*, experienced, united team will *deliver* a *strong* and stable government.'

successful lifestyle outcomes

Not a *lifestyle* flop. One with plumbing. As, 'Thornlands people appreciate the importance of a good relationship between functioning systems and *successful lifestyle outcomes*' (www.smartstateplumbing.com.au).

> 'The provision of a *flexible* suite of services that give older people a high level of self determination, as well as regard to privacy and respect, is critical to achieve *successful lifestyle outcomes*.'
>
> www.sutherlandshire.nsw.gov.au

supportive / supportiveness

(adj) Supporting, friendly, helpful, caring, thoughtful, generous, charitable, kind, loyal, faithful, solid, a brick, always ready to lend a hand, etc. offering or providing support; i.e. comfort, reassurance, money, guns, explosives, bodyguards, psychological and other counselling, sympathy, empathetic understanding, a hug, a cup of tea. Not neglective or merely acceptant. As, 'I want to thank my mum and dad for being *supportive*.' Some environments are *supportive* or provide *supportiveness*.

> 'So I am very, very *supportive* of the professionalism and the efforts of the Australian Defence Force, and the RAAF and the Army.'
>
> Bill Shorten, 27 August 2015

> 'He explained how he had been "emotionally *supportive*" of me, especially after I had "cried on his shoulder" in December 2003.'
>
> Mark Latham, *Australian Financial Review*, 9 August 2014

> 'Nuffer, Smith, Tucker is a public relations firm, founded in 1974, with expertise in the design and execution of *strategies* for the future, cultivating *supportive* stakeholder *relationships* and fuelling the quid pro quo exchange . . .'
>
> Nuffer, Smith, Tucker Public Relations

> 'And be *supportive*, in sickness and in health . . .'

> 'Wilt thou love her, comfort her, honour, and be *supportive* . . .'

sustainable / sustainability

1. What can be kept in existence, maintained; though merely uttering the word may satisfy one's purposes. As, 'Over the last 10 years OneSteel has embedded *sustainability* within strategy, management and operational practices. Our *people*'s *passion* and *commitment* is *driving* our *sustainability journey* and *delivering* tangible *value* for *stakeholders* . . . With over 200 *sustainability initiatives* underway, we are working hard to maximise the contribution to *sustainable* societies of today and tomorrow' (Geoff Plumme, CEO of OneSteel).

> 'The one day session on September 26th in Sydney will help participants understand carbon related *issues*, unravel the jargon and learn *strategies* on how to reduce an *events impact* on the climate, translating into cost savings and tapping into the growing demand for highly promotable *sustainable events*.'
>
> Spice News

> '. . . for richer, for poorer, in sickness and in health, to love and to cherish, *sustainably*.'

sustainable development

Development that can be sustained. Arose from *sustainability*.

> 'Northern Australia Environmental Resources – supporting the *sustainable development* of our unique northern landscapes.'
>
> Greg Hunt, Minister for the Environment,
> 25 September 2014

sustainable growth

Growth that can be sustained. Developed from *sustainable development* and interchangeable with it. As, 'Not temporary, flash-in-the-pan growth, but *sustainable growth*' (Glenn Stevens, 26 August 2015).

> 'So, our contribution to the Coral Triangle *Initiative* will *focus* on these *areas* of *leveraging* the private sector and *driving sustainable* economic *growth*.'
>
> Greg Hunt, 13 November 2014

sustained growth

Unending growth. Developed from *sustainable growth* and interchangeable with it and its antecedents. As, 'In this regard, we reaffirm the need to *achieve* economic stability, *sustained* economic *growth*, the promotion of social equity and the protection of the environment . . .' '. . . *enhance* food security and the livelihood of the poor and invigorate production and *sustained* economic *growth*' (The Future We Want, 2012 Earth Summit).

> 'But if *sustainability* means anything, it is surely the opposite of *sustained growth*. *Sustained growth* on a finite planet is the essence of unsustainability.'
>
> George Monbiot, *Guardian*, 22 June 2012

sustainable value

Value that can be sustained.

> 'We develop leaders with a global mindset who create *sustainable value* and are good citizens.'
>
> Macquarie Graduate School of Management

sustainably engaged

The gold standard for employee *engagement*: *engaged* to a very high degree, but not in a way that burns employees out or leads them to suicide. *Engagement* characteristic of the most productive companies. For example, 'Google . . . communicates an environment of playfulness from whimsical doodles to April Fool's Day jokes. Facebook is also overt about its *culture*, articulating its *values* on posters, in meetings and through other employee *communications* to ensure employee *values align* with the company' (Forbes, 14 August 2014).

> 'This issue of *Sustainably Engaged* will focus on the recent acquisition of Saville *Consulting* and how it complements *offerings* in employee *engagement* surveys.'
>
> Towers Watson

> 'Individuals who are *"sustainably" engaged* in waste management practices can see that their individual decisions can create a greater collective *impact*.'
>
> ableserve.com

> 'Their wake-up call, several of them said, was that over the last year, a series of colleagues in their division had died suddenly and prematurely, including two leaders who committed suicide, and two under the age of 50 who had heart attacks.'
>
> *Australian Financial Review*, 16 March 2015

swallow the frog

Do something unpleasant, make a hard decision, bite the bullet, screw your courage to the sticking place, etc. From

Huckleberry Finn, 'If you have to swallow a frog, don't look at it too long.'

synergise

Create *synergy*.

'Stakeholders *synergise* to make local footwear competitive.'
businessdayonline.com

'Creative Coalitions: a C20-C30-C40 "Coalition of the Working" of countries, companies and cities tackling climate change; a new cyber warning *platform*, CyberEx, to *synergise* awareness among governments and businesses of cyber threats and *build capacity* to thwart them; and a global Fit Cities network to fight the rise of non-communicable diseases.'
www.theage.com.au

synergistically

In the manner of *synergy*. In a *synergy* kind of way.
Not antagonistically.

'If things don't work out, there is always the perennial speculation of SABMiller hovering around as the white knight to take out the company. It makes sense *synergistically*.'
www.afr.com

'"They expect a single consistent experience gathering information, services and products at any time, any place as they need," he claimed. "With this in mind, our efforts today go *synergistically* in the direction of building an "experience economy".'
www.cmo.com.au

'Wagons ho, *synergistically*!'

synergy

Cooperation, combined effect, fruitful interaction of two or more elements – but much more profound. Said to occur when the sum of two parts together is greater than the sum of the two acting independently – hence '*synergistic* combination'. Organisational equivalent to certain forces in nature. As some believe salvation comes from a combination of divine grace and human will, others hold that *synergy* produces the same sort of *outcome*.

> 'We are leveraging *scale* to harvest global and *regional synergies* and maintaining *flexibility* to adapt to individual markets.'
>
> Annual report, 2003

> 'Achieve *synergies* intended by the amalgamation.'
>
> QSA Strategic Plan Consultancy

> '. . . targeted cross *synergies* between each business unit.'
>
> Annual report

> 'But really, the three things that have happened are Discoveries Need Dollars, which highlighted the fact the *community* is highly *supportive* of health and medical research; it does a lot for the *community* and the *community* really supports it so there's really a good *synergy* there.'
>
> The Conversation, 14 May 2014

> 'Love and marriage,
> *synergise* like a horse and carriage.'

T

takeaway / takeout

1. Food one takes away.
2. Life one takes away.
3. The 'take'. (n) The story, the gist, the main bit.

A journalist's term: 'What's the *takeout*?' 'My *takeaway* from it was, "Hey, we didn't play things properly on the front page . . ." ' (Erik Wemple, *New York Times*, August 2004). Also (v) To eliminate a person or target. As, ' "All day, you build up for the moment when you fire the shot," Field, 23, says as he and his partner take positions in a hostile zone. "Then there's a feeling of exhilaration, and you feel like you've really done something for your country. You've *taken* someone *out*" ' (*Chicago Tribune*, 25 April 2003).

taking out the trash

1. What governments and associated and similar parties do when they want to hide from the public view embarrassing or otherwise inconvenient news stories: during a terrorist attack on the World Trade Center for instance; or on a Friday evening, or after a famous person has just died, or even on a Friday evening when a famous person has just died. The Commonwealth Immigration Department took out the trash when, on the Friday that Malcolm Fraser died, it released a report detailing the abuse of children in detention on Nauru.
2. What Jesus does. As, '*Taking out the trash* begins with confession, and then counting on Jesus to get rid of it. "If we confess our sins, He is faithful and just to forgive us our sins and to cleanse us from all unrighteousness" (1 John 1:9). Today is garbage day. Take it out and then leave it there!' (getmorestrength.org)

talent matrix

Matrix for assessing talent; 'if you can't measure it, you can't manage it', e.g. 9 Box matrix, McKinsey matrix.

> 'So, why aren't organisations better at *engaging* their good talent? And by good talent, we don't just mean the high performing-high potential stars in box 9 on the *talent matrix,* we're including those in the "mighty middle" who consistently *deliver* but may not have *aspirations* beyond their current type of job and may not make much fuss about their dissatisfaction.'
>
> www.ldninternational.com

> '3 *facilitated* meetings with a reference group made up of a number of inspectors; Dianne Hyde and a rep from HR who acted as a sounding board on a range of *Issues* Including the Recruit for *Talent Matrix.*'
>
> Worksafe (WA) Inspector Attraction Project Interim report

talent pipeline

Imaginary long tubular thing through which talented people travel ever upwards, leaving the less talented at locations more suited to their modest abilities. Like all sophisticated equipment, *talent pipelines* sometimes experience *issues.* As, 'Not all *talent pipelines* are created equal, nor do all *talent pipelines* operate effectively. There are cracks, blockages and breaks that prevent the right talent from rising to the top and reaching their own – and the organization's – potential. This Ivey professor describes the *architecture* that allows an organization to *build* and maintain a *talent*-rich *pipeline* and to become a talent magnet' (*Ivey Business Journal*, 2006).

'How do these *needs map* to the organization's *talent pipeline*?'

Harvard Business Review, July–August 2015

'For to everyone who has will more be given, and he will have an abundance. But from the one who has not, even what he has will be taken away. And cast the worthless servant into the outer darkness.' The Parable of the *Talent Pipeline*.

Matthew 25:14

talk offline

Talk somewhere else; not here in front of everyone; somewhere less embarrassing to both of us. Shut up.

target / targeting

(n) Something to aim at – such as a tree, a terrorist or a monthly sales figure. An objective, *focus*, *goal*, esp. *key goal*. (v) To aim, *focus*, pursue, concentrate upon, make your main *mission*, the *achieved outcome* of choice, etc.

'We do what we call *targeted* roadside drug testing and based on that, we *target* offenders where there is a reasonable suspicion of drug use.'

Queensland Police

'CBC/Radio-Canada will identify important *target* segments, and be intentional about the specific purpose of each service for the respective segment. The *focus* is to engage *target* segments intensely with some, but not all, services; to engage Canadians in the public *space* in a way that is meaningful and personal to the individual.'

Elizabeth Renzetti, *Globe and Mail*, 28 June 2014

targeted localised shark mitigation strategy

Strategic mitigation of local sharks.

> 'This does not represent a culling of sharks. It is not a fear-driven hunt, it is a *targeted, localised shark mitigation strategy*.'
>
> WA Premier Colin Barnett, *WA Today*, 10 December 2013

team

A band of people playing or working to a common purpose: e.g., to kick goals, make or sell goods or services, pursue *agreed outcomes*, etc. *Teams* foster loyalty, create *synergy*, and sharpen the competitive edge, especially after a few *team-building* exercises. They are best *driven* by *passion* and inspired by *team* leaders. Great *teams* need *team players*. Don't join a *team* if you are not a *team player* and prepared to now and then 'take one for the *team*'.

> 'Gallup just came out with this month's poll, [and it's] pretty consistent with the last three or four years since the recession: Only 35% of the people polled feel they're *engaged* at work. Imagine going into a game with 65% of your *team* not turning on to play. It's a big problem'
>
> Jack Welch, Wharton School of the University of Pennsylvania, 8 May 2015

> 'Our *team* and we are thrilled by the excellent service, hotline availability and friendliness of the Apostore service *team*.'
>
> Apostore

> 'Operate as the leader of a *team*, supporting employees; lead the *achievement* of that *team's* business *outcomes*. As a member of the office *leadership team*, *achieve* business *outcomes* which *deliver*

high *quality customer* services in line with the Government's *agenda*, and lead the *implementation* of identified *strategic* priorities at the local level.'

Centrelink

'QPS has a proven and successful *track record* that is a direct result of QPS employees who are a *passionate*, experienced, organized and *driven team*.'

QPS

Team Australia

A *team* for everyone who lives in Australia. As 'Everyone has got to be on *Team Australia*' (Tony Abbott, PM, Captain of *Team Australia*).

'*Team Australia* is here in China to help build the Asian Century.'

Tony Abbott, PM, Address to BOAO Forum for Asia

'You don't migrate to this country unless you want to join our *team*.'

Tony Abbott, PM, 18 August 2014

'The great thing about *Team Australia* is that we welcome everyone who is prepared to have a go.'

Tony Abbott, PM

'I say to the Labor Party, join *Team Australia*. Get on board, and have the kind of *conversation*, have the kind of constructive *engagement*, with the government that is necessary . . . if you . . . are to be part of the *solution*.'

Tony Abbott, PM

> 'Australians all let us rejoice,
> That we're members of the *team* . . .'

Since May 2015 the team appears to have been disbanded. See *captain's pick/call.*

team building

Fostering *team* work, *team* spirit, *team* consciousness, *team* loyalty, *team* solidarity, *team* creativity, *team* fun, *team* bonding, *team* excitement, *team* hysteria, a sense of *team, gestalt, team zeitgeist*, etc., through often senseless, juvenile, embarrassing, sadistic, quasi-military exercises. As, 'If you wish to play an office prank on your colleagues then just try walking into the office and mentioning in passing that there is a company *team building event* planned soon. The looks of horror will cascade around the office as your colleagues picture the trust falls and group chanting in a secluded field somewhere around Dorset . . .' (www.content4reprint.com).

> 'No one really disputes that Chad Hudgens was waterboarded outside a Provo office park last May 29, right before lunch, by his boss. There is also general agreement that Hudgens volunteered for the "*team-building exercise*", that he lay on his back with his head downhill, and that co-workers knelt on either side of him, pinning the young sales rep down while their supervisor poured water from a gallon jug over his nose and mouth. And it's widely acknowledged that the supervisor, Joshua Christopherson, then told the assembled sales team, whose numbers had been lagging: "You saw how hard Chad fought for air right there. I want you to go back inside and fight that hard to make sales."'
>
> Karl Vick, *Washington Post*, 15 April 2008

team player

1. All-round good person who plays the *team* game. Not an egomaniac. Joiner-in. *Passionate*, creative, vocal, strong, synthesising, etc.
2. Toady, bootlicker, sycophant, myrmidon, tufthunter, lickspittle, sheep, office fodder, company stooge, boneless wonder, conga line of suckholes, etc., who 'exhibit positive *behaviors* that promote *teamwork*' (Peter Barron Stark).

> 'As a *strong* leader, act as a *"creative" change agent*, a vocal *team player*, and *passionate communicator driving* from conceptual ideas through to *execution* and ongoing maintenance and improvement. Synthesize cross-functional *input* to identify tradeoffs and make recommendations, balancing capabilities, constraints, and priorities.
>
> Job advert for HR Director on www.linkedin.com

> 'Yet another woman who worked closely with Mr Napoli for years said it was well-known that banker schools were being used *inappropriately* when "you wanted to pay for something on the quiet so there was no trace at head office".
>
> "If you asked questions you were told you were not a *team player*," she said.'
>
> www.theage.com.au

terms

1. *immediate to short*. Between now and when the short *term* starts.
2. *short term*. Not as long as the medium *term* and much shorter than the long. (As in: '. . . and the life of man, solitary, poor, nasty, brutish and short *term*'.)

3. *short to medium term*. This is self-explanatory.
4. *medium term*. A *term* that is not as long as the long *term* or as short as the short.
5. *medium to long term*. See short to medium. (As in: 'If you can look into the medium to long *term* / and say which grain will grow and which will not . . .')
6. *long term*. Longer than the medium *term*. Out there. Well down the track. Barely foreseeable *in terms of* the future, even with twenty-twenty vision.
7. *longer term*. Not as long as long term; even as short as short to medium.

think outside the square / box

Think of something different. To think differently. Don't think like everyone else. Think creatively. Think any thought that no one else in the team is thinking. Think outside the rut, hole, morass, etc. Think. (But don't do it too often or you'll get a reputation for not being a *team player*.)

> 'Ken Lay is emphatic about the need to *think outside the box* – to use *solutions* that complement law enforcement – an encouraging sign from the outset.'
>
> *Age*, 10 April 2015

> 'The twenty-first century challenge is to find a crosscultural methodology to speed up *ideation* for this purpose without sacrificing the creativity and humanity of our ideas. Creative Aerobics (CA) is an evolutionary *multi-cultural*, *time-sensitive*, *process driven* heuristic *paradigm* I designed that *utilizes* new methodologies to generate new *messages* in a fraction of the time required by traditional creative approaches. CA employs semiotics, the literary and less-than literary, and the art of *engagement*. By completing four mental exercises in succession

that increase the *flexibility* of information exchange between left and right brain, CA users develop multiple approaches, *strategies*, *markets* and *solutions* they can *utilize* for the assignment at hand – fresher, more persuasive *outside-the-box solutions*.'

Linda Conway Correll, University of Florida. From the workshop titled 'New Directions in Global Commercial Communication: Creative Aerobics: The Art of *Ideation*'

thought leader

Kim Il-sung, Mao Zedong, Joseph Stalin, Brian, Kylie, Jim . . .

'Ewan Morton, managing director of Sydney agency Morton, also has a chance to be named Industry *Thought Leader* for the third consecutive year.'

www.rebonline.com.au

'The Scrum Master will possess highly developed mentoring and coaching abilities and become a *thought leader* within the *agile* community.'

Australian Life Scientist

'A *paradigm shift* will require *thought leadership* in regards to *strategy* and *culture* . . .'

Equal Employment Opportunity Network of Australia

'Global *thought leader* and US scholar Mark Kramer was an exception to the rule with his call for *significant* Government involvement, suggesting the Australian Government could provide tax breaks to corporations using Shared *Value* principles and *addressing* social *need* through their *products* and services.'

www.probonoaustralia.com.au

'*Thought leadership* lives at our University.'

La Trobe University

'Take me to your *thought leader*.'

time (at this point in)

Now, then, before, earlier, later, next Wednesday, *at the end of the day*, etc. 'But at the end of the day we have to say it is not appropriate at this *point in time*' (after Alexander Downer); c.f. 'The whole life of man is but a *point in time* . . .' (Plutarch).

'At this *point in time* I lay me down to sleep.'

'Excuse me, can you tell me the *point in time*?'

time crunch

Not crunch time (As, 'Crunch Time Looms for PM', etc.). Time that is crunched (by, e.g., work and *family commitments*). Lack of time. No time. As, *7 Ways to Win the Time Crunch* by Ken Leonard Jr. and 'The *Time Crunch* Workout'.

'Sometimes, despite all of your planning and preparation, you get caught in a *time crunch* . . . so how do you manage this *time crunch*, without losing your mind?'

Kate Hamill, Freelancers Union

'Oh dear, oh dear,
I shall be in a *time crunch*.'

Alice's Adventures in Wonderland

time-poor

Short on time. Not much time. Out of time. Busy. Flat strap, etc.

> 'In an ever-increasing *time-poor* society, fitting in the desired amount of practice to improve your golf game, particularly at the driving range and course, becomes a *challenge* to all levels of player.'
>
> www.iseekgolf.com

> 'RMIT online masters *targets time-poor* medical scientists.'
>
> RMIT

tool

1. A useful implement such as a spanner or digging stick. As in: 'I think it's fair to say the computer is the most empowering *tool* we've ever created' (Bill Gates). '. . . thou shalt not build it of hewn stone: for if thou lift up thy *tool* upon it, thou hast polluted it' (Exodus).
2. Pretty well anything that might be *leveraged*: any asset inc. one's house, one's history, oneself, etc. As in: 'The *focus* is on discovery and using their heritage as a *key engagement tool*' (Heineken). 'He was a *tool* of the boss, without brains or backbone' (Kafka, *The Metamorphosis*).

> 'Educating to *Transform* Society: *Leveraging* Student *Tools* for Resilience and Resistance . . . These *tools* include: a strong sense of racial identity, solidarity, and collective obligation, critical consciousness; critical academic *achievement* identities; and activism *frameworks*.'
>
> Harvard University course

'We place high importance on accurately diagnosing and *aligning initiatives* to *key* organisational *strategic* priorities. Energy *Impact* Group has a palette of *tools* including an organisational energy diagnostic and survey *targeted* to measure individual personal energy.'

Energy Impact Group

top-down management

Old fashioned management. Autocratic, not democratic. Command and control. Taylorism. Not *bottom-up* management. Not outside-in. As, 'The opposite of *top-down* is not *bottom-up*, but outside-in' (Steve Denning). Iron fist. Shut up, and do as you're told. As, 'everyone has their face toward the CEO and their ass toward the *customer*' (Jack Welch). But fewer meetings; less cloyingly democratic; less phoney.

'"Managers are trained to manage," says [Bill] McKelvey. "This leads to *top-down* control and passive employee behavior. People are very engrained with point attractor thinking."'

UCLA Anderson

'Employees do not need another CEO pep-talk. We don't need cheerleaders, we need real *change* and that *change* needs to begin at the top, the very top, with the CEO and the Board. Leadership is *top down*! It's not middle or bottom up.'

John di Frances, comment,
knowledge.wharton.upenn.edu

See *bottom-up management*, *employee engagement*.

totality

1. State of being total. Not partial, fragmentary, narrow or slipshod. As, 'The trial looks at the *totality* of how we

can bring together in the interests of reducing *frictional unemployment* the provision of the technology and the vacancy database and improve the *penetration* of a greater range of jobs from a much wider range of sources than in the past' (Department of Employment and Workplace Relations employee at Senate Estimates Committee, 19 February 2004).

> 'It's very clear, I think, from the *totality* of the Opposition's question and the *totality* of the Prime Minister's answer exactly what the *context* of the answer was.'
>
> Tony Abbott, Leader of the Opposition

2. Extinguished. Put out.

> 'There are rains forecast this week for Wednesday and again on Saturday, and if those rains eventuate then we will be at the final stage of bringing this fire to its *totality*, where we can move the status from controlled to safe.'
>
> Victorian Fire Services Commissioner, ABC, 10 March 2014

> 'We got married in a fever, hotter than a pepper sprout,
> We've been talkin' 'bout Jackson, ever since the fire was brought to its *totality*.'
>
> Johnny Cash and June Carter

touch base

(US baseball) To make contact, speak to, phone, meet. As, 'I'll just *touch base* with the wife.'

> 'Pussy cat, pussy cat, where have you been?
> I've been up to London to *touch base* with the Queen.'

> 'Thus Zarathustra *touched base*.'

track record

Not the record at a particular track: as, 'Black Caviar broke the Flemington track record.' Rather, the historical record with 'track' in front of it: as, 'Hockey has a *track record* of putting his foot in it from time to time . . .' (*Business Insider*, 11 May 2015). *Track records* are often 'demonstrated'.

> 'The 2012 year has seen more tremendous results as we maintain our *track record* of delivering high quality research *outcomes* with our project *teams* continuing to work effectively.'
>
> CEO, DMTC, 2012 Annual Report

> 'The firm also has a demonstrated *track record* in the successful management of ADB, World Bank and UNDP technical assistance projects for *capacity building* of supreme *governance* institutions overseas.'
>
> Company document

> 'The investment *strategy* proposed is based on the following principles:
>
> • The "long" bias is optimized through a TAA process
>
> • We smooth TAA performance with DJ EuroStoxx 50 Options
>
> • We generate alphas through a sector rotation strategy
>
> • We implement truncated return *strategies* eliminating the worst (and best) returns for the fund *track record* using options or sector indexes.'
>
> Tactical Style Allocation (TSA), a new form of market-neutral strategy by Professor Noël Amenc, Edhec Risk and Asset Management Research Centre

trajectory

Something else to be *impacted*.

> 'Identifying Desired *Outcome*. Because HVT [*High Value Targeting*] operations can have unforeseen effects, governments tend to be most successful when they are clear about the desired *impact* on the insurgent group's *trajectory*.'
>
> CIA, *Best Practices* in Counter Insurgency, via WikiLeaks

> 'Having now affirmed JCU's long term *trajectory*, we owe it to our founders, our region, our nation and the tropical world to make this happen.'
>
> James Cook University

> 'We are still on a credible *trajectory* back to surplus.'
>
> Joe Hockey, Federal Treasurer, May 2015

transform

1. Change form. Transmute, transfigure, transmogrify, metamorphose. Change into something else. As, Dr Jekyll into Mr Hyde; wriggler into a mosquito.
2. Change a bit. Improve somewhat.

> 'INSPIRING INNOVATION TO ADVANCE COMMUNITIES
>
> Be part of our community to *transform* local government.'
>
> transformgov.org/en/home

'Reinventing Government *Customer Service* Conference 2015

The Reinventing Government *Customer Service* Conference 2015 will provide practical *solutions* for *transforming* government *customer service processes* and *performance*. The conference will *focus* on:

TECHNOLOGY AS AN ENABLER OF SERVICE DELIVERY:

• *Deliver* an integrated, omni-channel *customer service experience*

• *Transform customer service* using analytics, online, mobile and social media.'

www.govtechreview.com.au

'A *transformation* is as good as a holiday.'

transformational leadership

Not transactional leadership, which is a bit old fashioned and lacks *vision*. Infectious.

'*Transformational Leadership* starts with the development of a *vision*, a view of the future that will excite and convert potential followers. This *vision* may be *developed* by the *leader*, by the senior *team* or may emerge from a broad series of discussions. The important factor is the leader *buys into* it, hook, line and sinker . . . The *Transformational Leader* seeks to infect and reinfect their followers with a high level of *commitment* to the *vision*.'

Changing Minds

'. . . *transformational leaders* and their followers raise one another to higher levels of morality and motivation.'

James McGregor Burns

transformative moment

1. Big moment, transforming moment, metamorphosis. As, 'As Gregor Samsa awoke one morning from uneasy dreams he found himself *transformed* in his bed into a gigantic insect' (Kafka, *The Metamorphosis*).
2. Finding that each group's *strategic goals* are very much the same.
3. You could have knocked me down with a feather. Stone the crows. Etc.

> 'When the negotiators returned from their caucuses, we listed out each group's *strategic goals*, side-by-side, and found, amazingly, that they were very much the same. The graphic representation of these *goals*, repeated almost word-for-word beside one another, was a *transformative moment* in the *process*.'
>
> Strategic Solutions, Consultants

transition

(n) Passage from one place, time, type, state, tone or subject to another. As, 'There is no death, what seems so is *transition*' (Longfellow).
(v) Change, alter, evolve, shift, move, switch, adjust, vary, revise, morph, transform, convert, etc.

> '"We are *committed* to *transitioning* our energy mix through a deliberate and jobs *focused agenda*," she said.'
>
> Victorian State Government, *Age*, 17 June 2015

> 'The talk in Afghanistan is all about *transition*, the way in which *transition* will occur, the conditions that will lead to

transition . . . I dealt with this matter in the parliamentary debate and I've made it very clear that *transition* needs to be conditions-based . . . I've been very clear. I think it would be a bad error to *transition* out only to have to *transition* back in . . . I've got a very firm view that we need to be very clear that when we are *transitioning* our forces and *transitioning* leadership to local Afghan forces, that that needs to be irreversible. So there's some intellectual labour that needs to be brought to bear when we say we're going to engage in a conditions-based *transition*.'

Julia Gillard, PM, interview with Laurie Oakes, 7 November 2010

'You're the reason I'm *transitioning*
Don't think twice, it's alright.'

Bob Dylan

transition to greatness

Become great.

'Training Dynamics is your opportunity to *transition* to greatness under the guidance of a Master Trainer.'

Training Dynamics

'Some are born great, some *transition to greatness*, and some have greatness thrust upon them.'

Shakespeare

See *good to great*.

transparent / transparency

Readily understood, unconcealed, easily seen through, not murky, clear. Close relation of *accountable*.

> 'Without *transparency*, government *accountability* is not possible. Indeed, the ability of citizens to hold public officials *accountable* is directly proportional to the disclosure of information.'
>
> Tim Andrews, www.ipa.org.au

> 'At first blush, WikiLeaks' disclosure to newspapers of hundreds of thousands of State Department cables seems like a win for *transparency* and *accountability* in government. After all, these documents offer a never before seen window into U.S. diplomacy. But upon closer inspection, WikiLeaks' document dump illustrates the perils of going outside the system, and is likely to result in less *transparency* in the long run.'
>
> Anne L. Weismann, *Huffington Post*, 26 May 2011

> 'Now in his 12th year at the club, Stanton believed *transparency* within the group will be an important factor *moving forward*.'
>
> Brent Stanton is an Essendon footballer, EFC Website

turn up the dial

Turn up the heat, crack the whip, etc. Get more for less from employees.

> '"Organizations are *turning up the dial*, pushing their *teams* to do more for less money, either to keep up with the competition or just stay ahead of the executioner's blade," said

Clay Parker Jones, a *consultant* who helps old-line businesses become more responsive to *change*.'

New York Times, 17 August 2015

24/7

24 hours a day, seven days a week. Around the clock. Flat out. Burning the candle at both ends, etc. Show of *commitment*, *focus*, *actioning* the *agenda*, *back-ending*, *adding alpha*, *passion*, a *competitive* environment, living the *core values*, *enhanced implementation procedures*, *going forwards*, avoidance of an involuntary career event, etc.

'One of the most popular apps is Telstra *24x7*, which helps you manage your services at a time that suits you.'

'The Loan Ranger™ is here when you need him, *24/7*.'

www.loanrangercash.com.au

'Glamorous High Class Escorts Available *24/7*.'

U

Uber for X

A business model based on Uber on-demand taxi service. A start-up that connects services to *consumers* in the way Uber connects them to cars and drivers, i.e. through an app. As, Uber for ice-cream, Uber for podiatrist, Uber for relationship counselling, etc.

> 'Winter is coming, if you're a venture-backed on-demand *startup* with an aggressive pricing scheme and slow traction in the market. And the "*Uber for X*" graveyard may start to fill up faster than anyone expected.'
>
> Fusion

ultimate

Final, definitive, farthest in space and time, the last; beyond further analysis.

> 'When I look out tonight at an audience of people who work with timber, who work in forests, I don't see people who are environmental bandits, I see people who are the *ultimate* conservationists.'
>
> Tony Abbott, PM, *Sydney Morning Herald*, 5 March 2014

> 'We at Balmoral are in business to provide the *ultimate* coffee service whilst working with courtesy, enthusiasm and *professionalism*.'
>
> Balmoral Dispense, Kettering, UK

> '*Ultimate* Hair Design gives you a stylish look for your special occasions like wedding, parties, birthdays & debutante balls.'

un-Australian

Person, attitude or remark held to be inconsistent with or hostile to Australia's interests, essence, identity, traditions, customs or *zeitgeist*. Whatever is at odds with her *icons* or sport. To foul one's own nest or piss in one's own backyard. To be a smart-arse or wanker. *Caffè latte* drinker. *Elite*. *Out of touch*. Aka 'Not the Australian way'. Anti-American.

> 'Former Brisbane Roar goalkeeper Griffin McMaster has weighed into the Adam Goodes racism controversy by suggesting the dual Brownlow medallist and former Australian of the Year should be deported. McMaster also described the Indigenous sporting hero as "*unAustralian*".'
>
> *Sydney Morning Herald*, 29 July 2015

> 'People use the word *un-Australian* too often but I can't think of a better way to describe the behaviour of the crowd.'
>
> Nigel Scullion, Indigenous Affairs Minister, 3 August 2015

> 'Echoing the political philosophy of the two Josephs – Goebbels and McCarthy – [Shane] Stone claimed that the recent "negative outpouring against the Howard Government" was "*un-Australian*".'
>
> Mark McKenna, *Age*, April 2002

> '*UnAustralians* all let us lament,
> That we are young and free . . .'

under Operation Sovereign Borders

That of which he cannot speak.

unfortunate action

'Q: Minister, is there a boat in trouble off Christmas Island?

A: It is our standard practice as you know, *under Operation Sovereign Borders*, to report on any *significant events* regarding maritime operations at sea, particularly where there are safety of life at sea *issues* associated, and I am advised I have no such reports to provide.

Q: Is there a boat?

A: Well, I have answered the question . . .'

Immigration Minister Scott Morrison, *Sydney Morning Herald*, 4 July 2014

unfortunate action

Better if it had not been done. e.g. falsification of mammogram reports; displaying 'Show us your tits' banner at New Jersey firemen's convention; having sex with children; evicting old folk from their homes.

'Former Ga. technician falsified mammogram reports. Cary Martin, CEO of Houston Healthcare, which operates Perry Hospital, released a statement saying he is "pleased this component of Ms. Rapraeger's *unfortunate action* is concluded" and declined to comment further.'

news.yahoo.com

'Kurz apologized for the banner, which read "Show us your t---," that was hanging over a balcony, directly below the company's banner. "This was an *unfortunate action* caused by very poor judgment."'

www.nj.com/gloucester-county

'Marble Falls ISD worker, firefighter booked on child sex charge

The *unfortunate action* of any one individual is not a reflection of this great community.'

kxan.com

'Anger as "vulnerable and elderly" couple face eviction from Poplar Dock

"We have operated totally within our terms and conditions and this *unfortunate action* was a necessary business decision, however hard that may sound." '

www.wharf.co.uk

'Cry "Havoc", and let slip the dogs of war;
That this *unfortunate action* shall smell above the earth
With carrion men, groaning for burial.'

Julius Caesar, Shakespeare

unlock

1. Open, e.g. doors, windows, *value*, talent, cost savings, etc.

'CBA says it will need to axe 3700 jobs over the next three years to *unlock* the *targeted* cost savings.'

Australian Financial Review

'The new organisation structure is designed to *unlock* the depth of talent within Australia Post which will be *developed* and rewarded for *sustainable outcomes*.'

CEO of Australia Post, 21 April 2010

'Another way to *unlock value* is to recommend mechanisms to help an individual bridge a gap or *enhance* her capacity.'

Harvard Business Review, July–August 2015

'HR MANAGER: Jones, you're fired.

JONES: Why, sir?

HR MANAGER: To *unlock* the *targeted* cost savings.

JONES: Fair enough.'

unpacking

Getting to the bottom of it. Breaking it up into smaller parts to get the sense of it.

> 'In learning languages, the proficiency descriptors sit above the achievement objectives and, at each level, it is the descriptor that provides the primary focus for all teaching and learning. This means that, for most practical purposes, the descriptors fulfill the role that the achievement objectives have in other *learning* areas, and the function of the achievement objectives is to provide a level of *unpacking* of the descriptors.'
>
> New Zealand Curriculum Guides

update

(n) News, information, what's happening, breaking, etc. Statement, description, announcement, account, reporting, telling, informing, speaking, spruiking, etc. News *update*, updating, around the clock *updates*, etc.
(v) To provide any of the above. To bring up to date. To create an impression of progress, flux, movement or neurosis, and that life and business never stop. *Innovation*, moving on, *going forwards*, heading for *time crunch*, etc.

'Fox News staffers warn Trump to back off of Megyn Kelly after feud reignites; *Update*: "Unacceptable," "disturbing," says Ailes; *Update*: Hannity joins in; *Update*: Trump responds to Ailes . . .'

Fox News

'Mr Ballard also provided an *update* on the anticipated earnings position.'

Southcorp media release

'To *ensure* that the Commercial Manager is continually *updated* on *performance* improvements in order that we can improve our *added value* and/or be more *competitive* in the market place . . .'

Continuous improvement/quality manager,
Harrison Scott Europe Ltd

'Language shows most a man, *update* that I may see thee.'

Ben Jonson

upside

Potential for gain or advantage. What is a favourable in a deal or situation. Not the downside.

'"Those nine months really sucked," he wrote understatedly, "but they taught character, humility and patience". That one email got me thinking. Is there an *upside* to getting the sack?'

Sydney Morning Herald, 26 June 2015

'The ducks appear to be lining up in favour of our "buy 1" rating on CBA as we enter the 2004 year, given *restructuring upside*, valuation, *leverage* to wealth management and bias to rising rates.'

Jeff Emmanuel, *Australian Financial Review*, December 2004

'In our base case simulation there is an *upside* case that, er, corresponds on the flipside of the *downside* case in kind of an adverse direction.'

World Bank economist, 2008

'Seek and you will find the *upside*.'

uptake

Take up (e.g. drugs). As, 'The *Action Plan* identifies seven *key strategy areas* for preventing the *uptake* of illicit drug use . . .' (Department of Health and Aged Care). Buy, consume.

'The State Services Commission has appointed a Business *Development* and *Uptake* Manager to support SSC's new role as a provider of *mission-critical* all-of government services.'

www.e.govt.nz

'Though many industry *stakeholders* have predicted a long winter for the Indian *offshoring* industry, research firm Everest Group believes an *uptake* is around the corner . . . "We are seeing a lot of activity in people," Mr Samuel told *Business Line* in a recent interview.'

Hindu Business Line

'*Uptake* your cross and follow me . . .'

uptick

Not a down tick. An increase in a stock price. Positive tick *going upwards*. Tick up.

> 'An *uptick* in consumers' plans for major purchases at present was offset by a downtick for purchases over the next 12 months.'
>
> Automated Trader, 5 July 2010

> 'Money flow attempts to measure the capital moving in and out of a security by *adding the value* of higher, or *uptick*, trades and subtracting the value of downticks.'
>
> *Bloomberg Businessweek*, 21 June 2010

> 'Numbers: *Uptick* In Violent Deaths & Threatened Teacher Reports At School'

> 'Poll Shows *Uptick* In Obamacare Favorable Rating'

user-centric

Centred on the user. Centric for users.

> 'At the recent Gartner Security and *Risk Management* Summit, Hafaele told the audience identity and *access* can no longer be a one-size-fits-all approach. We need to create a *user-centric consumer experience* while maintaining sufficient security.'
>
> www.cso.com.au

> In particular, we hope to: *leverage* cloud-based services, both *consuming* them for increased operating efficiencies and provisioning them to enable more efficient exchange of information between government, business and the *community*; and

provide *user-centric interfaces* to government information and *processes*, putting greater *focus* on the *customer*.'

glodigital.com.au

utilise

To use, make useful, turn to profitable account.

'I *utilise* a range of modalities including Shiatsu, Bowen Therapy, Traditional Chinese Medicine and Relaxation/ Remedial techniques etc.'

Masseur's advertisement

'Project *outcomes* are achieved from the *utilisation* of the *outputs delivered* by a project. Not to be confused with Agency Budget *Outcomes* and treasury arrangements.'

Tasmanian Government

'Leicester to *utilise* Cambiasso's knowledge of Mourinho.'

www.sportal.com.au

'As Walsh identified, Port's ability to *utilise* its talls would be dependent on the side moving the ball quickly to them.'

www.afl.com.au

'We will be *utilizing* a team of Pact "*brand* ambassadors" comprised of Pact staff to help connect all Pact employees with the *branding process*.'

www.pactworld.org

V

value-adding / value-added / value-addeds / value add

Washing the potatoes before selling them, or turning them into crisps, frozen chips, French fries; salting, packaging, branding, marketing them. Advertising, design – anything that adds to the *value* (and price) of a *product* is *value-adding*. What employees, technology, organisation, etc. do; what *passion* and *commitment delivers*. Etc.

> 'The Australian Bureau of Statistics doesn't even report on *productivity* in the public sector because not only is it difficult to economically measure the *output* of public servants but Government spending is hardly an economic *value add*.'
>
> Joe Hockey, 21 August 2015

> 'An educated labour force allows the population to take full advantage of the *growth* and *value add* opportunities in the economy, whether it be in natural resources, tourism, manufacturing or services.'
>
> Kevin Rudd, 26 October 2011

> 'That the organisation identifies which *performance management* activities provide the most *value-add in terms of* individual and organisation *performance*.'
>
> Centrelink

value propositions

Buy ours, not theirs.

> '*Product leadership* or lowest-cost *value propositions* remain valid sources of *competitive advantage*, however for many businesses it is *customer* intimacy that affords them "*blue ocean*" in their competitive waters.'
>
> Churchill Consultants

'Resonating with the revolutionary *changes* taking place in the information industry, Huawei continuously *innovates* to meet *customer needs* and advance our technological *leadership*. We openly cooperate with industry *partners*, *focus* on *building* future-proof information *pipes*, and continuously create *value* for our *customers* and society at large. Based on these *value propositions*, Huawei is dedicated to enriching life and improving efficiency through a better connected world.'

Huawei

Death of a Value Propositioner by Arthur Miller

value (your call, we)

We are so not indifferent to your call. To it we have ascribed a *value* which bears no relation to the time we are taking to pick up the phone. If we wanted you to piss off, do you think we'd be playing you 'Moon River'? For your further enjoyment we will now advertise our services.

values

Principles, ethics, morals, etc. Guiding beliefs or ideals, especially of those who cannot live by them: c.f. 'So, a leader doesn't have to possess all the virtuous qualities I've mentioned, but it's absolutely imperative that he seem to possess them' (Machiavelli). Desirable qualities (integrity, transparency, efficiency, profitability, commitment to stakeholders, etc.).

Values are held to define the nature of an individual or organisation and determine *behaviours* (esp. *core values*): so long as the *behaviours* are *aligned* with the *values* and the *values* with the *goals*, and the *goals* with the *mission* (and/or *vision*) which the *values* support. *Misalignment* might lead to *inappropriate behaviours* or *strategy*, mismanagement, workplace bullying and declining profits; in which case the *goals*, *mission*, *vision* or *values* will likely need adjusting – a task for which a *consultant* is recommended.

Some *values* are intrinsic, but they can also be *achieved*, as in: 'Vivo is proven to improve student *engagement*, raise attendance, improve grades and help *achieve* school *values*'. They can *drive* a *mission*, as: 'The dynamic, entrepreneurial and pioneering *values* which drive UL's *mission* and *strategy ensures* that we capitalise on local, national and international *engagement* and connectivity' (University of Limerick).

> 'Core *values* guide our professional and personal *actions*.
>
> Service. We put country first and Agency before self. Quiet patriotism is our hallmark. We are dedicated to the *mission*, and we pride ourselves on our extraordinary responsiveness to the needs of our *customers*.
>
> Integrity. We uphold the highest standards of conduct. We seek and speak the truth – to our colleagues and to our *customers*.'
>
> CIA: Clandestine Service. Last *Updated*: Jan 23, 2013 09:20 AM

> ' "We will be a problem-solving government based on *values*, not ideology," the new Prime Minister added.'
>
> Tony Abbott, ABC, 19 September 2013

> 'Authentic leaders have clarity about the personal *values* that guide them. Use these True Growth™ *Values* Cards to discover the *values* you hold most deeply. Each deck contains 54 cards pre-printed with individual *values* and

corresponding *behaviors*. Also included is an exercise that helps leaders discover their five most important *values*. $89.50.'

Byrd Baggett CSP

values and transformation modalities

Found in any good *skill set*.

'Apart from an extensive design and *brand* experience, Monika Evers is also trained in a number of *values and transformation modalities*: NLP; Dip Shamanism; WOM; MBTI. Her understanding of the unconscious, *values* and beliefs underpins her unique MetaBrand System® of *processes* and *strategies* in *brand*, influence and loyalty.'

Monika Evers, Office of Influence, evers.com.au

values-based

The right approach, and the right thing to say if you're a manager. Based on, determined by, *values* – as Gandhi and Pol Pot were in their *behaviours*.

'We genuinely approached it as a board and senior exec as a *values-based* approach that we believed that the right thing to do, knowing it was probably going to get pretty difficult throughout the year, was to call it late in the year – to put a shield up and go whatever happens, we're going to do it late in the year.'

Carlton FC president, *Age*, 26 May 2015

'There comes a time when one must take a position that is neither safe, nor politic, nor popular, but he must take it because conscience tells him it is the *values-based* approach.'

M. L. King

> 'Do the *Values-based* Thing'.
>
> Spike Lee

vertical and horizontal associations

Up and down associations. Allows a higher as well as a broader understanding of *social capital.*

> 'A broader understanding of *social capital* accounts for the positive and negative aspects by including *vertical as well as horizontal associations* between people, and includes behaviour within and among organisations, such as firms.'
>
> World Bank

vibrant

Vibrating, pulsing; vibrant with life and energy. Thrilling, tremulous, vigorous, resounding, etc. Absolutely buzzing. Arts, communities, cultures, multicultures, (*vibrant multicultural societies*), business *cultures*, business addresses are *vibrant.* As, 'Delfin Lend Lease is committed to the development of employment and investment opportunities by encouraging *vibrant* business addresses where business can grow and prosper.'

> 'Wherever you are in Australia, whoever you are, you should be able to be your best. Australians should have a tax system that does not hinder that goal. It should reflect the hopes and aspirations of a modern, *vibrant* nation.'
>
> Joe Hockey, 24 August 2015

'To be a *vibrant*, attractive and thriving District by developing sustainable *lifestyles* based around our unique environment; the envy of New Zealand and recognised worldwide.'

Whangarei District Council, New Zealand

vision

What is seen by visionaries. *Vision* thing. What is widely assumed to be lacking in all but a very few politicians. As, 'Political leaders will need to again set out a *vision* for Australia that includes having one of us as our head of state' (George Williams, *Sydney Morning Herald*).

'Resistance is not enough – Britain needs a whole new political *vision*.'

Zoe Williams, *Guardian*, 13 July 2015

'In particular, it elaborated Keating's *vision* of a *culture*-led economic future in a globalised society.'

epress.anu.edu

'The University of Tasmania has a strong *vision* for its future. We encourage you to come along on this *journey* with us.'

University of Tasmania

'An essential part of any national *vision*, such as ours, is galvanising the people around it and instilling the collective ownership of *buy-in* of everyone in the country, regardless of their political affiliations. Thus, the prerequisite for the success of a national *vision* is an active citizenry that identifies with and owns the *vision* and mission, and which sees itself as a central agent in the success of national goals – a nation

> that is driven by its *vision* and which in turn drives that *vision* through enacting the *mission*.'
>
> David Ntshabele, 'South Africa has work to do, but is well on the way to an ideal society', 17 March 2015

visioning / vision setting

Not, as one might think, looking, seeing or foreseeing. Not as, 'Can I help you, ma'am?' 'No thank you, I'm just *visioning*.' More like getting everyone to see the same thing, or at least to pretend that they do. As:

> 'Here are a few starting points to help *leaders* begin a *process* that results in employee *buy-in*:
>
> • Create the *vision* by telling a company story that sets the rationale – the economic, psychological and moral imperative to fulfill this *vision*.
>
> • Foster excitement, motivation, and *engagement* around the *vision* by articulating the WIFM (What's In It For Me) factor.
>
> • Let your employees know how they will benefit from embracing the *vision*. Explain and reinforce the financial rewards when the goals of the *vision* have been *achieved*, such as bonuses, recognition, and career *development* . . .
>
> • *Develop* visuals, such as tables, charts and photos, which highlight milestone accomplishments of the *vision*.
>
> • Create and *align* company goals with the *vision*, and *align* individual and *team goals* with company *goals*.
>
> • Identify a cross-functional *change management team* that can anticipate the *impact* of the *vision* . . .
>
> • Talk it up . . .

• Celebrate meaningful *benchmarks* along the way.'

Bonni Carson Dimatteo

'[*visioning*] . . . creates a *Mission*, *Values* and qualitative, timebased *Vision* using a SWOT (Strengths, Weaknesses, Opportunities and Threats) Analysis to define the *strategic* context.'

The Growth Connection, www.growconnect.com.au

'The *Team* will *facilitate* a *Visioning* Session with each neighborhood in their hometown. The session's purpose is to encourage and foster collaborative efforts among all critical neighborhood *stakeholders* involved in the successful *implementation* and management of the principals, *strategies* and recommendation's [sic] of the Neighborhood Revitalization *Action Plan*.'

Private firm contracted by the State of Michigan, US

'COMMUNITY VISIONING MASTER CLASS.'

engage2.com.au

'THE GOLD COAST TOURISM VISIONING PROJECT BUS0021

Secondly, the *visioning* statement produced at the end of the *process* should be couched in terms that enable it to provide a meaningful foundation for the *strategic planning* process. Beyond this, however, the *visioning* exercise itself should be used as a *catalyst* for bringing about the permanent changes in the structure of the destination planning and management *process* that are necessary for the Gold Coast to become a "learning organisation" at the destination level.'

www.crctourism.com.au

vision statement

Envisioned statement. Stated *vision.*

'As an effective learning community, our learning and teaching is grounded in our *Vision Statement*; Mary Immaculate, a community embracing learning in and beyond the classroom in the spirit of Christ and the humanness of all.'

'It is the business visionary who, having focused his *passion* on the *mission* of his business and created a *mission statement*, then seeks to formulate and implement his desired future with a clearly stated *vision statement*.'

Don Midgett, author of *Mission* and *Vision Statements*: Your Path to a Successful Business Future

'During 2006–07 we reviewed the Department's *vision* and *mission statements*. Everyone in the Department had the chance to be involved through workshops conducted in Treasury's offices throughout the State. The result is a powerful *vision* and *mission* that differentiates Treasury from other organisations. Our *vision statement* is a description of what we strive to achieve – a picture of the future we seek to create. It enables staff members to clearly imagine where the Department is heading.'

Department of Treasury and Finance, Tasmania

'And on a clear day, on that clear day
You can see where the Department is heading . . .'

Barbra Streisand

visitation

Visit: particularly of an official, ordained, calamitous or supernatural kind.

> ' "VTIC has long advocated for greater support for regional tourism and, as recently as yesterday, we called for government funding for activities to *drive visitation* throughout Victoria," said VTIC Chief Executive Dianne Smith.'
>
> VTIC, 14 August 2015

> 'Council Arts Development Officer says *visitation* to the toilet block has risen significantly since the installation of the murals.'
>
> Surf Coast Shire Bulletin, 2003

> 'Excuse me, I must pay a *visitation* to the lavatory.'

> 'On the way home I decided to *visitate* aunt Hilda.'

weaponise

Adapt the unwarlike for war; equip with weapons, or so alter as to make a weapon – e.g. information into misinformation. C.f. Mark Twain, 'The human race has one really effective weapon, and that is laughter.'

> 'Mr Miliband said he would "*weaponise*" the NHS during a briefing he gave to up to 15 executives at the BBC.'
>
> *Daily Telegraph*, UK

> 'The *weaponization* of information, *culture* and money is a vital part of the Kremlin's hybrid, or non-linear, war, which combines the above elements with covert and small-scale military operations.'
>
> The Menace of Unreality: How the Kremlin *Weaponizes* Information, *Culture* and Money by Peter Pomerantsev and Michael Weiss, Institute of Modern Russia

> 'When it comes to the controversial idea of police taser drones, North Dakota is leading the charge in *implementing* new laws that would allow *weaponized* drones to carry pepper spray, rubber bullets, and taser weapons.'
>
> www.inquisitr.com

wellbeing (enhanced)

Being well. *Lifestyle*, health, complexion, joie de vivre; whatever can be *enhanced* with lip balm and a spray of Evian water.

> 'This functional bag contains specially selected *products* chosen for their ability to *enhance* your *wellbeing*.'
>
> Qantas toiletry bag

'Hawkesbury-Hills Division of General Practice's Mission Statement is "Advancing General Practice in North West Sydney to *optimise* health and *wellbeing* in our community". Hawkesbury Division of General Practice's *mission* and *values* show good *alignment* with the identified national health priorities . . . All activities within this plan have been checked against these *values* and fulfill at least one, and in many cases multiple, *value/s*.'

www.phcris.org.au

'Dear Bruce, I hope you are *wellbeing* . . .' etc.

window of opportunity

If it were a door you might not be able to see the opportunity. An opportunity that might not be there tomorrow, or one you can reach only if you move quickly. A fleeting opportunity. A glimpse. Go for it. Chance for a *quick fix*.

'The IPA warns that Abbott has a tiny *window of opportunity* to change the nation.'

Sydney Morning Herald, 28 June 2015

'So the sooner we can have this matter resolved, and there are some *windows of opportunity* there that I will certainly be involving myself in to make it happen.'

Warren Entsch MP, ABC, 12 August 2015

'Many of these events have an association with those time periods when a person's immune system is weakened or stressed. If compromised a person's immune system, which under normal circumstances is able to keep the herpes virus particles in check, is overwhelmed and a *window of opportunity* for cold sore formation is opened.'

www.animated-teeth.com

'If a *window of opportunity* appears, don't pull down the shade.'

Tom Peters

'Gather ye rosebuds while ye have ye *window of opportunity*.'

win-win

Ideal *outcome*. Both sides happy. All *relevant stakeholders* delighted.

'Deputy Premier and Minister for State Development, Infrastructure and Planning Jeff Seeney told a public meeting in Bowen that the Abbot Point Beneficial Reuse *Strategy* would protect the natural wonder and allow for the *sustainable development* of the port. "Our Government believes this landmark *plan* offers the strongest and most exciting opportunity yet to achieve a *win-win* for the environment and economic growth," Mr Seeney said.'

statements.qld.gov.au

'Becoming a Brand You is a *win-win* strategy; good for individuals and good for their organizations.'

Tom Peters

'Regulatory reform creates winners and losers in many different parts of the economy. Advocating powerfully and consistently with Government for *win-win* regulatory reforms will help you achieve your commercial objectives either by mitigating *impacts* of *reforms* or by opening up new opportunities in your sector.'

connectgr.com.au/services

workshop

1. (n) A place of work.
2. (v) To take to a committee; ring around; think about; *dialogue*; talk to a standstill. (As in: 'OK, I think we need to *workshop* that.')
3. A *facilitator's* natural environment.

> 'Facilitated *workshop* on practical solutions and *the way forward* regarding your *issues* in senior executive *leadership*.'
>
> Benchmarking Partnerships

> 'If there's one word that sums up everything that's gone wrong since the War, it's *Workshop*.'
>
> Kingsley Amis

> 'Delegates will be able to select a concurrent skills *workshop* that explores specific *tools* and *processes* for integrated *sustainability*. Delegates will be *engaged* in small group *workshops* to consider how each tool will support and potentially expand their *capacity* to *develop* an integrated approach.'
>
> NSW Department of Environment and Climate Change

> 'Hi, ho! Hi, ho!
> It's off to a *facilitated workshop* we go!
> Hi, ho! Hi, ho . . .' etc.
>
> *Snow White and the Seven Facilitators*

work with the customer

1. Work with the *customer*.
2. Fleece the *customer*, etc.

> 'This usurer-relief campaign has been increasingly successful, with lawmakers in Arizona, Florida, Indiana, Kentucky, Missouri, and North Carolina buying the argument that lenders such as OneMain actually "*work with their customer,*" as demonstrated by low default rates . . .
>
> When a borrower does default, companies like OneMain "back up a truck to the house and take the furniture and the TV set." However, the company much prefers to keep *customers* on the hook by repeatedly and expensively refinancing their loans – which helps to explain the low default rates.'
>
> Andrew Cockburn, 'Saving the Whale Again . . .' *Harper's*, August 2015

See *consumer finance*

world class

Among the best. None (or not that many) finer.

> 'The *delivery* of the *world class* commissioning *vision* and *competencies* will take place within a commissioning assurance system. This will *drive performance* and *development*, and reward PCTs as they move towards becoming *world class* commissioners.'
>
> M. Sobanja, What is *World Class* Commissioning? (Note: World class commissioning has been decommissioned.)

Y

your call is important to us

Please hold the line.

Z

zero kilojoule hydration option

Water. As in: 'People willing to pay for the convenience of a *zero-kilojoule hydration option* when they're out and about' (CEO, Australasian Bottled Water Institute).

> '*Zero kilojoule hydration options* everywhere, nor any drop to drink.'
>
> Coleridge

This book owes much to the many people who sent examples of workplace words to weaselwords.com.au. We thank them all.